Trusts

EDWARD C. HALBACH, JR.

Late University of California, Berkeley and Reporter for the Restatement (Third) of Trusts

CARLA SPIVACK

Justice Joseph Josiah Brewer Distinguished Professor of Law, Albany Law School

KAREN J. SNEDDON

Dean and Professor of Law, Mercer University School of Law

Fourteenth Edition

Gilbert Law Summaries is a trademark registered in the U.S. Patent and Trademark Office

© 2008 by Thomson/West
© 2023 LEG, Inc. d/b/a West Academic
    860 Blue Gentian Road, Suite 350
    Eagan, MN 55121
    1-877-888-1330

West, West Academic Publishing, and West Academic are trademarks of West Publishing Corporation, used under license.

Printed in the United States of America

ISBN: 978-1-68561-141-5

Summary of Contents

CAPSULE SUMMARY V

GILBERT EXAM STRATEGIES XXXIX

Chapter One. Introduction 1
    Key Exam Issues 2
    A.   Definition of Fundamental Terms...2
    B.   Classification of Trusts 3
    C.   Trusts Distinguished from Similar Relationships...6

Chapter Two. Elements of a Trust...11
    Key Exam Issues 12
    A.   Introduction 13
    B.   Expression of Trust Intent—Express Trusts 14
    C.   Trust Property (Res) 17
    D.   Parties to the Trust 21
    E.   Trust Purposes 39

Chapter Three. Creation of Express Trusts 49
    Key Exam Issues 50
    A.   Methods of Trust Creation 51
    B.   Creation of Inter Vivos Trusts 52
    C.   Creation of Testamentary Trusts 69
    D.   Revocable Inter Vivos Trusts as Will Substitutes—Special Problems 73

Chapter Four. Rights of the Beneficiary and the Beneficiary's Creditors in the Beneficiary's Interest 81
    Key Exam Issues 82
    A.   Beneficiary's Rights in the Trust 82
    B.   Voluntary Transfers by the Beneficiary...83
    C.   Rights of Beneficiary's Creditors to Reach Beneficiary's Interest 84

Chapter Five. Charitable Trusts 93
    Key Exam Issues 94
    A.   General Nature and Treatment of Charitable Trusts 95
    B.   Requirement of Public, Not Private, Benefit...97
    C.   Charitable Purpose Defined 99
    D.   Limitations on Charitable Trusts...109
    E.   Modification of Charitable Trusts—the Cy Pres Doctrine..112

Chapter Six. Duties, Powers and Liability of the Trustee...117
    Key Exam Issues 118
    A.   General Responsibilities and Authority of Trustees...119
    B.   Trustee Duties 120
    C.   Powers of the Trustee 126
    D.   Trustee's Liabilities and Beneficiaries' Remedies 137
    E.   Trustee's Liability to Third Parties 142
    F.   Duties and Liabilities of Beneficiaries 144
    G.   Liabilities of Third Parties..146

Chapter Seven. Accounting for Income and Principal..149
    Key Exam Issues 150
    A.   Introduction 150
    B.   Specific Rules of Trust Principal-Income Accounting 153

Chapter Eight. Modification and Termination of Trusts...161
    Key Exam Issues 162
    A.   Revocable Trusts 162
    B.   Irrevocable Trusts 164

Chapter Nine. Trusts Arising by Operation of Law...173
    Key Exam Issues 174
    A.   Introduction 174
    B.   Resulting Trusts...176
    C.   Constructive Trusts 179

REVIEW QUESTIONS AND ANSWERS 183
    Review Questions 184
    Answers to Review Questions 194

EXAM QUESTIONS AND ANSWERS..207

TABLE OF CASES..221

INDEX 223

Capsule Summary

I. INTRODUCTION

A. DEFINITION OF FUNDAMENTAL TERMS

1. Trust

A trust is a fiduciary relationship *with respect to specific property*, to which the trustee holds legal title for the benefit of beneficiaries, who hold equitable title.

2. Settlor

A settlor is the person who creates the trust by will or inter vivos transfer. (The settlor may also be called the "trustor," "donor," "transferor," "grantor," or "testator.")

3. Trustee

The trustee is the individual or entity that holds legal title to the trust property.

4. Trust Property

The trust property (or res) is the interest the trustee holds for the beneficiaries.

5. Beneficiary

A beneficiary ("cestui que trust") is a person for whose benefit the trust property is held by the trustee.

B. CLASSIFICATION OF TRUSTS

1. Methods of Classifying

Trusts may be classified according to the (i) *duties* imposed on the trustee (*i.e.*, active vs. passive); (ii) *purposes* of the trust (*i.e.*, private vs. charitable); (iii) *manner of creation* (*e.g.*, express, resulting, constructive); and (iv) *time of creation* (*i.e.*, inter vivos or testamentary).

2. Active vs. Passive Trusts

In an *active* trust, the trustee has some affirmative management duties. In a *passive* trust, the trustee has no real duties but is a mere holder of the legal title.

a. Statute of Uses

Uses were historical predecessors of trusts and were usually *passive*. The Statute of Uses was enacted in 1536 to eliminate this method of holding or passing title to land. The Statute transformed an *equitable interest into a legal interest*. The Statute as construed was held inapplicable to some uses (*e.g.*, personal property and most active uses were *not* covered). The Statute of Uses concept is still recognized in most American jurisdictions.

3. Private vs. Charitable Trusts

A *charitable* trust bestows a benefit upon the public at large or upon a broad segment of the public. Other trusts are *private* and are subject to more restrictive rules.

4. **Express Trusts vs. Implied Trusts**

   a. **Express Trusts**

   An express trust is created as a result of a ***manifestation of intention*** to create the relationship that the law recognizes as a trust.

   b. **Implied Trusts**

   Implied trusts are created by operation of law. They are sometimes called remedial trusts.

   (1) **Resulting Trusts**

   A resulting trust is an ***equitable reversionary interest*** based on the ***legally presumed intention*** of a property owner. It arises by operation of law where an express trust fails in whole or in part or where its beneficial provisions are incomplete.

   (2) **Constructive Trusts**

   A constructive trust is a ***remedial device*** imposed by a court of equity to prevent a person who has obtained property by wrongful conduct or unjust enrichment from deriving the benefits thereof.

C. **TRUSTS DISTINGUISHED FROM SIMILAR RELATIONSHIPS**

   1. **Characteristics, Not Terminology, Controlling**

   Other legal relationships may resemble trusts but lack one or more trust elements.

   2. **Bailment**

   Where an owner of tangible personal property gives ***possession*** of the chattel, ***but not title***, to another, the relationship is a bailment. A bailment ***differs*** from a trust in that:

   a. It applies only to ***chattels***;

   b. Both legal and equitable ***title remain in the bailor***;

   c. A bailee ***cannot convey title***;

   d. ***Rents, profits***, etc., belong to the ***bailor*** (as opposed to a beneficiary in a trust relationship); and

   e. Bailment ***remedies are usually legal***, while trust remedies are equitable.

   3. **Agency**

   An agent is a fiduciary with many responsibilities similar to those of a trustee, but an agency ***differs*** from a trust in that:

   a. Holding title to the property is ***not an essential aspect*** of the agency;

   b. The agent is ***subject to control*** by the principal;

   c. The agent's authority is ***strictly construed***;

   d. The agent acting within the scope of authority is ***not personally liable*** (while a trustee is liable to third parties for acts on behalf of the trust); and

   e. The agency ***terminates upon the death or*** (traditionally) ***incapacity*** of the principal.

4. **Debtor-Creditor Relationship**

Although a creditor has a claim against a debtor, an unsecured creditor has *no interest in specific funds or property*. The crucial distinction between this type of relationship and a trust is usually whether the parties intended to create a relationship with regard to specific property. Note that payment of *interest* is virtually conclusive that the relationship involves a debt.

5. **Conditional Fee**

A condition in a grant for the benefit of the grantor or a third party may at times suggest a trust relationship, but also may be construed as a trust, an equitable charge, or a conditional fee. Because failure of the condition terminates a conditional fee estate, courts usually favor construing conditional language *as a trust*.

6. **Other Relationships**

Other fiduciary relationships (*e.g.,* guardianships) may appear similar to trusts, but they differ in one or more key aspects.

II. ELEMENTS OF A TRUST

A. INTRODUCTION

The usual elements of a trust are: (i) *trust intent*; (ii) *specific trust res*; (iii) properly *designated parties*; and (iv) a *valid trust purpose*. Consideration is *not* required.

B. EXPRESSION OF TRUST INTENT—EXPRESS TRUSTS

1. **In General**

The settlor must objectively manifest a final, definite, and specific intention that a trust (*i.e.,* a fiduciary relationship) should immediately arise with respect to some particular property.

2. **Form of Expression**

Manifestation of intent may be by *words* or *conduct*. Some external manifestation is required, but no specific words need be used, and words of trust need not be construed as creating a trust. The settlor's failure to communicate intent to beneficiaries will not prevent a trust from arising.

3. **Precatory Expressions of Intent**

Precatory language of the settlor (*e.g.,* "I wish," "I hope," etc.) *presumptively does not create a trust* under the modern view. However, such language *may* be construed as creating a trust in light of other factors such as:

a. *Detailed instructions* to an alleged trustee;

b. *Language addressed to a fiduciary*;

c. An *unnatural disposition of property* resulting if no trust;

d. *Timing and placement* of precatory terms; and

e. A *preexisting relationship* between the parties or other expressions of the settlor that would seem to indicate a trust relationship was intended.

4. **Time When Trust Intent Must Be Expressed**

The general rule is that the intention to create a trust must exist and be manifested at a time when the settlor owns or is transferring the trust property.

a. **Gifts**

The owner may not convey property as an outright gift and later convert the gift into a trust.

b. **After-Acquired Property**

Where a voluntary trust intent is manifested prior to acquisition of the property to be put in trust, courts will usually find sufficient trust intent if there is some further *manifestation* of such intent *after* the property is acquired and *consistent* with the prior expression.

5. **Trust Must Be Intended to Take Effect Immediately**

The settlor must intend that the trust take effect immediately, even if subject to revocation, and not at some future time.

a. **Subsequent Action**

If there is an appropriate subsequent act (*e.g.,* a transfer) consistent with the previously stated intent *coupled* with an intent that the trust presently take effect, a valid trust will *then* arise.

b. **Effect of Postponing Designation of Essential Elements**

If the settlor purports to create a trust but postpones designating the beneficiaries, trustee, or trust property, the incomplete terms of the "trust" indicate that a trust is intended to arise in the future. Thus, there is *no valid present trust*.

c. **Trust of Future Interests and Promises**

A future interest *may* be the proper res of a present, valid trust, as may an *enforceable promissory note*.

(1) **Effect of Consideration**

Although an unenforceable promise to create a trust in the future does not create a trust, if consideration was given for an otherwise enforceable promise, the intended beneficiaries' rights can be enforced.

d. **Savings Bank Trusts ("Totten Trusts")**

These are generally held to be valid, revocable, inter vivos trusts.

e. **Testamentary Trusts**

Trusts created by will meet the immediate effect requirement because the trust intent is expressed at the time the will "speaks" (*i.e.,* at the testator's death).

C. TRUST PROPERTY (RES)

1. **Requirements—in General**

The property must be (i) an *existing interest* in property; (ii) capable of *ownership* and usually of *alienation*; and (iii) sufficiently *identifiable or identified*.

2. **Interest in Property**

The res must be an existing interest in existing property.

a. **Mere Expectancy**

A mere expectancy (*i.e.,* an interest that has not yet come into existence) is *insufficient*. If *consideration* is involved, the courts may find a contract to create a trust; or if the property is later acquired and the settlor then remanifests an intent to create a trust, a trust will come into existence at that time.

b. **Equitable Interests**

Equitable interests (*e.g.,* the interest of a trust beneficiary, if assignable) may constitute a trust res.

3. **Alienability**

In general, the interest to be placed in trust must be alienable, as trusts are created by some form of transfer. At early common law, some future interests were not alienable and could not be transferred into a trust; this is no longer true in most jurisdictions. Certain other types of property (*e.g.,* tort causes of action) are frequently held to be personal to the holder and thus may not be transferred.

4. **Identified or Identifiable**

The trust res must be specific property that is actually identified or described with sufficient certainty that it is identifiable, *i.e.,* can be ascertained from existing facts.

a. **Fractional Interests**

Fractional interests in *specific* properties *may* be the res of a trust.

b. **Fungible Goods**

Some doubt may still exist where a trust is sought to be created in a portion of fungible goods (*e.g.,* cash, commercially equivalent goods), but this should not be a problem if the broader collection is itself identifiable.

c. **Obligor as Trustee**

Generally, when a person makes an agreement with a creditor to pay a third person, the person does not become a trustee of what is simply the person's own debt, as there is no identifiable res.

d. **Obligee as Trustee**

A bank is not normally a trustee of unsegregated funds, but a bank depositor (obligee) may hold or transfer the deposit (*i.e.,* debt) in trust for another. The deposit (a *chose in action*) is an identifiable res.

5. **Exception to Funding Requirement—Pourover Wills**

D. **PARTIES TO THE TRUST**

1. **Settlor ("Trustor")**

Generally, a property owner may create a trust of that property and become a settlor.

a. **Capacity**

The settlor's legal capacity to create a trust is measured by the same standards applied to similar nontrust conveyances (*e.g.,* legal age, sound mind, etc.).

b. **Rights in Trust Property After Creation of Trust**

Once the trust is established, the settlor generally has only such rights or interests in the trust property as are reserved by the trust terms or as are not disposed of by the trust terms (reversionary interests). But a growing number of states provide that trusts are revocable unless expressly declared to be irrevocable. A trust may, however, be set aside or reformed in case of fraud, duress, undue influence, or mistake. A settlor who retains no powers or beneficial interests is usually held to have no right to enforce the trust.

c. Settlor's Creditors

The settlor's creditors may reach retained beneficial interests. Despite this, the traditional but declining view is that creditors may *not* reach the *corpus* of a revocable trust unless its creation was a fraud upon creditors.

2. Trustee

The trustee must have capacity to *take and hold title*. At common law, partnerships were precluded from being trustees, but this is no longer the case. Corporations may be trustees, but several states limit or condition the ability of *foreign* corporations (*i.e.,* those incorporated in other states) to engage in trust administration. (*Note:* The constitutionality of some of these statutes is questionable.) To continue serving as trustee, the designated trustee must *also have capacity to administer the trust*. Each co-trustee must have the requisite qualifications.

a. Bonding

Many states require trustees of testamentary trusts to post faithful-performance bonds.

b. Failure to Name Trustee or Failure of Named Trustee to Serve

If the settlor fails to name a trustee or the named trustee fails to survive or qualify, where the trust is otherwise validly created, *"equity will not allow a trust to fail for lack of a trustee."* A court will appoint a trustee to save the trust, except in rare cases where the settlor clearly manifests intent that the named trustee is the *only* acceptable trustee. The absence of a trustee, however, may cause an intended *inter vivos* trust to fail for *lack of effective transfer*.

(1) Trustee Disqualified

If the trustee is technically disqualified by law from *taking title* initially, there is a split of opinion as to whether courts should salvage an inter vivos trust despite the apparent defect in the intended transfer for lack of a transferee. In testamentary trusts, this problem does not exist.

c. Nature of Trustee's Interest

The trustee generally is said to have *"bare" legal title* (*i.e.,* devoid of beneficial ownership—holding property for beneficiaries in accordance with the trust). The trustee of an inter vivos trust derives title from the trust instrument. Courts are split on whether a testamentary trustee derives title from the will or by the judicial appointment that confirms a "nomination" in the will, with title relating back to the settlor's death. The trust instrument usually spells out the nature and extent of title conveyed to the trustee. If there is no instrument, the court will determine the quantum of the estate. In such cases, the trustee traditionally takes title to real property only to the extent necessary to carry out the trust, but today this normally requires full title.

(1) Trust Estate Not Liable for Trustee's Personal Debts

The trustee's personal creditors cannot satisfy their claims from trust property.

(2) Effect of Trustee's Death

If the sole trustee dies, title to the trust property is held to pass to the trustee's estate *subject to the trust*; the court will then transfer title to a successor trustee. Co-trustees are presumed to hold as *joint tenants* with right of survivorship. Unless the needs of sound administration or the terms of the trust indicate that a successor co-trustee should be appointed, the court will allow the surviving trustee(s) to serve alone.

d. Disclaimer or Resignation by Trustee

(1) Disclaimer

A trust cannot be forced upon a designated trustee who has not previously accepted the trust or contracted in advance to do so. With some exceptions, a trustee cannot accept in part and disclaim in part.

(2) Resignation

A trustee may not resign unless the trust terms give the trustee the right to do so or all beneficiaries consent to the resignation. A trustee must obtain a court order relieving the trustee of the duties.

e. Removal of Trustees

Unless a trust instrument states otherwise, only a court of competent jurisdiction has the power to remove a trustee. A trustee may be removed only for "good cause." Animosity between the trustee and beneficiaries is not in and of itself a sufficient ground for the removal of a trustee unless it jeopardizes the trust. *Note:* Courts are less willing to remove a settlor-appointed trustee than a court-appointed trustee.

(1) Removal by Beneficiaries

If the trust terms allow the beneficiaries to modify or terminate the trust, the beneficiaries have the power to remove the trustee.

f. Merger of Title

Where a *sole trustee and sole beneficiary are one and the same person*, the result is a merger of legal and equitable titles, defeating the trust and creating a fee simple in the person. *Note:* Interests must be *exactly* the same for merger to occur.

3. Beneficiaries

a. Necessity of Beneficiaries

(1) Private Trusts

To create a *private* trust, a settlor must name or otherwise describe as beneficiary one or more persons who are or will become capable of taking a property interest and becoming an obligee. Without a beneficiary there is no one capable of enforcing a trust. Accordingly, the attempt to create a trust will fail. The *trustee* need not know who the beneficiary is as long as the beneficiary is identifiable or will become ascertainable within the period of the Rule Against Perpetuities (*infra*). If a private trust fails for lack of a beneficiary, there is a *resulting trust* in favor of the transferor or the transferor's estate.

(2) Honorary Trusts

Many jurisdictions allow the voluntary carrying out (but usually not enforcement) of some "trusts" that are neither charitable nor private (*e.g.,* for care of a person's pets or for some other noncharitable purpose). Some jurisdictions prevent such "honorary trusts" from being implemented, even voluntarily by the transferee, with a resulting trust for the transferor, the transferor's estate, or the transferor's successors in interest. *Note:*

Honorary trusts are different from special purpose statutory trusts, such as pet trusts.

b. Who May Be a Beneficiary?

Generally, any person, natural or artificial, who is capable of *taking and holding title* to property may be a beneficiary of a private trust. This includes minors and incompetents, and under modern law, unincorporated associations. Trusts for the continuing benefit of noncharitable, unincorporated associations may fail because of the Rule Against Perpetuities.

c. Incidental Benefits

Not every party who stands to benefit by operation of the trust is a beneficiary. One whose benefits are only incidental is not a beneficiary and cannot enforce rights under the trust (*e.g.*, where trust terms require investment in a particular corporation, the corporation is not a beneficiary).

d. Reasonably Definite Class Requirement

Beneficiaries must be ascertained or ascertainable when the trust is created or become ascertainable within the period of the Rule Against Perpetuities. Thus, persons must be identifiable as beneficiaries or members of a "reasonably definite and ascertainable class." The beneficiaries need *not* be ascertainable at the time the trust is created, but the instrument must then provide a formula or description by which the beneficiaries can be identified at the time when their enjoyment of interest is to begin. That time must be within the perpetuities period.

(1) Status Until Beneficiaries Ascertained

A few cases have held that there is no trust if all beneficiaries are presently unascertained. The *majority* view is contra, provided the beneficiaries will be ascertained within the period of the Rule Against Perpetuities; until the beneficiaries are ascertained, there is a *resulting trust* for the benefit of the settlor, subject to an *executory limitation* in favor of the beneficiaries.

(a) "Heirs" of Settlor

In most jurisdictions today, a remainder to the settlor's "heirs" is enforceable. In the few jurisdictions that still follow the Doctrine of Worthier Title, there is a reversion in the settlor. An analogous problem arises in those few jurisdictions adhering to the Rule in Shelley's Case.

(2) Caution—Formalities Must Be Satisfied

Whatever formal requirements are applicable must be followed in the instrument identifying the beneficiaries; *i.e.,* testamentary trusts must meet the requirements of the Statute of Wills, and inter vivos trusts must meet any applicable requirements of the Statute of Frauds.

(3) Class Gifts

Trusts for the benefit of a class of persons are valid, provided the class membership, as described, is or will become reasonably definite and ascertainable within the period of the Rule Against Perpetuities. A trustee can have the power to select among members of a class if the class is sufficiently definite. If not, under the traditional view, such power does *not* make the beneficiaries sufficiently ascertainable to validate a trust. If, however, the power can be exercised in favor of the trustee (although other class members are indefinite), the court will probably treat the "trust" as an outright gift to the trustee.

(a) Reasonably Definite Class

The class of beneficiaries must be definite enough for a court to determine by whom or on whose behalf the trust may be enforced, and, where the trustee has the power of selection, to determine not only whether a selection is proper but also who is to take if no appointment is made. Specific class terms such as "children," "issue," "heirs," and "next of kin" are sufficiently definite. "Family" has been so construed, but terms like "relatives" have caused problems for the courts. Modern construction usually equates "relatives" with "next of kin" if no selection of other relatives is made by the trustee.

E. TRUST PURPOSES

1. Requirement of Lawful and Appropriate Purpose

A trust may not be created for a purpose that is illegal or contrary to public policy. Some statutes provide that a trust may be created for any purpose for which a *contract* could be made. Except for the special case of "honorary trusts" (*supra*), a trust *must* be either private or charitable.

2. Impermissible Trust Purposes

A trust, or a provision therein, may be challenged as invalid if it appears that the settlor was attempting to accomplish an objective that is illegal, requires the commission of a tortious or criminal act, or otherwise offends public policy. Examples of prohibited trust purposes include: to perpetrate a fraud on existing creditors; to reward a person for committing an illegal or immoral act; or to unreasonably restrain marriage or to encourage divorce. Courts usually try to *excise* the illegal purpose or condition and enforce the trust without that illegal purpose or condition, unless doing so would defeat the overall purpose of the settlor in establishing the trust.

3. Related Question of Permissible Duration

The law is concerned about the period of time during which the "dead hand" of a settlor may tie up property to restrict or impair the freedom of those beneficially interested in the property. Historically, private trusts designed to last indefinitely will run afoul of various rules of property law.

a. Rule Against Perpetuities

This is the most significant limitation in most states. The common law Rule (significantly modified, or even abolished, in a growing number of states) provides that, to be valid, an interest must vest, *if at all*, no later than 21 years after some life in being at the time of creation of the interest. *Note: A number of states have significantly modified the Rule Against Perpetuities meaning that in some instances, private trusts may be considered to be "perpetual trusts."*

(1) Requirements of Vesting and Certainty—Class Gifts

An *entire* class gift is generally void if the interest of *any* single class member may vest beyond the period.

(2) Charitable Trusts

Charitable trusts have long been exempted from the restrictions of the Rule against Perpetuities. The property rights *may* validly shift from one charity to another beyond the period, but an interest may *not* shift from charitable to private (or vice versa) beyond the period of the Rule.

(3) Effect of Remoteness

The Rule against Perpetuities strikes down only the offending interests. The trust is generally carried out without the offending interests—unless the settlor's purpose would be defeated. Statutes in a significant number of states, often by adoption of a Uniform Act, *reform* the interest to comply with the Rule against Perpetuities.

b. Statutory Rule Against Suspension of Power of Alienation

Usually a transfer that violates the Rule Against Perpetuities also violates the statutory rule against suspension of the power of alienation in a few states. Occasionally a trust conveyance that does not violate the perpetuities period violates this rule.

c. Rule Against Accumulations

Trust income may not be accumulated beyond the perpetuities period in most states, and in a few states the law is more restrictive. The rule is generally *not* applicable to charitable trusts.

d. Trusts May Continue Beyond Perpetuities Period

Most states do not restrict trusts to the perpetuities period if all interests are vested; however, after the period has expired, beneficiaries may join to terminate the trust and any restraints on alienation cease.

III. CREATION OF EXPRESS TRUSTS

A. METHODS OF TRUST CREATION

The principal methods of creating a trust are by: (i) *declaration*, (ii) *transfer* (during lifetime or by will), (iii) exercise of *power of appointment*, and (iv) *contract*.

B. CREATION OF INTER VIVOS TRUSTS

1. Requirement of Effective, Present Transfer or Declaration

To create an inter vivos trust, there must be an effective and present transfer of the trust property. (A declaration substitutes for a transfer.)

a. Present vs. Future Transfer

A mere promise to hold or transfer property in trust *in the future* does *not* create a trust (at least in the absence of consideration).

b. Delivery to Trustee

A transfer requires adequate delivery of the trust property to the trustee. Chattels should be *physically passed* to the trustee or a *deed* (a writing stating the gift) should be delivered to her. In cases of real property, the settlor must effectively *convey title* to land. Where the settlor is also the trustee, a *declaration of trust* accompanied by segregation or identification of trust property substitutes for delivery.

t of No Trustee

e there is no trustee for an inter vivos trust, the transfer requirement
met. Under special circumstances, courts may save the trust by
g the settlor (or the settlor's successors) *constructive trustee* until
urt appoints a trustee.

nd Acceptance by Trustee

ve transfer has been made, a valid trust exists even if the trustee is
f it. (*Example:* An effective delivery made to the trustee's agent,
t inform the trustee.) The trustee's acceptance is *presumed* until
s shown. After acceptance, the trustee is bound by the terms of the
fiduciary requirements. A trustee's acceptance usually *"relates*
ime of the trust's creation.

er

not fail if the trustee disclaims *before acceptance*; a substitute
appointed.

Acceptance by Beneficiary

cceptance by the beneficiary are not required for creation of a
e beneficiary is presumed to accept. A trust may *not* be forced
ry, who has the right to *disclaim* within a reasonable time. It is
hat the beneficiary may not accept in part and disclaim in part,
ably only true where there are both benefits and burdens
eneficiary may *withdraw a renunciation* of a trust interest
ce to others is involved.

s

at have adopted the Uniform Probate Code ("UPC"), trustees
st with the probate court at the "principal place of
e to register does not invalidate the trust, but the trustee is
ial of compensation, or surcharge by the court. Non-UPC
ire registration of inter vivos trusts, but testamentary trusts
inuing probate court jurisdiction.

cessary for a valid trust. Many trusts are gratuitous.
create a trust in the future, even if in writing, cannot be
ation was given for the promise. Where consideration is
enforced even though the requisite transfer was defective,
uired property.

erty are valid in most states, but trusts of land must be
ng.

Property

r the trust is of real property or personal property, the
nal status of the trust property (equitable conversion
uoctrine generally is *not* applied).

b. Type of Writing Required

If a writing is required, the writing need not be in the form of a deed of conveyance, but the writing must be reasonably complete and definite and must reasonably indicate essential terms of the trust (*i.e.*, the property, beneficiaries, and basic trust purposes).

c. By Whom Must the Writing Be Signed?

Typical procedures would have both the settlor and trustee sign the trust document. Otherwise, a required writing must be executed (at or before time of transfer) by a party who has the *power to create the trust* or by the grantee who thereafter receives the property. The signature of the *beneficiary* is *not* sufficient or required to create an enforceable trust.

d. Part Performance Doctrine

Acts of part performance by the parties that tend to prove the existence of a trust may be sufficient to take the matter out of the Statute of Frauds. Generally, the beneficiary must have been allowed to take *possession* of the property *plus* (in many jurisdictions) done *some other act* (*e.g.,* repair, payment of taxes), or the beneficiary must have been allowed *beneficial use* or otherwise been distributed fruits of the trust property. The trustee must be involved in (or approve) the acts relied upon to show the *trustee's acknowledgment* of the trust. Acts of part performance may also cure certain ineffective transfers.

e. Effect of Statute—Bar to Enforcement

An oral trust of real property is not void; it is merely unenforceable against the title holder. If the trustee is *willing* to perform the trust, others have no right to object. Nonetheless, transfer of legal title to a *bona fide purchaser cuts off latent equities* (*i.e.,* a beneficiary's interest).

f. Constructive Trust Remedy

If the trustee is not willing to perform and the trust is unenforceable under the Statute of Frauds, the intended beneficiaries or the grantor may have a constructive trust remedy. A constructive trust may be imposed if the conveyance was obtained by *fraud, mistake, duress, undue influence, abuse of confidential relationship,* or in *contemplation of the transferor's death.* Parol evidence *is* admissible to prove the trust intent and wrongful conduct.

(1) No Wrongful Conduct

Where no fraud or special circumstances can be shown, the courts are split as to whether a constructive trust can be imposed merely to prevent unjust enrichment. The position of many states allows the trustee to keep the land, but the modern trend is to favor imposition of a constructive trust.

5. Parol Evidence Rule

Where a writing *clearly establishes* or *clearly precludes* a trust, parol evidence is *inadmissible*. If an instrument is *ambiguous* as to whether there is a trust, parol evidence is *admissible*. If the instrument is *silent* as to a trust, the majority (and Restatement) position admits parol evidence to *supplement* an incomplete writing.

C. CREATION OF TESTAMENTARY TRUSTS

1. Requirements of Wills Act

A testamentary trust is one created by the will of a decedent. The will (plus other evidence that satisfies the wills act) must provide *all essential elements* of a trust (although the court will appoint a trustee, if necessary). In addition to the will itself and any codicils, the trust terms may be proved through the doctrines of *facts of independent significance* and *incorporation by reference*.

2. Secret Trusts—Oral Trust of Outright Bequest or Devise

Where a decedent's will devises property in reliance on a devisee's oral promise to hold property in trust for others, a "secret trust" arises. The oral trust agreement is *unenforceable* under the wills act but may be voluntarily performed by the devisee-trustee.

a. Constructive Trust Remedy

If the devisee fails to perform, a constructive trust will be imposed in most states. No proof of fraud, undue influence, etc., is required. The majority would impose the trust in favor of the *intended beneficiaries*, but a minority of cases impose a constructive trust in favor of the *decedent's estate*.

b. Distinguish—Semi-Secret Trusts

There is a *split of authority* where the will indicates that the property is devised to someone *in trust*, but *fails to specify a beneficiary*. Many courts would find a resulting trust for the testator's heirs. Other courts would impose a constructive trust for the intended beneficiary.

c. Breach of Agreement by Intestate Heir

Secret trust principles also apply where the decedent died intestate, forgoing the opportunity to make a will in reliance on a promise by an heir to hold property in trust for another.

D. REVOCABLE INTER VIVOS TRUSTS AS WILL SUBSTITUTES—SPECIAL PROBLEMS

1. Historical Issue—Is a Revocable Trust "Testamentary"?

Revocable trusts pose a special problem. Because the settlor often retains benefits along with the right to revoke, a court may find the trust "illusory" and hold that no trust was presently created. In such a case, the trust having failed, the assets become part of the would-be settlor's probate estate. The issue then becomes whether the trust document could serve as a testamentary instrument, which it likely cannot unless it was executed with testamentary formalities and testamentary intent. The courts often ask whether *any interest really has passed* to beneficiaries in the settlor's lifetime and look for the settlor's *intent* to create more than a "mere agency."

2. Modern Approach

Modern authority recognizes that the settlor can validly create a nontestamentary trust even while retaining extensive powers or serving as trustee. There *must*, however, be an *intention* to create a trust, a specific trust *res*, and the trust must create some interests in some category of beneficiaries *other than the settlor* (although these may be future interests, vested or contingent, and they may be revocable).

3. Special Types of Revocable Trusts

a. Life Insurance Trusts

A transfer of a life insurance policy to the trustee of a revocable or irrevocable trust is valid, with the policy itself being the trust property. Despite the similarity of *revocable* life insurance trusts to testamentary dispositions, the courts have consistently *upheld* them, even with no transfer of the policy but with a mere (even revocable) designation of the trustee as payee of the policy proceeds. They are upheld on the basis that such trusts are no more testamentary than other revocable trusts, and either that the property is the trustee's right as a beneficiary of the policy (chose in action) or that the trust is created at the insured's death by operation of contract.

b. "Totten Trusts"—Savings Deposit or "Tentative" Trusts

Where money is deposited in a bank or savings institution in the depositor's own name *"in trust for" another*, questions arise as to real trust intent or testamentary nature of the "trust." Most authorities presume that this creates a *valid, revocable trust*. Revocation occurs to the extent the depositor writes a check or otherwise *withdraws funds*. These Totten trusts differ from other trusts in that the depositor's creditors *can* reach the assets in most states, and the trust *terminates* if the named beneficiary predeceases the depositor-settlor. On the depositor's death, funds left in the account belong to the beneficiary and are not part of the depositor's estate. Evidence, including the depositor's statements and conduct, is admissible to show the depositor's intent.

3. Revocable Trusts and Substantive Policies

a. Elective Share of Surviving Spouse

Sometimes a settlor will transfer property into a revocable trust to attempt to avoid the surviving spouse's statutory forced share (also called an elective share). The majority view at common law *allows* this, provided the trust is not illusory or a "mere agency." Many states have adopted statutes and a number have decisions allowing the surviving spouse to assert rights in the property even if the trust is not illusory. Even in states that allow the use of a revocable trust to avoid the forced share, rights of dower or curtesy and community property rights *cannot* be circumvented.

b. Taxation, Creditors, and Charitable Restrictions

Under the Internal Revenue Code and most state laws, transfers of property into a revocable trust achieve *no beneficial change in tax position*. Absent legislation, property in a revocable trust is generally *not reachable by creditors*. The few statutes that now limit bequests to *charity* are generally held *not* to invalidate revocable inter vivos trusts for charitable purposes.

IV. RIGHTS OF BENEFICIARIES AND BENEFICIARIES' CREDITORS IN THE BENEFICIARIES' INTEREST

A. MANDATORY VERSUS DISCRETIONARY LANGUAGE

1. Mandatory Language Effect on Beneficiary's and Creditor's Rights

If the trustee fails to make mandatory distributions as outlined in the trust instrument, the beneficiary can likely successfully sue the trustee for breach of the trustee's duties. Because the beneficiary has a right to demand mandatory distributions, a creditor of a beneficiary, who will stand in the beneficiary's shoes, can petition a court to seize the distributions.

2. Discretionary Language Effect on Beneficiary's and Creditor's Rights

If a trustee does not make discretionary distributions as permitted in the trust instrument, the beneficiary does not have a right to force a distribution. Likewise, because the beneficiary has no right to demand discretionary distributions, a creditor of a beneficiary generally has no access to the property either.

a. Standards of Support

Watch for language that may limit the trustee's discretion, such as standards of support. In such instance, the beneficiary (and hence the beneficiary's creditors) may compel a distribution if the trustee does not comply with the standard.

b. Exception Creditors

Special creditors, such as a spouse, former spouse, or child with a support order, may be able to compel a distribution—even in a discretionary trust.

B. RESTRAINTS ON ALIENATION—SPENDTHRIFT AND RELATED TRUSTS

1. In General

Most states allow the beneficiaries' interests to be conditioned or limited to prevent or impair transferability.

2. Spendthrift Trusts

Spendthrift trusts prevent voluntary transfer or involuntary transfer of a beneficiary's interest in the trust. Thus, the beneficiary cannot sell, assign, or give away the beneficiary's rights, nor can the beneficiary's creditors levy on or attach such rights. These trusts are to protect the beneficiary from the beneficiary's own improvidence. Spendthrift trusts are valid in *nearly all* states. No special wording is required as long as the settlor's intent is clear.

a. Effect of Spendthrift Provision

Spendthrift provisions are generally given literal effect, except that some states require that limits on involuntary transfers be coupled with limits on voluntary transfers. Some statutes also allow creditors to reach a percentage of the beneficiary's interest or any excess over the amount needed for support.

(1) Effect of Attempted Transfer

If the beneficiary tries to assign the beneficiary's interest, the assignee *cannot enforce* the assignment over the beneficiary's objection; *i.e.*, the purported assignment is, in effect, *revocable*.

(2) Creditor's Rights

If there is a valid spendthrift provision, creditors are generally *barred from reaching* the beneficiary's interest in the trust. Once monies are *paid* to the beneficiary from the trust, creditors *can* attach and execute on those monies paid to the beneficiary.

(a) "Breaking Through" Spendthrift Restraints

Some classes of creditors may "break through" spendthrift provisions. Although states may differ on which creditors may "break through," the Restatement lists: (i) the federal or state *government* (*e.g.*, tax claims); (ii) a spouse (or ex-spouse) or child seeking *support*; (iii) providers of *necessaries*; and (iv) one who *"preserves the interest"* of a beneficiary (*e.g.*, attorney). *Note: Some* or all of these creditors can "break through" in *most* states. A limited number of states may permit some tort creditors to "break through."

b. Spendthrift Clause Cannot Protect Settlor's Retained Interest

The owner of property cannot create a spendthrift trust for themself. Interests retained by the settlor are reachable by the settlor's creditors.

(1) Spouse-Beneficiary Who Elects Against Trust

The fact that the beneficiary is the settlor's surviving spouse and had the right to (but did not) reject the testamentary trust and demand a share of the settlor's estate does not make the spouse a settlor so as to allow the spouse's creditors to reach the trust interest.

c. Arguments for and Against Spendthrift Trusts

(1) Against

There is a violation of the concept of "symmetry of estates" (*i.e.,* there is no reason to treat equitable estates differently from legal estates), and public policy favors having propertied persons pay their creditors.

(2) For

The donee and the donee's creditors had no right to the property, which the settlor was free to withhold; therefore, the settlor should have the right to dispose of the property with qualifications.

3. Protective Trusts

A protective trust ordinarily pays out income regularly but, upon attempted voluntary or involuntary alienation of the beneficiary's interest, becomes a discretionary trust. These trusts are widely used in England and sometimes in American states that do not allow or significantly limit spendthrift trusts.

4. Support Trusts

What is sometimes called a "support trust" directs the trustee to make distributions as necessary for the *education and maintenance* of the beneficiary, and to expend trust funds *only for that purpose*. Traditionally, in some states, the beneficiary's interest is neither assignable nor reachable by creditors.

5. Blended Trusts

Where the trust is for the benefit of a group of persons, and no member of the group has an interest separate and apart from the others, the interest is said to be "blended" with that of every other beneficiary. Such interests are not assignable and are unreachable by creditors.

6. Distinctions Questioned

Most trusts that grant trustees discretion regarding distributions contain standards usually related to support. Thus, the distinctions above are highly artificial and increasingly disfavored.

V. CHARITABLE TRUSTS

A. GENERAL NATURE AND TREATMENT OF CHARITABLE TRUSTS

1. Creation and Purpose of Trust

A charitable trust is created in the same manner as a private trust (by will, inter vivos transfer, or declaration), but it is established for a purpose that the law regards as charitable (*i.e.,* benefiting the public or a reasonably broad and appropriate segment thereof).

2. **Charitable Purposes**

Purposes recognized as charitable include: (i) relief of *poverty*; (ii) advancement of *knowledge or education*; (iii) advancement of *religion*; (iv) promotion of *health*; (v) *governmental or municipal purposes*; and (vi) other purposes *beneficial to the community*.

3. **Charitable Trusts Favored**

Charitable trusts are favored by the law and receive special privileges.

B. REQUIREMENT OF PUBLIC, NOT PRIVATE, BENEFIT

1. **Indefinite Beneficiaries and the Public Benefit Requirement**

A charitable trust must be for the public benefit generally or for some members of a class of the public that is *indefinite in number*. A charitable trust, unlike a private trust, does *not* require definite, designated beneficiaries. The state attorney general is usually authorized to enforce charitable trusts on behalf of the community. A co-trustee, successor trustee, or person having a "special interest" in the performance of the trust (which traditionally does *not* include the settlor) also has standing to enforce the trust.

    a. **Effect of Limited Number of Direct Beneficiaries**

    Problems arise where a trust requires selection of a limited number of actual recipients or where the eligible group of potential recipients is limited. The modern view allows such trusts if the category from which the individual(s) are chosen is *substantial in size* and *indefinite in membership* and if the benefit to the recipient is *sufficiently within the general public interest*. The outmoded view held that the benefit had to be "substantial," and where only a few persons were benefited the substantiality test was *not* met.

2. **Effect of Trust Having Noncharitable Co-Beneficiaries**

Where the trust has both charitable purposes and noncharitable purposes or where the purposes are broader than those allowed for charitable trusts, it does not qualify as a charitable trust unless a separate amount, share, or interest is provided for the charitable purpose (*i.e.,* a trust *cannot* have intermingled charitable and private purposes and qualify as a charitable trust).

C. CHARITABLE PURPOSE DEFINED

1. **Meaning of "Purpose" and "Charitable"**

The purpose of the charitable trust (or charitable portion) must be *exclusively charitable*. The *purpose* for which the trust is created (the ultimate objective of the trust) is the controlling factor, rather than the settlor's *motive* for establishing the trust. The term "charitable" does not include everything that a settlor may consider to be useful and worthwhile, but only what courts consider *sufficiently desirable to the public*. A trust to promote a cause that is *illegal, immoral, irrational*, or otherwise *contrary to public policy* will *not* be upheld as charitable. The purpose must be sufficiently well-defined so that the court can determine (i) what the settlor intended, and (ii) whether the purpose is exclusively charitable. Trusts "for charity" are upheld, but terms like "for benevolent purposes" have sometimes been held to be unduly broad. The modern tendency is to construe potentially broader terms as limited to charitable purposes.

2. **Particular Charitable Purposes**

    a. **Relief of Poverty**

    This is a charitable purpose per se. A trust that significantly benefits indigents is acceptable even if some nonindigents may share (*e.g.,* trust for parentless children).

    b. **Education**

    A trust to improve the minds of indefinite members of the public is valid. This may be done through support of schools, museums, etc. Those receiving the benefits of an educational trust need *not* be impoverished. Trusts that provide for the education of one's *own descendants* are *not* charitable, nor are trusts for the financial benefit of *profit-making institutions*.

    (1) **Politics and Change of Law**

    The modern trend is to approve trusts for the dissemination of particular *political views*, but a trust for the promotion of a *particular political party is noncharitable*. Trusts for general *"improvement of the law"* are valid, but trusts to bring about *particular* changes in the law may or may not be.

    c. **Religion**

    Maintenance and support of religion by providing for religious services, places of worship, salary of clergy, etc., are charitable purposes per se. Most states also allow trusts providing for masses to be said for the soul of the settlor. The usual problem with religious trusts is determining what constitutes a "religion." Practically any doctrine having numerous adherents in the community is acceptable, but certain beliefs (*e.g.,* spiritualism) have sometimes been found to be irrational and of no widespread interest, and trusts to promote *atheism* might be found to be nonreligious (although they may be educational).

    d. **Health**

    The cure of disease and promotion of health are charitable purposes per se. Nonindigents may benefit from such a trust, but such a trust may not be designed to enhance profit-making.

    e. **Governmental Purposes**

    A trust for governmental or municipal purposes is charitable because there is general community interest in the functioning of government. Trusts for prevention of suffering of *indefinite groups* of domestic or wild *animals* are valid, but trusts for maintenance of particular animals (*e.g.,* my cat) are not (unless as honorary trusts).

3. **Other Charitable and Noncharitable Purposes**

The general standard for charitable purposes, applied subjectively by courts, is a *benefit to the public or indefinite members thereof*. Perpetual care of graves is a questionable trust purpose but is usually permitted by statute. It is not certain that trusts "for the elderly," if not limited to poor persons, are of appropriate benefit to the community. Trusts to aid private social clubs or lodges, for the preservation and display of the settlor's collections (when not of general community interest), and for the erection of monuments to the settlor have been held to be noncharitable. If a trust fails as a charitable trust, it may nevertheless qualify as a *private trust* if it meets private trust requirements regarding definiteness of beneficiaries, Rule Against

Perpetuities, etc., or possibly as an *honorary trust* if it is for an allowable honorary purpose.

4. **Profit-Making or Private Purpose Not Charitable**

Although the *trustee* of a charitable trust may be a profit-making institution (*e.g.*, a bank), the *purposes* must not be for the benefit of a profit-making institution. It is not objectionable if benefits for a profit-making institution are *only incidental* or trust funds for charitable purposes are *segregated*.

a. **"Split-Interest" Trusts**

It is not objectionable if property is to be devoted to private purposes for one period of time and exclusively to charitable purposes for another. Split-interest trusts are common in the form of *charitable remainder trusts* and *charitable lead trusts*.

5. **Conditional Gifts to Charity**

If conditions of gift might prevent the charitable interest in the property from being used exclusively for charitable purposes, the trust will *not* qualify as charitable. *Exceptions:* A condition that an activity supported by a trust be named after the settlor, and a conditional amount of gift (*e.g.*, matching funds) do not affect the charitable status of the trust.

D. **LIMITATIONS ON CHARITABLE TRUSTS**

1. **Charitable Limitations**

Few, if any, states currently restrict dispositions that may be left by will to charity. Such statutes have generally limited amounts given or devises to charity if the will was made shortly before the testator's death. Such statutes *were not generally applicable to inter vivos trusts*, even if the trust instrument was executed shortly before the settlor's death or the settlor retained a life interest and the power to revoke. Such legislation was, however, applicable to *constructive trusts* that might be imposed upon property passing by will. Some states had similar legislation applying only to charitable corporations.

2. **Charities and the Rule Against Perpetuities**

The Rule against Perpetuities does *not apply* to the *duration* of charitable trusts, but the Rule *does* apply to the *vesting* of charitable gifts. Benefits of a charitable trust may shift from one charity to another even after expiration of the perpetuities period, provided that the trust has "vested in charity."

3. **Constitutional Limitations on Charitable Purposes**

A state agency may *not* serve as trustee for a trust that furthers racial or other prohibited discrimination. "State action" may, in fact, be inherently characteristic of *all* charitable trusts today, although this question is unsettled.

E. **MODIFICATION OF CHARITABLE TRUSTS—THE CY PRES DOCTRINE**

1. **Nature and Requirements of Cy Pres**

Because a charitable trust may endure indefinitely, it sometimes outlives the purposes for which it was established. Courts may *modify* the trust to apply the trust in a manner approximating the settlor's plan. To invoke the doctrine: (i) the settlor's purpose must be *fulfilled or frustrated*; and (ii) traditionally, the settlor must have had a *general charitable intent*. In such cases, a court will apply the trust benefits to a charitable purpose reasonably similar to that set forth by the settlor.

2. Application of Cy Pres

Merely finding that a "better" purpose is available for the trust benefits is not sufficient to apply cy pres. At the very least, pursuit of the trust's original charitable purpose(s) must be "impracticable." If a settlor has provided a valid *express gift over* in case the charitable purpose fails, that provision will be honored if it does not violate the Rule Against Perpetuities. Because cy pres traditionally is to be applied only where consistent with the probable wishes of the settlor, it may *not* be invoked if the settlor really intended to benefit only a *particular* charity or charitable purpose *and no other*. Once a court decides to apply cy pres, it must modify the trust in such a way as to approximate *as nearly as reasonable* the settlor's original purpose. *Note:* Today, courts will presume a general charitable intent and the party opposing cy pres will need to establish a specific charitable intent.

VI. DUTIES, POWERS AND LIABILITY OF THE TRUSTEE

A. TRUSTEE DUTIES

1. In General

A trustee's conduct must conform to standards of law and to the requirements of the trust instrument. Questions to ask are whether the act was *authorized*, and if the act was, whether performance was consistent with *fiduciary standards and duties*.

2. Duty to Administer Trust According to Its Terms

A trustee is under a duty to carry out the trust and to administer the trust estate in accordance with the terms of the trust and applicable law.

a. Duty to Perform Personally—Question of Delegation

A trustee may delegate *ministerial* functions; *discretionary* functions may be delegated only when *necessary* (under the traditional view) or when *reasonable and prudent* under the circumstances (under the modern view). Discretionary powers over *distributions* are nondelegable even under the modern view. No matter what type of function is delegated, the trustee must act with prudence—proper care, skill, and caution—in the *selection and monitoring* of employees and in arranging the terms of the agency. A trustee may seek advice related to nondelegable duties (*e.g.,* of lawyers or investment counselors), but the trustee must make the decisions.

(1) Liability for Losses Caused by Agents

If a trustee delegates a *nondelegable* duty, the trustee is *absolutely liable* (*i.e.,* as a guarantor) to the beneficiaries for any resulting loss. If the duty is *delegable* and the trustee has used proper care, the trustee is ordinarily *not liable*. The trustee is normally liable in the trustee's representative capacity (not personally, absent fault) to *third parties* for the agent's negligence, although ordinarily not for the agent's dishonesty or if the delegation was to an independent contractor.

b. Duty with Respect to Other Trustees

Each co-trustee is responsible for all functions in the administration of the entire trust, and each must use reasonable care to prevent a co-trustee from committing a breach of trust. A trustee is generally *not* liable for breaches of a predecessor trustee, *unless* the trustee *knew or should have known* of the breach and failed to redress the breach *or negligently failed* to rectify a breach.

c. **Duty Under a Directory Provision**

Where the trustee is directed to follow instructions of a third party (*e.g.,* a particular investment advisor), the trustee has a **duty** to do so. A trustee, however, must be watchful to avoid committing a breach of trust on improper instructions.

3. **Duty of Prudence—Standard of Care, Skill, and Caution**

A trustee must exercise that degree of care, skill, and caution that a **reasonably prudent person** would use in administering **similar property for similar purposes**, although some courts still use (and purport to distinguish between) a standard a prudent person would use in administering either "their **own** property" or "the property of **others**."

a. **Trustees with Special Skills**

If a trustee has (or holds out as having) special or superior skills, knowledge, or facilities, the trustee is under a duty to exercise such advantages. A professional fiduciary (*e.g.,* a bank) is generally held to higher standards than a lay trustee.

4. **Duty of Loyalty to Beneficiaries**

A trustee has a duty of **absolute loyalty** to beneficiaries and must not engage in self-dealing or enter into conflict-of-interest situations. (The exception involving unavoidable conflicts of loyalty to diverse beneficiaries is discussed as a **duty of impartiality**, *supra*.)

a. **Transactions with Trust Estate**

A trustee may not deal personally with trust estate assets; if the trustee does, beneficiaries have the power to **set aside** such transactions.

(1) **Compensation**

A trustee may be entitled to compensation for services rendered and reimbursement of reasonable expenses if the trust is silent. The trust instrument may define the permissible compensation. Such payment of compensation or reimbursement of reasonable expenses is not a prohibited transaction with the trust. Note that the trust instrument may prohibit compensation.

b. **Transactions with Beneficiary**

Although such transactions are not flatly prohibited, a trustee must act with **utmost fairness and openness** in personal dealings with trust beneficiaries, and has the burden of proving that such action was fair.

c. **Specific Types of Transactions**

(1) **Loans**

It is improper for a trustee to **borrow from the trust** estate. While the trustee is generally not permitted **to lend** funds to the trust, the rule appears to be that the trustee may do so only if there is a legitimate need for cash and **other sources** of money are **not reasonably available**.

(2) **Compensation from Third Person**

A trustee may **not** accept compensation from a third person for an act done in administering the trust, **unless** (under appropriate circumstances) the compensation is paid for the trustee's additional services or services on the board of directors.

(3) Self-Employment

A trustee ordinarily may not be compensated for services to the trust beyond those ordinarily required of a trustee. If services performed are not an aspect of the trustee's duties as trustee, it is often prohibited self-dealing for the trustee to engage the trustee themself for the rendering of such services. In many states, the view is that a trustee with special skills (*e.g.,* an attorney) is expected to use those special skills at least in routine circumstances, and that those services may be taken into account in determining reasonable compensation as trustee.

d. Special Problems of Corporate Trustees

A trustee bank may not purchase its own shares but may be allowed to retain such shares if expressly or impliedly authorized (*e.g.,* specific bequest of those shares to the trust). Generally, a trustee bank may not deposit trust funds in its own bank, although some states allow this if the prevailing rate of interest is paid.

(1) Commingled Investment of Trust Funds

Under modern authority, it is permissible for a trustee of two or more trusts to pool assets or to purchase common investments.

e. Exceptions to Loyalty-Based Prohibitions

Self-dealing may be allowed *if* permitted by trust terms (expressly or by clear implication), authorized by court order, or consented to by all possible beneficiaries.

5. Duty to Collect and Safeguard Trust Estate

A trustee has a duty to take and keep control of trust property in accordance with trust terms. The trustee has an affirmative duty to *collect and take possession of* trust assets, to *preserve* the assets of the trust (*e.g.,* inspect periodically, pay taxes, etc.), and to *defend* the trust from attack (even by the settlor). The trustee is entitled to *indemnification* for expenses reasonably incurred in defending the trust.

a. Duty to Insure

A trustee has a duty to obtain insurance on trust assets (including liability insurance) when it is prudent to do so.

6. Duty to Segregate and Identify (Earmark)

A trustee must keep trust assets *separate* from the trustee's individual assets and earmark property so as to identify it as property of the particular trust estate. *Exception:* Corporate trustees are generally permitted to hold property of numerous trust estates in common funds for investment purposes.

a. Liability in Event of Loss

Under the traditional rule, a trustee is *absolutely liable* for any loss that befalls trust property that is not properly earmarked, but a modern trend is to hold a trustee responsible only for losses *caused by failure* to earmark.

7. Duty to Account

A trustee owes a duty to keep records and render clear and accurate reports with respect to the administration of the trust.

8. Duty to Invest and Make Property Productive

A trustee normally has a duty promptly and continuously to make trust property productive. Reasonable care and skill must be used to procure a reasonable rate of yield for income beneficiaries (except as accounting techniques may compensate for inadequate or excessive income productivity). This duty includes the duty to rid the trust of unproductive, underproductive, or overproductive ("wasting") assets, at least if such property would render the trust estate as a whole underproductive or overproductive of trust accounting income.

a. Standards for Trust Investments

Under the traditional analysis of investments, the basic questions have been: (i) was the investment a proper *type* for trust holding, and (ii) was a *particular* investment selected with the requisite degree of care and skill? Trust instruments may specify that particular types of investments are authorized or prohibited. *Statutory lists* of approved fiduciary investments still exist in a few states for a few purposes.

(1) "Prudent Person" Rule

The "prudent person" (historically termed the "prudent man") rule over time came to be adopted by nearly all jurisdictions but few, if any, still follow it today. The trustee was and is today held to a standard of good faith and of care, skill, and caution in making investments. But under the "prudent person" rule, subrules generally evolved to establish that certain categories of investments were or were not permissible for trust investing.

(2) "Prudent Investor" Rule

The Third Restatement and the Uniform Prudent Investor Act advanced a quite different and modernized rule for trust investment law. The so-called "prudent investor" principles now prevail, in one form or another, in the trust law of all states. The "prudent investor" rule judges an investment not in isolation but as a part of the *trust portfolio as a whole*, with suitable levels of risk depending on the contents, terms, and purposes of the particular trust and the circumstances of that trust and its beneficiaries. This rule gives increased emphasis to diversification and is much more flexible with respect to suitable levels of risk while preserving the duty of loyalty and attempting to clarify the duty of impartiality. Prudent delegation is authorized, and the rule also adds emphasis to the trustee's duty to be cost conscious in investing.

b. Standards Under Rules of Prudence

The trustee has a *duty of impartiality* and therefore must consider the interests of *remainder beneficiaries* as well as income beneficiaries. Propriety of investment is determined as of *time of investment*, and the trustee must dispose of investments that are or later become "unsuitable" to the trust; the trustee will be personally liable for losses resulting from unreasonable retention even of original ("inception") assets. A trustee must also *diversify* investments. While the traditional view has emphasized the nature of *each particular investment* rather than the content and management of the trust fund as a whole, the modern theory calls for substantial diversification on an *overall portfolio basis*. The terms of a trust may alter the rule's application to the particular trust.

c. Specific Types of Trust Investments

The modern rule asserts that no investment is per se or even presumptively imprudent. An investment's propriety depends on its role in the trust portfolio and all of the trust's holdings and circumstances at the time.

(1) Common or Commingled Investment Devices

The modern rule allows the creation and use of common (*i.e.,* pooled) trust funds by corporate trustees and investment in mortgage participations, mutual funds, real estate investment trusts ("REITs"), and the like by all trustees.

B. POWERS OF THE TRUSTEE

1. Meaning and Nature of Trustee "Powers"

The term "power" refers to the authority expressly or impliedly conferred upon the trustee by trust provision or by law—*i.e.,* acts the trustee may perform. Authority to perform a particular act, however, does not remove the possibility of violating a duty (*e.g.,* by exercising that authority negligently, unreasonably, or arbitrarily).

2. Powers Generally

If a trustee has *no powers*, but merely holds title to the res, the trust is *passive*. If it appears that the settlor intended to create more than a passive trust and no powers are stated in the trust instrument, powers appropriate (some have said "necessary") to carry out the trust purposes are *implied by law*. Nonetheless, powers will *not* be implied if doing so would be contrary to the terms of the trust (except for court-authorized deviation under certain circumstances).

3. What Powers Are Implied as "Appropriate"?

Unless a trust instrument so forbids, the following powers are generally held to be implied: power to *sell, lease,* and *incur reasonable management and other expenses* (normally including the power to make *improvements*). Traditionally, there is *no* implied power to *encumber* (*e.g.,* mortgage) trust assets, but this and other limits are increasingly being abandoned. The law does not confer an implied power to invade the trust corpus for the benefit of a life income beneficiary.

4. "Imperative" vs. "Discretionary" Powers

Most trust powers are *discretionary* (*i.e.,* trustee is expected to use the trustee's *judgment* as to whether and how to exercise). If, however, the trustee is required to perform a particular act, the power is *imperative* (or "mandatory") and a court will order performance upon petition by the beneficiary. Courts limit review of discretionary powers to whether the trustee has *abused* its discretion.

5. Who May Exercise Trust Powers

a. Co-Trustees

Co-trustees hold powers *jointly* unless the trust instrument or a statute states otherwise. Under traditional doctrine, co-trustees must act *unanimously*, but the modern trend allows three or more trustees to act by *majority* vote. Each co-trustee owes a duty of prudent participation and is liable to beneficiaries for the co-trustee's own improper or negligent acts and for failure to prevent or remedy acts of another co-trustee. If administration is stalled because of an inability of co-trustees to agree, a court may direct the trustee action.

b. Delegation of Powers to Third Persons (Agents)

Under the modern view, a trustee has power to employ agents to perform various acts and exercise management powers granted to him as long as the delegation is consistent with the general duties of care, skill, and caution. If power is delegable, a trustee has a duty of care in *selecting, contracting with, and supervising* (or monitoring) agents.

c. Successor Trustees and "Personal" Powers

Unless the trust instrument provides or circumstances clearly indicate otherwise, powers granted to a trustee are *not personal* to the particular trustee originally named. Accordingly, trust powers may be exercised by successor or substitute trustees.

C. TRUSTEE'S LIABILITIES AND BENEFICIARIES' REMEDIES

1. Standing to Enforce Trust

Usually, only *beneficiaries* (or co-trustees, successor trustees, or other fiduciaries on the beneficiaries' behalf) have standing to complain of a breach of trust and to surcharge the trustee for the trustee's actions.

2. Beneficiaries' Remedies

Equitable remedies for breach of trust include injunction, removal of trustee, and constructive trust. Where *damages* are sought, a trustee is personally liable to the trust estate or to the beneficiaries (*i.e.,* is "surcharged") for any *loss or depreciation in value* of the trust estate and *loss of income* resulting from that breach of trust. (Some cases, in which the trustee has made an improper investment, have compared income and corpus values of the trust with the values that would have resulted from proper investment, thus surcharging the trustee for lost appreciation based on the performance of similar trust funds or some index deemed appropriate.) *Gains* from improper investments *cannot* properly be offset against losses, unless both arise from the *same* breach of trust. A trustee may be charged *interest* on amounts owing to the trust or beneficiaries because of a breach of trust. Any personal profits made by the trustee through a breach must be disgorged to beneficiaries.

a. Relief from Liability

(1) Exculpatory Clause

If an exculpatory clause (also called an exoneration clause) is included in a trust instrument, it will generally relieve the trustee of liability for *negligence*, but *not* for intentional breach of trust or gross negligence. Such clauses are *narrowly construed*.

(2) Consent of Beneficiaries

Where *all* beneficiaries consent to a trustee's action, the trustee may be free from liability. In cases where not all beneficiaries consent, those who *do* consent are ordinarily estopped from pressing their claims.

(3) Limitations Periods

Statutes of limitations (where applicable to equitable claims) or the doctrine of *laches* may bar action if a beneficiary is dilatory in pursuing a claim.

(4) Trustee's Insolvency

In bankruptcy or other insolvency proceedings, questions of priority among beneficiaries may arise. Bankruptcy will *discharge* a trustee's liability, but not with respect to losses caused by fraud, embezzlement, or other intentional misappropriation. Generally, beneficiaries share *pro rata* in the available recovery against an insolvent trustee.

(5) Good Faith

A few cases have considered a trustee's reasonable and good faith effort to understand and perform the trustee's duties in mitigating recovery by the trust or its beneficiaries.

D. TRUSTEE'S LIABILITY TO THIRD PARTIES

1. Contract Liability

Traditionally, the trustee (as principal), rather than the trust estate, is *personally liable* to all parties with whom the trustee contracts in the trustee's fiduciary capacity (unless liability is limited in the contract or a statute provides otherwise). A trustee who signs a negotiable instrument "as trustee" has probably negated personal liability, and the holder has an action against the trust estate (*i.e.*, against the trustee only in the trustee's *fiduciary capacity*). Statutes in most states and a few decisions, absent a breach of trust, eliminate the personal liability of the trustee and only the trust estate is liable.

a. Indemnification

Under the traditional rule, a trustee has the right of indemnification against the trust estate, providing the trustee has acted properly in making the contract. The right of indemnification includes the right to pay the liability directly from the trust fund (*"exoneration"*), or from the trustee's own funds and then obtain *"reimbursement"* from the trust estate. A trustee may be indemnified for the reasonable costs of legal defense, *unless* the suit arises out of a breach of duty by the trustee. An insolvent trustee's indemnification rights *may* generally be *reached by the trustee's creditors*.

2. Tort Liability

Traditionally, a trustee is *personally liable* for torts committed by the trustee or the trustee's agents, with a right of *indemnification* from the trust estate if the trustee is not personally at fault. It has been held that trustees of *charitable* trusts were not personally liable for the acts of agents selected with due care; but the modern trend of authority (especially by statute) is, again, that absent personal fault on the part of the trustee, liability is only in the representative (*i.e.,* fiduciary) capacity.

E. DUTIES AND LIABILITIES OF BENEFICIARIES

1. Beneficiaries' Duties Generally

Unless a beneficiary is also a trustee or unless an obligation is imposed by the trust instrument, a beneficiary owes *no affirmative duties* to co-beneficiaries or the trust estate.

a. Breach of Trust

A beneficiary does owe a duty to other beneficiaries not to participate in a breach of trust by the trustee or to profit (even innocently) from the trustee's breach. *Mere consent* is generally *not* considered to be *"participation"* in a breach of trust. An innocent beneficiary who profits from a breach of trust is liable only to the extent of the improper benefit—*i.e., "unjust enrichment"* (unless such beneficiary has changed position in good faith reliance). A beneficiary who *participates* in a breach is also liable for damage to the trust estate or other beneficiaries.

b. Indemnification

A beneficiary has *no duty* to indemnify a trustee, unless the beneficiary has contracted to do so.

2. Remedies Against Beneficiary

A beneficiary may be personally liable if the beneficiary has benefited from or participated in a breach of trust. The beneficial interest in the trust is then subject to a *lien or charge*. Thus, except as "inequitable," the benefits are suspended and impounded until the trust estate is restored and obligations to other beneficiaries have been paid.

a. Creditors and Assignees

Creditors and donees of a beneficiary who has acted improperly are generally *subordinated* to the rights of the trust estate and other beneficiaries.

F. LIABILITIES OF THIRD PARTIES

1. Generally and for Breach of Trust

a. Debts Owed

Where a third party is indebted to the trust estate, commits a tort with respect to the trust estate, or is in breach of contract with the trust, the *trustee* has a right to maintain suit against the third party. Under modern doctrine, a *beneficiary* may, by joining the trustee, sue the third party if the trustee fails to pursue the claim.

b. Breach of Trust—Third Party Participation with Trustee

A third party who participates with a trustee in a breach of trust may be liable to the beneficiaries if the third party had *notice* of the trustee's intent to misapply money or other property.

2. Third Party's Acquisition of Trust Property

If a transfer of property by the trustee to a third party involved a breach of trust by the trustee, *donee-transferees* and *non-bona fide purchasers* take *subject to* the beneficiaries' rights. *Bona fide purchasers* (*i.e.,* purchasers who take for value without notice of breach) take good title *free of* other beneficial interests.

VII. ACCOUNTING FOR INCOME AND PRINCIPAL

A. INTRODUCTION

1. General Nature of Principal-Income Problem

In the typical trust, interests are divided between *income beneficiaries* and *remainder* beneficiaries. Economically conflicting rights turn on whether receipts or expenditures are classified as "income" or "principal." The problem is moot in cases of wholly discretionary trusts.

2. Sources and Priority of Accounting Rules

The terms of a trust govern principal-income accounting questions. For matters not covered by the trust instrument, all states have enacted principal-income legislation, most by adopting a version of either the 1962 Revised Uniform Principal and Income

Act or the 1997 Uniform Act. Trust accounting rules often differ from general accounting principles. Trust terms may give the trustee private "rulemaking" authority; such discretion tends to be broadly construed by some courts and narrowly by others. The law is designed, and a trustee's judgment is expected, to reflect the fiduciary duty of *impartiality*. (The 1997 Act grants the trustee the power of *equitable adjustment* to compensate a beneficiary whose interest suffers under the trustee's investment plan in a manner inconsistent with the duty of impartiality.)

B. SPECIFIC RULES OF TRUST PRINCIPAL-INCOME ACCOUNTING

1. Allocation Rules Are Default Rules

Where the trust instrument is silent, some specific rules are applied.

2. Allocation of Benefits (Essentially Receipts)

The general rule is that *ordinary* receipts are "trust income," while *extraordinary* receipts are trust capital.

a. Timing of Receipts

An income beneficiary is generally entitled to net income from the *date of creation* of an *inter vivos trust* and from the *date of the testator's death* in the case of a *testamentary trust*. A frequent issue between successive beneficiaries is whether income received after the testator's death or life beneficiary's death should be allocated on a basis of when *received* or when *accrued*. Under the common law, receipts were allocable to whomever was income beneficiary when the trustee received the income (*exception:* interest), but modern statutes may *apportion* all income except dividends.

b. Dividends

Ordinary cash dividends are treated as *income*. Extraordinary dividends (including stock dividends) are generally treated as *principal* but still generate a split of authority.

(1) "Massachusetts Rule" (Modern Statutory View)

Stock dividends (in stock of declaring corporation), as well as stock splits, are *principal*. Extraordinary cash dividends and stock dividends in stock of other companies are subject to refined rules and distinctions and are treated differently by various decisions and by the 1962 and 1997 Acts. Mutual fund distributions are typically *principal* to the extent they represent capital gains and are *income* to the extent they represent ordinary dividends or interest.

(2) "Pennsylvania Rule" (One-Time Minority View)

This was an apportionment rule under which extraordinary dividends were principal to the extent they reduced the book value of shares from what it was when the stock was acquired by the trust; otherwise, they were income. The test was the "intact value" of the retained shares.

(3) Other Corporate Distributions

Other corporate distributions (*e.g.,* stock rights and options) are allocated to *principal*.

c. Allocation of Proceeds from Sale of Trust Assets

Generally, proceeds from a sale of trust assets are *principal*. A small minority may still follow the Pennsylvania Rule of apportionment based on intact value and dates of earnings for proceeds from a sale of corporate stock. In some states, if a trustee delays selling un(der)productive property which the trustee had a duty to sell, the trustee must allocate as *income* an amount from proceeds based on a formula granting the income beneficiary a portion reflecting what would have been received had the property been reasonably productive (based on an average trust rate of return); this rule also is eliminated by many statutes.

d. Treatment of "Wasting Assets"

Wasting assets are those *depletable or perishable through use* (*e.g.,* timber, minerals, also depreciable assets). Often, where a wasting asset becomes part of a trust through a *general* testamentary bequest (*e.g.,* "all my estate"), the trustee must amortize or sell the property and invest in permanent securities. In the case of a *specifically* devised wasting asset, an income beneficiary is usually entitled to all receipts. Legislation and cases vary and are in flux on these matters, even regarding retirement annuities.

e. Bond Premium and Discount

The 1962 Act forbids amortization except for noninterest-bearing bonds. The Second Restatement allows (but does not require) amortization in the case of interest-bearing bonds purchased at a premium.

3. Allocation of Burdens (Essentially Expenditures)

The general rule is that a trustee should pay *ordinary, current expenses* out of income, while *"extraordinary" expenses* or those *solely beneficial to remainder beneficiaries* should generally be paid from the capital account.

a. Losses from Operation of Business

Losses sustained in the operation of a business owned by the trust are charged to *principal*.

b. Taxes, Assessments

Ordinary property taxes are paid from *income*. Assessments for "capital" or *permanent improvements* are generally charged to *principal*, with the income account sometimes charged with interest, depreciation, or amortization.

c. Upkeep

Current repairs and maintenance are charged to *income*. Insurance premiums are charged to *income* in some states but *apportioned* in others. However, expenses incurred when a trust is initially established, for the purpose of putting property in an income-producing condition, are charged to *principal*. Capital improvements are either *apportioned* or charged to *principal* and *depreciated*.

d. Mortgage Payments

The interest part of payments is charged to *income*, and the principal portion to *principal*.

e. Trustee's Fees and Administrative Expenses

According to some cases, trustee's fees and other administrative expenses are charged to *income*, but statutes and cases now tend to *apportion* these fees and expenses.

f. Depreciation Reserves

There is a split of authority (in the absence of direction in the trust instrument) on whether a trustee may, must, or must not set up depreciation reserves to protect remainder beneficiaries. Absent a statute, some states require depreciation reserves in most instances (especially if the depreciable property was purchased by the trustee), while others either forbid such reserves or leave it to the trustee's discretion.

VIII. MODIFICATION AND TERMINATION OF TRUSTS

A. REVOCABLE TRUSTS

1. Settlor Can Revoke Anytime

In a revocable trust, the settlor has retained the right to revoke the trust so long as the settlor retains capacity to do so.

2. Beneficiaries and Settlor Can Agree to Revoke at Any Time

The settlors and all of the beneficiaries may consent to revoke the trust at any time.

B. IRREVOCABLE TRUSTS

1. Claflin Doctrine

Without the settlor's consent, all of the beneficiaries may agree to modify or terminate a trust (even an irrevocable trust) so long as such modification does not interfere with the "material purpose" of the trust. Note that obtaining consent of all beneficiaries may prove challenging.

2. Equitable Deviation

A petitioner, who may be the trustee or a beneficiary, establishes "changed circumstances" that were not anticipated by the settlor and compliance with the original term would defeat or substantially impair the purpose of the trust.

3. Judicial Power to Deviate from or Modify Administrative Provisions

Under the traditional view, a court of equity may authorize a trustee to deviate from or modify the *administrative* terms of a trust where, due to *changed circumstances unforeseen by the settlor*, deviation is *necessary* (not merely convenient) because compliance with the original terms would defeat or substantially impair a trust purpose; by the modern view, it is sufficient that the deviation will "further the purposes" of the trust in the event of "unforeseen circumstances." The mere fact that a trust instrument specifically forbids the act in question (*e.g.,* prohibits sale of certain property) does not preclude deviation. Where a trustee *should know* of circumstances justifying deviation from the original terms of the trust, the trustee may be liable if the trustee *fails to seek court approval to so deviate* and blindly follows the trust terms.

4. Power Regarding "Distributive" Provisions

Under the traditional majority view, a court *cannot* alter any of the *distributive* provisions in a way that may result in taking from one beneficiary and giving to another. An increasing number of cases and statutes are contra. Acceleration of indefeasibly vested rights may be permitted in the rare situation where there are *no other potential beneficiaries' interests to be affected*. Some courts following the majority view have been able to find, by construction, that the power to invade is *implied* by the terms of the trust instrument. (*See also* cy pres for charitable trusts, *supra.*

5. Abandonment or Removal of Material Purpose

If the settlor consents to a request of all the beneficiaries, there is no "material purpose" barring termination under *Claflin*. The settlor's opposition, however, does not prevent modification if a court finds that there is no material purpose barrier.

a. Trustee's Abandonment

If all beneficiaries request modification or termination and, despite a material purpose, the trustee acquiesces, it has been held that the beneficiaries are *estopped* from later suing the trustee for premature distribution, and the settlor probably lacks standing to do so.

b. Purpose Frustrated or Impermissible

Where a beneficiary whose interest was protected dies or no longer holds an interest, that material purpose barrier ordinarily is deemed to be removed. Restraint upon freedom of beneficiaries to terminate ends by operation of law when the perpetuities period expires.

C. TERMINATION OF TRUSTS BY OPERATION OF LAW

Trusts will terminate by their own provisions if the period specified for the duration of the trust *expires*. Trusts will terminate by *operation of law* if: (i) the trust purpose is *fulfilled or prevented*; (ii) there has been a *merger* of legal and beneficial interests; or (iii) the trust estate has been *destroyed or consumed*.

D. DECANTING

Today, a trustee may transfer (*i.e.*, decant) assets from one trust to another. The trust instrument may specifically authorize decanting. An increasing number of states have adopted statutes authorizing decanting. If permitted, judicial authorization is not required.

E. TRUSTEE REMOVAL

Trustee removal is a remedy. Nevertheless, removal of a trustee with replacement of another trustee may act as a form of modification is the new trustee were to take a different interpretation of the trust terms or exercise the powers in a different manner.

IX. TRUSTS ARISING BY OPERATION OF LAW

A. INTRODUCTION

1. General Nature

Constructive trusts and resulting trusts are not based on any real expression of trust intent, but rather upon operation of law (*i.e.,* implied by law or imposed by courts). *Resulting trusts* are a reflection or implementation of reversionary interests. *Constructive trusts* are devices imposed to remedy wrongs or avoid unjust enrichment.

2. Statute of Frauds Not Applicable

The Statute of Frauds does *not* apply to trusts arising by operation of law.

3. Retroactivity, Tracing, and Accounting

Usually a decree establishing a constructive trust, and occasionally a resulting trust, is retroactive to the *date the transferee acquired title*.

4. Duty to Convey Title

In most instances, constructive trusts and resulting trusts are passive or "dry" trusts, and the trustee's *sole duty* is to convey title.

B. RESULTING TRUSTS

A resulting trust is equity's way of recognizing an *equitable reversionary interest* (*i.e.,* an interest remaining in a transferor who made an incomplete or defective disposition of the beneficial ownership). A resulting trust may arise if: (i) there is *no express or implied intent as to some or all beneficial interests* (*e.g.,* excessive trust property for trust purposes, unanticipated circumstances for which no interest is expressed); (ii) an express trust is *unenforceable* (*e.g.,* improper form prevents proof of beneficial interests); or (iii) a *trust fails in whole or in part* for other reasons (*e.g.,* illegality, impossibility, disclaimer).

C. PURCHASE MONEY RESULTING TRUSTS

1. Development and Status of Doctrine

At early common law, the courts adopted a *strong presumption against a gift* so that the "use" (beneficial enjoyment) was deemed to go to the person who paid the consideration.

2. Statement of Doctrine Under Modern Law

Where the purchase money for property is paid by one person but, at that person's direction, title is transferred by the seller to another, and there is *no close family relationship* between payor and grantee, it is *presumed* that no gift was intended. There is instead a *rebuttable presumption* that the payor intended the grantee to hold legal title upon a "resulting" trust for the payor. (The purchase money resulting trust has been abolished by statute in a minority of states).

D. CONSTRUCTIVE TRUSTS

1. Remedial Device—Not Really a Trust

A constructive trust is not really a "trust" at all. It arises by operation of law as an *equitable remedy* to redress wrongful conduct or prevent unjust enrichment. It is imposed when an equity court is convinced that the person who acquired title to the property should not in equity be allowed to retain the property but should convey it to another, because the acquisition was through fraud, duress, mistake, etc., or the title holder will be *unjustly enriched*.

2. When Oral Trust Unenforceable

A constructive trust is frequently applied when property was transferred with a trust intention that is unenforceable. If a transferee refuses to carry out an unenforceable oral trust, *e.g.,* courts may in some circumstances impose a constructive trust.

3. As Remedy for Breach of Fiduciary Duty

A constructive trust may be imposed when property is obtained through breach of fiduciary duty owed to another (*e.g.,* trustee absconds with trust funds and misuses money to buy land or stock). This is not limited to wrongdoing of trustees, but encompasses other fiduciaries (*e.g.,* guardians).

4. As Remedy in Nontrust Situations

A constructive trust remedy is generally available to rectify wrongs and prevent unjust enrichment arising from fraud, mistake, etc.

5. Effect of Transfer to Third Person

If a wrongdoer sells the wrongfully obtained property to a *bona fide purchaser*, the wronged party may no longer have a constructive trust imposed upon that property.

The wronged party may, however, have a constructive trust imposed upon the **proceeds** of the sale (and profits) in the hands of the wrongdoer.

Gilbert Exam Strategies

Problems in the field of trusts invariably require you to determine the nature of the relationship that has been created and the rights and obligations of the parties in light of that relationship. The following analysis may be helpful in resolving such problems. (Remember that the key exam issues are highlighted at the beginning of each chapter.)

1. **Nature of Relationship**

   As a first step, consider whether the relationship that has been created is in fact a trust. Except where the law implies a trust, there must be some effective expression of *intent* by the owner of property to create the particular status that the law regards as a trust. The parties' own expressions of intent are, of course, significant, but also consider:

   a. Is there a *bifurcation of title*, so that legal title is held by one party and beneficial ownership by another?

   b. Is there in fact a *fiduciary relationship* between the holder of legal title and the claimed beneficiary?

   c. Is the relationship one with respect to *property*, rather than one involving merely personal obligations?

   d. Does it impose equitable *duties* upon the holder of legal title?

2. **Enforceability as a Trust**

   Assuming that the relationship intended is in fact an express, private trust, consider whether it is enforceable as such:

   a. **Are the Essential Elements of a Trust Present?**

      There must be: (i) a present *intent* to create a trust, (ii) designation of trust property (*i.e., res)*, (iii) identification of *beneficiaries* and *trustee* (inter vivos trust only), and (iv) a statement of *valid trust purpose(s)*.

   b. **Has the Trust Been Effectively Created?**

      (1) Inter Vivos Trust

      If created by the settlor during the settlor's lifetime:

      (a) Is there an *effective, present* transfer of the trust res?

      (b) Is the *Statute of Frauds* applicable? If so, is there a sufficient writing; or if not, is there some way around the Statute of the Fraud (*e.g.,* part performance, estoppel, purchase money resulting trusts)?

      (c) Is the trust *"testamentary"* in effect such that the Statute of Wills is applicable to the creation of the instrument and the funding of the trust?

      (2) Testamentary Trust

      If created in a decedent's will, is the trust executed in compliance with applicable wills law and, if relevant, what is the consequences of a "pour over"?

c.   **Is the Trust Purpose Valid?**

Consider not only the expressed trust purposes, but also whether the terms of the trust would violate any rule of property law, *e.g.,* the ***Rule Against Perpetuities***, the rule against suspension of power of alienation, the rule against accumulations, etc.

(1) Charitable Trust

If the trust is ***exclusively for the benefit of the public*** or some large segment thereof, it may be held charitable, in which case special (and typically liberal) rules are applied (*e.g.,* no identification of ascertainable beneficiaries required, may last perpetually, cy pres doctrine may apply), and some restrictions may apply as well (*e.g.,* Mortmain acts). Remember, however, that to be considered a charitable trust, the purpose must either fall within one of the ***generally accepted categories of charity*** or be sufficiently ***of interest or beneficial to the community***.

3. **Rights, Duties, and Liabilities as Between Parties to the Transaction**

The rights and remedies available to the parties to the transaction turn on whether an enforceable trust relationship exists.

a.   **Where There Is an Enforceable Trust**

The rights and duties are those created under the trust instrument and by law. Consider the rights of each party separately:

(1) Rights of Beneficiary

(a) To obtain an equitable decree ***compelling trustee's performance***;

(b) To obtain ***removal of trustee*** for breach of trust;

(c) To obtain ***damages against trustee*** (*see* below);

(d) To ***compel modification or termination*** of trust under appropriate circumstances; and

(e) To obtain an ***accounting as to the beneficiary's share***; consider allocation of income to trust and expenses of trust administration in determining share of income beneficiary and remainder beneficiaries.

(2) Rights of Settlor

(a) To exercise any ***right reserved by the settlor*** in creating the trust (to revoke, modify, etc.) or inferred by law; and

(b) To ***compel trustee's performance*** where trust created by contract between settlor and trustee.

(3) Rights, Duties, and Liabilities of Trustee

(a) Rights of Trustee

1)   Right to exercise ***powers*** created by trust instrument or inferred by law:

a)   Consider the ***source and scope*** of trust powers; and

b)   Consider whether exercise is ***mandatory or discretionary*** and the scope of judicial review.

2)   Right to ***compensation*** for services and ***indemnification*** from trust estate for expenses and liabilities incurred in proper administration.

(b) Duties Owed to Beneficiary

1)   Duty to ***act with care, skill, and caution*** (*i.e., prudence*)—in administration, investment, and management of trust estate; and

2) Duties of *loyalty and impartiality*—in avoiding conflict of interests in personal transactions with beneficiary or trust estate, self-dealing, earmarking and segregating assets.

(c) **Trustee's Liabilities**

1) *Measure of liability* for breach of trust duties—profits, losses, and interest; and

2) *Defenses to liability*—consent or ratification by beneficiaries having capacity to consent.

b. **Where There Is No Enforceable Trust**

Consider whether the apparent trust intent can be enforced, and if not, consider what other remedies may be available.

(1) **Contractual**

If *consideration* was given for the unenforceable trust promise, is specific performance available to compel effective trust transfer and render the trust enforceable? In any event, damages or other relief may be available.

(2) **Resulting Trust**

Where an express trust is totally invalid or excessive trust res is conveyed, a resulting trust may be imposed in favor of the grantor to effectuate the grantor's *presumed intention*.

(3) **Constructive Trust**

Where an express trust is merely unenforceable, and the grantee's retention would constitute *unjust enrichment*, a constructive trust may be imposed. But consider whether it should be imposed in favor of the grantor or the intended beneficiary.

4. **Rights of Third Parties**

The question may also involve third parties who have dealings with the trustee or the trust estate, or who seek to reach the beneficial interest under the trust.

a. **Assignee of Beneficiary's Interest**

In determining the rights of someone to whom the beneficiary has made a voluntary assignment of the interest, consider whether there is a valid *spendthrift restraint*; also consider priority as between successive assignments of the same right.

b. **Beneficiary's Creditors**

In determining whether creditors can reach the beneficiary's interest, consider the validity and effect of spendthrift or similar restraints, and the scope of protection afforded thereby (principal and/or income).

c. **Settlor's Creditors**

Consider whether creditors can reach the trust estate (i) on the theory that the settlor has *reserved powers* over the trust, or (ii) on the theory that the trust transfer was a *fraudulent conveyance*.

d. **Contract Creditors**

Consider whether the trustee is *personally liable* on contracts executed by the trustee on behalf of the trust, the effect of any *disclaimer of liability*, the trustee's right of *indemnification* from the trust, and whether the contract creditors can reach this right.

e. Tort Creditors

Consider whether the trustee is ***personally liable*** for torts committed by the trustee or the trustee's agents in the course of trust administration, the scope of such liability, the trustee's right of ***indemnification*** from the trust, and whether the tort creditors can reach this right.

Author's Note: References are made throughout this Summary to the Uniform Trust Code ("UTC"), which was promulgated in 2000 by the National Conference of Commissioners on Uniform State Laws. The 1959 Restatement (Second) of the Law of Trusts, referred to in this Summary as the "Second Restatement" or "Rest. 2d," is being replaced by a new Restatement ("Third Restatement" or "Rest. 3d"). A preliminary volume on the "Prudent Investor Rule" was published in 1992 by the American Law Institute and has been codified directly or by adoption of the 1994 Uniform Prudent Investor Act ("UPIA") in nearly all states; another three volumes (§§ 1–92) have now been published. The third of these volumes ends with Chapter 17 (§§ 90–92), which incorporates, in proper sequence, the Prudent Investor Rule (originally §§ 227–229 in the Second Restatement and 1992 preliminary volume). The fourth and final volume is now under way.

Trusts

Fourteenth Edition

Chapter One
Introduction

CONTENTS	PAGE

Key Exam Issues 2

A.   Definition of Fundamental Terms 2

B.   Classification of Trusts 3

C.   Trusts Distinguished from Similar Relationships 6

Key Exam Issues

When the nature of a legal relationship involving property in your exam question is not stated or self-evident, you will need to determine whether that relationship is properly classified as a trust or as something else. Although the basic definition of a trust may seem clear, the variable nature of the trust means that it can be challenging to identify in many situations. Other comparable relationships may resemble a trust (*e.g.,* a bailment, an agency) and must be distinguished in order to make a determination of whether there is a trust. And remember. "Magic words" are necessary to create any of these relationships; you will have to determine the nature of the relationship from the substance, that is, the relationship between the parties.

This determination of trust (or a determination of no trust) may itself be the answer to your exam question, or it may be only one step in determining the ultimate issues of the rights and duties of the parties (which depend upon the classification of a trust or nontrust relationship and possibly upon the type of trust).

(*Note:* This chapter introduces the basic concept of the trust and its various forms, but more elaborate definitions and descriptions appear elsewhere in this Summary.)

A. Definition of Fundamental Terms

1. Trust

A *"trust"* is a fiduciary relationship **with respect to specific property**, to which the trustee holds (usually at least) the legal title for the benefit of one or more persons, the beneficiaries. who hold equitable title. Thus, two forms of ownership interests—legal and equitable—exist in the same property at the same time. [Rest. 3d § 2]

Example: A testamentary trust created by Settlor's will leaves "the residue of my estate to Trustee in trust, to hold, invest, and manage the property and to pay the net income annually to Beneficiary for as long as Beneficiary lives, and upon Beneficiary's death to distribute the principal to Beneficiary's then living issue by right of representation." Other terms of Settlor's will spell out in some detail other rights of the beneficiaries and Trustee's powers and duties.

a. Legal and Equitable Interests

Legal title confers upon the trustee the ability to manage the property—that is, buy. sell, invest, and distribute it to the beneficiaries. The beneficiaries' equitable interest means that they, and they alone, can benefit from the property—that is, use it for themselves, spend it for themselves, or maybe live on it if is real property. The trustee may not use the trust property for his own benefit, and the beneficiaries have no ability to manage or distribute it.

b. Property

Because a "trust" is a relationship with respect to *property*, and because the beneficiary acquires an *interest* in the property, the normal rules for transfer of property and for the creation of property rights apply to the creation of trusts (*e.g.,* conveyancing rules apply in creating trusts of land). An exception is the "declaration of trust" by which a property owner can make ("declare") herself trustee of the property for the benefit of others. Most trusts are created by will or by gift and do not require consideration to be enforceable and effective.

c. Reasons to Create a Trust

The reasons to create a trust will vary. Trusts provide professional, ongoing asset management. Some trusts may avoid the probate process. Some may protect minors, the disabled, or those with substance abuse problems who are in a position to receive property outright. Some trusts preserve privacy, some trusts may minimize tax liability, some trusts may provide asset protections, and some trusts provide a flexible organizational structure for an enterprise. Trusts are flexible devices with many uses that would appeal to a number of property owners.

2. Settlor

The *"settlor"* (sometimes called the "trustor," "donor," "transferor," or "grantor") is the property owner who creates the trust—*i.e.,* who intentionally causes it to come into existence by inter vivos transfer (or declaration) or by will.

3. Trustee

The *"trustee"* is the individual or entity (often a bank or other corporation) who holds legal title to the trust property. There may be co-trustees (*i.e.,* more than one trustee), and the trustee (or one or more of the co-trustees) may also be a beneficiary or settlor of the trust.

4. Trust Property

The *"trust property"* (or "res" or "corpus") is the interest the trustee holds for the beneficiaries. It may consist of real or personal property, or both. The most common subject matter today is intangible personalty in the form of securities (stocks and bonds). Although it is generally stated (*e.g.,* above) that the trustee has legal title to trust property, some or all of the trust property could itself be an equitable interest assigned to the trust.

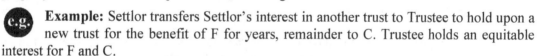 **Example:** Settlor transfers Settlor's interest in another trust to Trustee to hold upon a new trust for the benefit of F for years, remainder to C. Trustee holds an equitable interest for F and C.

5. Beneficiary

A *"beneficiary"* (sometimes called "cestui que trust" or simply "cestui") is a person for whose benefit the trustee holds the trust property. Most trusts have a number of beneficiaries: usually one or more life beneficiaries, and one or more remainder beneficiaries, often consisting of a class (or several classes) of which some or all of the members are likely to be unborn or presently unascertainable (*e.g.,* remainder to "S's descendants living at termination, and if none, then to X's then living descendants").

B. Classification of Trusts

1. Methods of Classifying

Because trusts can be so varied, it is helpful to classify the major types of trusts. A trust may be classified in several different ways, according to:

a. The *duties* imposed on the trustee—"active" trusts vs. "passive" trusts.

b. The *trust purposes*—"private" trusts vs. "charitable" trusts.

c. The *manner of creation*—express or by operation of law (*i.e.,* the remedial trusts, which are resulting trusts and constructive trusts).

d. The *time of creation*—inter vivos ("living") or testamentary trusts; living trusts may be irrevocable or revocable (and amendable) in whole or in part.

EXAM TIP   🔖GILBERT

The classifications above are important, as the classifications may affect the **substantive rules** that govern the validity, creation, and operation of the trust and the rights of the parties.

---

2. Active Trusts vs. Passive Trusts

a. Based on Duties

Trusts are classifiable as "active" or "passive" according to the duties imposed on the trustee.

(1) Active Trusts

Trusts in which, in addition to holding title to the trust property, the trustee has some *affirmative duties* of management and administration to perform (and this is the typical modern arrangement with which the subject of trusts is primarily concerned) are "active" trusts.

(2) Passive Trusts

Trusts in which the trustee has *no real duties* but holds (*i.e.,* is a mere receptacle of) the legal title on behalf of another are "passive" trusts.

b. Active Trustee vs. Passive Trustee

(1) "Active" Trustee

In general, a trust will be treated as "active" if by its terms the trustee has any power or duty that involves the *exercise of discretion in active management or in determining the rights of the beneficiaries*. The typical modern trust involves a broad array of management authority and responsibilities and some discretion over distributions, such as a power to invade principal for the life beneficiary.

(2) "Passive" Trustee

If the only acts the trustee must perform are *purely mechanical and formal* in nature, the trust will be regarded as "passive" and the trustee's legal title will pass through to the beneficiary, who will hold both legal and equitable title; then there is no trust.

(a) Duty to Hold and Convey

Where a trustee's duty is merely to hold and convey title, the duty to convey is not considered by most authorities to be an "active" duty and the trust is usually regarded as passive.

3. Private Trusts vs. Charitable Trusts

Where the trust purpose is to confer certain benefits upon the public at large, or upon some *significantly large segment of the public* to be deemed charitable, the trust is classified as a "charitable trust," and language and rules are liberally interpreted and applied to give effect to the settlor's wishes. Other trusts are considered to be "private" trusts and are subject to more restrictive substantive rules.

4. Express Trusts vs. Those Created by Operation of Law

Trusts are also classified according to the manner or basis of their creation. Some trusts are intentionally created by the parties, this legally ascertained intent being expressed or inferred (*i.e.,* found in the settlor's words or conduct). Others arise from operation of law and are actually not trusts at all. Rather, they are equitable remedies put in place to deal with the assets left in a failed trust, or to transfer assets someone has wrongfully acquired,

a. Express Trust

An express trust is created by the ***manifestation of an intention*** by a person or persons having the power to do so, to create that fiduciary relationship with respect to property that the law recognizes as a trust. In other words, an express trust arises when a settlor either transfers property to someone else to hold and manage for a beneficiary or declares himself a trustee over his own property for the benefit of the beneficiary. This person need not use "Trust" phrasing and terminology, or even know it. The required "manifestation" of intent appears in the settlor's oral or written words, conduct, or a combination of these, viewed in an overall context. Most matters discussed in this Summary primarily involve express trusts of the active variety, private or charitable, testamentary or inter vivos, revocable or irrevocable.

b. Resulting Trusts

A resulting trust arises by operation of law when an express trust fails in whole or in part or where the beneficial provisions of an express trust are incomplete (*i.e.,* the settlor has failed to make full disposition of the equitable interests). For example, a trust is to pay for A's college tuition. A graduates from college with money left in the trust, and the settlor failed to provide for any further use for the assets. In this situation, the law decrees that the trustee holds the assets upon a" "resulting trust" for the settlor or the settlor's successors in interest. That is, the assets are no longer trust assets and will return to the settlor or the settlor's heirs in fee simple. The term "trust" is really a misnomer: here it is really a way to solve the problem of excess assets in the trust after the trust's purpose has been served.

c. Constructive Trusts

A "constructive trust" is also a misnomer. It is not, again, a trust at all. A constructive trust is a ***remedial device*** invoked by a court in the exercise of its equitable powers. Its purpose is to compel a person who has obtained property by wrongful means (including, in most jurisdictions, through unjust enrichment as the result of mistake or the wrongful behavior of another) to turn the property over to the party entitled to it. This restitutionary device is broadly applicable to transactions having nothing to do with express trusts, but it is also applied in cases where an intended express trust cannot be enforced as such but where the law will intervene to prevent a transferee (the intended trustee) from benefiting from that unenforceability by keeping the property, such as where an oral promise to hold in trust is unenforceable by reason of the Statute of Frauds.

C. Trusts Distinguished from Similar Relationships

1. Characteristics, Not Terminology, Controlling

Similar arrays of rights and responsibilities, including fiduciary duties and obligations, appear in a variety of other relationships that are, in varying degrees, similar to trusts but which lack one or more of the essential characteristics of a trust. It is often difficult to ascertain whether the parties involved intended to create a relationship that the law recognizes as a trust, because the use or the failure to use trust terminology is not conclusive of the parties' intent. [*See generally* Rest. 3d § 5]

2. Bailment

Where the owner of tangible personal property gives *possession but not title* to another, the relationship is one of bailment. If the property owner delivers a chattel to another to benefit the owner or a third party, this may come close to a trust, but it may actually constitute some other form of relationship.

a. Guide for Distinguishing

A court will first attempt to determine whether the owner *intended to pass title* as well as possession in assessing whether the recipient is a trustee or bailee. If the owner's intention is unclear, an important factor is whether the owner's *purposes* in delivering the chattel could have been affected by a transfer merely of possession.

b. Principal Differences Between Bailment and Trust

(1) Nature of the Property

A bailment pertains only to *chattels* (although a comparable interest in land might be a leasehold). A trust may exist with respect to real or personal property, whether tangible or intangible.

(2) Title

The bailor (owner) *retains both legal and equitable title*; the bailee merely has a right to possession. In a trust, legal title is in the trustee; the settlor does not retain title (unless it is an equitable interest retained as a beneficiary, or unless she also serves as trustee and thereby takes title in her fiduciary capacity—a transaction, however, that would obviously raise no bailment question).

Example: Transferor hands her diamond bracelet to Transferee, telling Transferee to "give this bracelet to my daughter when she returns from Europe." If Transferee is a bailee, the Transferee merely has a right to possess the bracelet; the bailor retains title. If Transferee is a trustee, the Transferee has legal title to the bracelet.

(3) Transfers

Lacking title to the chattel, a bailee *cannot ordinarily convey title* to another; *i.e.,* even a sale to a bona fide purchaser would not cut off the bailor's interest under common law principles. (In other words, the BFP cannot keep the asset.) A wrongful sale of the trust res by a trustee to a bona fide purchaser, however, usually does cut off the equitable interests of the beneficiaries. (In other words, the BFP gets to keep the asset.)

(4) Income

Rents, issues, and profits from the trust res belong to the beneficiary, whereas the rents, issues, and profits from bailed chattels ordinarily belong to the *bailor*.

(5) Remedies

The rights between bailor and bailee are usually enforced *at law*, although if unique chattels are involved, equitable relief may be appropriate and available. The duties of a trustee are enforced in equity.

EXAM TIP

A bailment involves the transfer of possession of personal property for a limited period of time for a limited purpose. Think coat check or car valet. Thus, in the example above, the transfer of the bracelet is likely a bailment, since it seems to be for a fairly short period of time.

---

3. Agency

An agency often appears very similar to a trust, and the duties and obligations of an agent holding property for a principal are similar to those of a trustee.

a. Guide for Distinguishing

BUT an agency relationship with regard to property differs from a trust relationship in several important ways. These distinctions are important both as possible consequences of the distinction and as possible aids in understanding and identifying which relationship is involved.

(1) Title

A trustee has title to the trust property; an agent may or may not hold title on behalf of the principal, but the holding of title is *not an element* of an agency as such.

(2) Control

An agent is *subject to the control of the principal*, but a trustee is not subject to the control of either the beneficiaries (although they have power to enforce the trust) or the settlor as such (although the settlor's reservation of powers of revocation, amendment, or direction may give the settlor effective control, or some measure of control, over the trustee).

(3) Powers

An agent's *authority is limited* to what is granted by the principal and tends to be quite strictly construed. In addition to powers expressly granted by the terms of the instrument, a trustee's powers tend to be rather broadly construed; except as limited by the settlor or by law, a trustee generally has powers necessary or appropriate to carry out the purposes of the trust and, under the modern view, all of the powers of an outright owner. [Rest. 3d § 85]

(4) Liability

An agent acting within the scope of the agent's authority (and who discloses the agency) normally *incurs no personal liability*; rather, the principal alone is liable for any contracts or debts thus incurred by the agent. In most jurisdictions today, and under the Third Restatement and UTC § 1010, the trustee's liability is not personal but "representative" (of the trust), meaning that she is not personally liable for contracts or debts incurred in her fiduciary capacity.

(5) Termination

An agent's power *terminates on the death or* (except in the case of a "durable power of attorney") *incapacity* of the principal; a trustee's power does not depend on the settlor's competence or survival.

> **e.g.** **Example:** O delivers $25,000 to N to distribute to certain of O's relatives. N fails to do so prior to O's death. If N is only an agent, the $25,000 belongs to O's estate and N no longer has power to make distribution among the relatives. In contrast, if N is a trustee, the distribution is to be made despite O's death.

4. Debtor-Creditor Relationship

A debt differs from a trust in that, although the creditor may have a claim against the debtor personally, the creditor has no interest in any specific property of the debtor (at least until judgment or unless the creditor has a security interest, in which case the rights are still quite different from those of a trust beneficiary). [*See* Rest. 3d § 5 cmt. i]

a. Guide for Distinguishing

Notwithstanding some obvious distinctions, it is sometimes difficult to tell whether a debt or trust relationship was intended in a given situation. The crucial distinction is usually whether the parties intended to create a relationship with respect to *specific property*.

> **e.g.** **Example:** Transferor hands Transferee a bundle of $20 bills totaling $500 and indicates that she wants the money returned at a specified date. If, as is likely, Transferor does not care whether she gets back that particular group of bills, or even property directly traceable to them, the arrangement cannot be a trust but is simply a debt. As a result, Transferee can repay Transferor any $500 and is free to dispose of the particular bills received.

> **e.g.** **Example:** An employer "withholds" a portion of each employee's pay with the understanding that the employer is obligated to deposit certain amounts in an employee pension fund. The employer probably has a debt for this amount, rather than holding certain properties in trust; as long as the withholding did not involve identifying and setting aside particular dollars, the expectation would be that the employer is to make the deposit at the appropriate time from any funds available.

> **cf.** **Compare:** When a party is obligated to hold for the benefit of another specific funds received from a third party, the result will usually be that the funds constitute property held in trust.

(1) Note—Interest Payment Denotes Debt

If the transferee is obligated to pay *interest* or some agreed substitute, this is virtually conclusive that the relationship is a debt. (The fact that the interest or the principal is to be paid to a third party is not likely to matter.) If, however, the transferee only promises to pay whatever interest or income the money earns when deposited in a savings account or invested, the relationship is more likely to be a trust.

b. Consequences of Distinctions Between Debt and Trust

(1) Insolvency

If Transferee is merely indebted to Transferor and Transferee becomes insolvent, Transferor would have the **same status as any other creditor**. If, however, Transferee is trustee of funds received from Transferor, Transferor could claim those funds or trace them into other identifiable assets. If the Transferor is able to do that, the Transferor may obtain priority over other creditors, and in fact have an exclusive right to that property.

(2) Profits

If a debt is involved, any profits realized on Transferee's investment of the funds **normally belong to Transferee**; Transferee merely has an obligation to repay the amount owed to Transferor, including any agreed interest. On the other hand, if the funds were held in trust, the profits would belong to the beneficiaries and not to the trustee.

(3) Losses

If the relationship between Transferee and Transferor is a debt, Transferee owes the amount in question to Transferor **regardless of any losses sustained** through the investment or theft. If the relationship is a trust, losses from investments or theft merely diminish the trust res (*i.e.,* the beneficiaries bear the loss), and Transferee is not personally liable as long as he conformed to the appropriate fiduciary standards of care, etc., in managing and caring for the property. (If Transferee had been negligent as trustee, Transferor could hold him liable by way of surcharge; if the loss resulted through no fault of Transferee, the party who will bear the loss will depend on whether the relationship was one of debt or trust.)

5. Conditional Fee

A *condition* in a grant for the benefit of the grantor or a third party may at times suggest a trust relationship. For example, a conveyance from P "to C upon condition that C support D for the rest of D's life" could conceivably be construed to: (i) impose a trust; (ii) create an equitable charge on the land; or (iii) create a determinable fee or fee subject to a condition subsequent.

a. Consequences of Distinction

Where title is held as a determinable fee or a fee subject to a condition subsequent, any failure ("breach") of condition subjects the estate to termination and entitles the transferor or his successor in interest to recover the property. A failure of a trust duty, however, entitles the beneficiary to sue in equity to compel the trustee to perform the trustee's duties.

b. Rule of Construction

Generally, courts are reluctant to give words of condition literal effect where forfeitures on failure of the condition would result. (*See* Property Summary.) Hence, unless the language makes clear that a condition was intended, a grant will usually be construed as creating a *trust or equitable charge* rather than a conditional fee. [Rest. 3d § 5 cmt. h]

6. Other Relationships

Various other fiduciary relationships may at times appear similar to trusts, *e.g.,* guardianships, receiverships, the positions of executors or administrators of estates, even corporate directorships, partnerships, or limited liability companies. [Rest. 3d § 5 cmts. e, d, g] Each of these differs from a trust in some or all of the following respects: the nature and character of title held by the fiduciary; the duties and powers of the fiduciary; and the remedies available for enforcement. Other bodies of law also deal with special uses of the trust device, such as real estate investment trusts ("REITs"), voting trusts, Massachusetts business trusts, and employee benefit trusts, none of which are dealt with specifically in this Summary.

DISTINGUISHING CHARACTERISTICS OF TRUST AND NONTRUST RELATIONSHIPS			GILBERT
TYPE OF RELATIONSHIP	**DISTINCTION**	**EXAMPLE**	**WHO HOLDS TITLE?**
TRUST	Transferee holds legal title to *specific property* for benefit of one or more persons, who hold equitable title	X devises property "to T in trust for Y"	T holds legal title; Y holds equitable title
BAILMENT	Transferee has *possession but not title*	X leaves her car with a mechanic for service	X retains both legal and equitable title
AGENCY	Transferee is *subject to control* of transferor	X tells Y to deliver a diamond necklace to Z	X until delivery is complete
DEBTOR-CREDITOR	Transferee is entitled to unrestricted use and disposition of property (*i.e., no duty to segregate*), subject to repayment to transferor	X loans Y $10,000 with repayment plus 10% interest due in 12 months	Y; X's rights are as a creditor
CONDITIONAL FEE	Failure of condition results in forfeiture or termination of estate with *no legal or equitable remedy* for transferee	X conveys "to Y upon condition that no alcohol is served on the premises"	Y, but if alcohol is served on the premises and X exercises her right of reentry (*see* Property Summary), Y's interest terminates and X regains full title; Y has no recourse

Chapter Two
Elements of a Trust

CONTENTS	PAGE

Key Exam Issues 12

A.   Introduction 13

B.   Expression of Trust Intent—Express Trusts 14

C.   Trust Property (Res) 17

D.   Parties to the Trust 21

E.   Trust Purposes 39

Key Exam Issues

To determine whether a trust relationship exists, look for the essential elements of a trust listed in UTC § 402:

1. **Trust Intent**

   a. If an exam question leaves any doubt about the required intent to create a trust, remember that the manifestation of intent must be *timely* and use of the term "trust" or the term "trustee" are not necessary to create a trust. Do, however, watch for questions that involve *precatory* language such as "hope," "wish," etc.: such wording today is presumed not to express the intent required to create a trust. Consider that some phrasing may be ambiguous such as "it being understood." Because no magic language is needed to create a trust for the sake of counterargument, be sure to analyze the question's facts and circumstances carefully because those facts and circumstances could indicate that a trust exists despite the language used. The key issue is: did the Grantor intend to impose a fiduciary duty on himself or someone else?

2. **Trust Property**

   There can be no trust without trust property; it must be *presently existing "property"*, and it must also be *specific* and *identifiable*. Trust property is often called *res*. Other words for res are corpus or trust assets; they are interchangeable, and we use "trust property" and "res" throughout. [UTC § 103(12) (defining property)]

3. **Parties to Trust**

   A trust must also have a *trustee* and one or more *beneficiaries*.

   a. But remember that *courts will appoint trustees* if necessary: Because of this, the maxim is that "no trust will fail for lack of a trustee." In questions about trustees be sure to consider both legal and practical capacity to serve and watch for the existence of grounds for removal (as well as liabilities considered in chapter VI of this Summary).

   b. For *private trusts* there generally must be *identifiable beneficiaries*. UTC § 402(a)(3) (But see discussion of UTC § 408 and § 409 below) Questions in this area are likely to focus on: (i) the requirement that if the trust beneficiaries are to be selected by a trustee they traditionally must come from a reasonably definite class, and (ii) whether the holder of a power of appointment has a *duty* (*i.e.,* imperative) to select distributees or merely a nonmandatory *power* to do so (which is not a trust and does not require definite beneficiaries and therefore can offer salvation, even under traditional doctrine, when a class is indefinite).

   c. Absent identifiable beneficiaries, look for a *charitable purpose* (*see* chapter V) or in some states for the limited possibility of sustaining an arrangement as an "honorary trust," or as a trust for an allowable noncharitable purpose.

4. **Trust Purpose**

   A trust must have a valid purpose. For private trusts, watch for the existence and consequences of trust purposes that are *impermissible* because they are illegal, tortious, or contrary to public policy. For charitable trusts, the purpose must be charitable.

   a. Such issues tend to focus on invalid conditions, which attempt to impose *improper restraints or inducements* on a continuing basis through the trust device.

b. If your exam encompasses perpetuities matters, watch for any problems of *remoteness of vesting* or accumulations.

A. Introduction

1. Requirements—in General

The usual elements of a trust are:

(i) *Trust intent* (at least in express trusts);

(ii) A specific trust *res* (aka trust property);

(iii) Designation of the *parties* (settlor, trustee, and beneficiary); and

(iv) A valid trust *purpose*.

2. Exceptions

a. As discussed, the word "trust" sometimes refers to an equitable remedy for wrongly held or acquired property. In these cases, it does not refer to an actual trust, but Trusts and Estates often cover these cases as well, which can be confusing.

b. The temporary absence of a trustee or a beneficiary will not destroy a trust. A court will appoint a trustee if necessary, and a future beneficiary satisfies the beneficiary requirement.

c. **BUT**, the lack of trust property (res, or corpus) will destroy a trust.

3. Consideration

Consideration is *not required* to create a trust. In fact, most trusts are gratuitous. (We discuss below the role of consideration when there are contracts to create trusts is noted below.)

◢ GILBERT
CHECKLIST OF ELEMENTS OF VALID PRIVATE TRUST
TO DETERMINE WHETHER A VALID PRIVATE TRUST HAS BEEN CREATED, LOOK FOR THE FOLLOWING CHARACTERISTICS:
☑ *Intent* to create a trust (manifested by settlor's words or conduct)   ☑ *Trust property* (res)   ☑ *Settlor* with capacity   ☑ *Trustee* (but a trust generally will not fail for lack of a trustee)   ☑ *Identifiable beneficiary(ies)*   ☑ *Valid trust purpose* (one that is not illegal, tortious, or against public policy)

B. Expression of Trust Intent— Express Trusts

1. In General

It is essential to the creation of an express trust that the settlor objectively manifest a final, definite, and specific intention that a trust should immediately arise with respect to some particular property.

2. Form of Expression

There must be some external manifestation of intention *by words* or *by conduct*. It is not enough that the settlor's intent was formed in the settlor's own mind if the settlor gave no external manifestation thereof. Nor are vague expressions of donative intent sufficient; the settlor must manifest a specific intent to create, as to some particular property, a relationship known in the law as a trust. [**Palozie v. Palozie**, 927 A.2d 903 (Conn. 2007)]

a. Wording

No particular words—even the word "trust" itself—are necessary. Nor is it essential that the settlor (or any of the other parties involved) know or understand that the intended relationship is legally defined as a "trust." If the court finds that the parties intended to form a relationship with respect to the property involved that the law defines as a trust, then the parties' intention to enter into that relationship provides the requisite trust intent.

(1) Use of Term "Trust"

Conversely, parties may refer to their relationship as a trust, but if the requisite intentions are lacking or an essential element is missing and not to be provided by a court, there is no trust.

(2) Use of Other Terms

Even if the parties proclaim their intention to create a bailment, agency, guardianship, or other relationship, the court may find their "real" intent was to create what the law defines as a trust. [Rest. 3d § 13 cmt. b]

b. Communication

Provided there is some "external expression" (essentially, some admissible evidence), the settlor's failure to communicate the trust intention to the beneficiaries or others does not prevent the trust from arising.

Example: An envelope found in a safe deposit box and marked "held for my nephew N" constituted a sufficient manifestation of intent to declare a trust of the contents of the envelope.

3. Precatory Expressions of Intent

a. Intent Uncertain

Usually, the settlor directs the trustee to manage the trust property for another, but on occasion the settlor may simply express a "hope," "wish," or suggestion that the property be so used. This type of expression is called "precatory" language. Today, courts are unlikely to find that precatory expressions create trusts. Rather, they are usually found to create only unenforceable moral obligations—or no obligations at all.

Example: A devises Blackacre to F "with the expectation that F will use the property to take care of N." Because the language "with the expectation" is precatory, it is unlikely that a court will find this to be a trust with an enforceable obligation on F. F may disregard it and certainly there is no trust.

b. Other Evidence of Trust Intent

Don't forget to look at the context and any *other* factors that may support a counterargument that there is a trust despite the precatory language.

EXAM TIP GILBERT

If you encounter a fact pattern on your exam in which the settlor expresses a "hope," "wish," or mere suggestion that the property be used in a certain way, you should raise the issue of whether a trust was formed. Such precatory language generally raises a presumption that the settlor *did not intend for there to be a trust*. But other facts may overcome that presumption.

---

4. Time When Trust Intent Must Be Expressed

The general rule is that the settlor must express the intention to create a trust (by words or conduct) at a time when the *settlor owns* or *is transferring* the intended trust property. This prior or contemporaneous expression of trust intention may also be made by the transferor and transferee together, or by the transferee with reliance thereon by the transferor. (Of course, after a transfer the *transferee*, as owner, may declare himself trustee.)

a. Gifts

The settlor cannot convey property as an outright gift and later execute a trust instrument declaring that the gift was actually in trust.

b. After-Acquired Property

Where someone expresses trust intent *prior to the acquisition* of the intended trust property, courts will probably find this to be a sufficient manifestation of intent to create a trust *if* there is some *further manifestation* of trust intent by that person, either by conduct or by words, *after* acquiring the property and *consistent* with the prior expression. For example, such subsequent conduct might occur by segregation of the property and making income payments to the intended beneficiary of a trust thus established by "declaration," or it might take the form of subsequent delivery of the property to *another* as the designated trustee.

5. Trust Must Be Intended to Take Effect Immediately

Another factor you should consider in determining whether a trust exists is the time when the trust was intended to take effect. The settlor must intend the trust to take effect *immediately* (at least with regard to property the settlor already owns), even if subject to revocation, and not at some future time. In the case of an intended declaration of trust, if the settlor's manifestation indicates an intention only to become trustee in the future, there is no effective declaration of trust. Similarly, in the case of a trust to be created by transfer, if the settlor merely manifests an intention to establish it by a transfer in the future, there is no trust, for lack of a present transfer, and lack of a trust res. [Rest. 3d §§ 13, 16] Note that under either of these circumstances, a trust does not arise later without further action at the contemplated future time. Note the close interrelationship between that requirement and the requirement of trust intent.

Examples: S writes to B: "As soon as the harvest is completed, I want you to have my farm, which you are to hold in trust for your children"; or "When I return from Europe, I shall make myself trustee of the cash in my safe for your children and shall invest it for them until the youngest reaches age 21." Neither of these statements is enough to create a trust because the intended trust is to take effect only at a future time.

a. Subsequent Action

If, however, there is an appropriate *subsequent* act (of *transfer* or, in the case of a declaration, of *segregating the res*) that is consistent with the previously stated intention and with an intent that the trust presently take effect, a valid trust will *then* arise. Thus, in the first example above, if S delivers the deed to the farm to B after the harvest is completed (which would be a present transfer accompanied by the manifestation of present trust intention that is implied from this conduct together with the prior expression), this would cause a valid trust to arise at that point (but with no relation back). Or, in the second example above, if S on S's return put the cash in an envelope marked "for B's children," there would be an effective declaration of trust at that moment, even if S should die before investing the funds.

b. Effect of Postponing Designation of Essential Elements

If the owner of property executes an instrument purporting to create a trust but providing that the beneficiaries, trustee, or trustees are to be designated later, the incomplete terms of trust are evidence that the settlor intended a trust only in the future, and there is no present trust. Note the distinction between this scenario and one in which the settlor creates a valid trust but fails to name a trustee and makes no provision for naming one at a later date: in this case, there will be a valid trust and a court will simply appoint a trustee. Remember the rule that no trust fails for lack of a trustee. What's the difference between the two scenarios? In the first one, the settlor's provision that she will appoint the trustee in the future shows that she does not intend to create a trust at the present time. In the second one, the settlor did intend to create a trust, but just failed for whatever reason to name a trustee. In the latter case, a court will put someone in that role.

c. Trust of Future Interest

As long as the trust takes effect immediately, the trust property itself may consist partly or entirely of a presently existing future interest.

Example: Grantor deeds Redacre "to Grantee for life, remainder to T in trust for F." A valid present trust is created because F has enforceable rights as beneficiary and T has present rights and duties as trustee (*e.g.,* to prevent waste by Grantee, the life tenant).

Example: A devises Blueacre "to First Bank in trust, to pay the income to B for life, remainder to C." C assigns C's remainder "to Second Bank in trust for D." C has also created a valid present trust because A has enforceable rights as beneficiary and Second Bank has present rights and duties as trustee (*e.g.,* to prevent breach of trust by First Bank).

A promise that is otherwise enforceable at law (*e.g.,* by damages) or in equity (*e.g.,* by specific performance), can be the res for a trust.

Example: O owns an enforceable promissory note from D for $10,000 and transfers it to Q as trustee for stated purposes and beneficiaries. Here, there is a trust and a res (a chose in action)

d. Promise to Create a Trust in the Future

An unenforceable (*i.e.,* gratuitous) promise to create a trust in the future does not create a trust. There is neither a present transfer nor an intention to create a present trust.

Example: S executes and delivers to P a promissory note stating, "I hereby promise to pay P $10,000 to be held by P in trust" for certain stated purposes and beneficiaries. Assuming the promise is not for consideration, there is no trust.

e. Savings Bank Trusts ("Totten Trusts")

Courts have developed unique rules where a person deposits that person's own money in a bank account in that person's own name "as trustee" for another. Realistically, such a deposit may *not* in itself manifest a clear intention presently to create a trust. The depositor may have intended to create no immediate interest in the designated beneficiary but merely to have the funds go to him only in the event of the depositor's death. Nevertheless, most courts hold that, presumptively, such a deposit presently creates a valid, although revocable, inter vivos trust, sometimes understandably called a "tentative trust."

6. Trusts Created by Wills

Trusts that are to be created by will are effective despite the fact that they are not intended to take effect until the testator dies. There *is* an expressed present intention to create a trust at the time the transfer occurs and the time at which the will "speaks"—*i.e.,* the date of death.

⬛GILBERT
CHECKLIST TO DETERMINE SUFFICIENT TRUST INTENT
TO DETERMINE WHETHER A SETTLOR HAS THE REQUISITE INTENT TO CREATE A TRUST, ASK YOURSELF THE FOLLOWING QUESTIONS:
☑ Is the intent manifested *by words or by conduct* (need not use the word "trust")?
☑ Is the intent expressed as a mere hope, wish, or suggestion (*precatory language*)?
☑ Is the intent manifested *while the settlor owns or is transferring* the intended res?
☑ Is the trust intended to take effect *immediately*?

C. Trust Property (Res)

1. Requirements—in General

The following are the three generally stated requirements for the trust property or "res": it must be (i) an *existing interest* in property; (ii) *capable of ownership and alienation*; and (iii) *sufficiently identifiable or identified*.

2. Interest in Property

The property must be an existing interest in existing property, real or personal, tangible or intangible. The interest held in trust may be a present or future interest, possessory or nonpossessory, vested or contingent. [Rest. 3d § 40]

a. Mere Expectancy Insufficient

An interest that has not yet come into existence—a mere expectancy—cannot be a trust res because the settlor does not have an enforceable claim to the property. [Rest. 3d § 41] This is unlike a presently existing future interest, which is vested the moment it was created,

Example: D declares that D holds "any properties I may inherit from F" (who is still alive) in trust for C's children. D has not created a valid trust; nor can D transfer such an expectancy to Trustee in trust.

Compare: If F had been dead when the transfer was made, however, there would be a valid trust because D's interest in the estate would be existing property, even if F's estate had not yet been administered.

EXAM TIP   GILBERT

Watch out for an exam question in which the trust property consists of property that the settlor *does not currently possess*. A *future interest* such as a remainder *can* be a trust property because it is a presently existing, legally protected right in property, although possession may be postponed until the future. However, a *mere expectancy* (*i.e.*, not yet in legal existence) *cannot* be held in trust.

(1) Manifestation Again After Acquisition

In the example above, if D again manifests D's present intention by declaring a trust of the inherited property *after* it is acquired, this will create a trust at that time; but the later declaration is not retroactive to the earlier expression of intention—a potentially important point because it fixes the date for the existence of the trust rights and duties. [*See* **Brainard v. Commissioner of Internal Revenue**, 91 F.2d 880 (7th Cir. 1937)]

(2) Consideration

In the example above, if F had paid *consideration* for D's declaration of a trust in assets to be subsequently acquired, however, the courts would probably treat the transaction as a contract to create a trust; when the assets are actually acquired, the contract can be specifically enforced even if D has changed D's mind.

EXAM TIP   GILBERT

Remember that consideration is *not* required to create a trust, but it can cause an otherwise unenforceable gratuitous *promise* to create a trust in the future to be *enforceable under contract principles*.

b. A Trust Beneficiary's Interest in One Trust Can Be the Res for Another Trust Interests in Trust

The property may consist of an equitable interest; *e.g.,* the interest of a trust beneficiary, if assignable, can be transferred into another trust and held as the res of that second trust for the benefit of others.

3. Alienability

Because trusts arise from by some form of transfer by the settlor (even if in the form of a declaration passing title from the settlor individually to the settlor in the settlor's fiduciary capacity), it is an informal maxim of trust law that the interest held in trust must be alienable. [Rest. 2d § 79]

a. Inalienable Property

Certain other types of property are not alienable, and hence cannot be transferred into a trust—*e.g.,* certain tort causes of action in some states, or the interest of a beneficiary of a spendthrift trust.

4. Identified or Identifiable

The trust res must be specific property that is actually identified or is described with sufficient certainty that it is identifiable, *i.e.,* can be ascertained from existing facts. [Rest. 3d § 40 cmt. e] Thus, it is often said that the trust property must be "segregated," but this is not technically true. It is more accurate to say that a trust requires a certain identifiable res. It does not mean that the trust property must be literally physically separate.

Example: S declares herself trustee of "the bulk of my securities." The description is too indefinite and creates no trust. But a declaration as to "all of my securities, except my Pear Stock" would be sufficient, because by taking inventory of all of S's securities on the date of the declaration and excluding the Pear Stock, the identity of the trust estate could be established.

a. Fractional Interests

The trust property may consist of a fractional undivided interest in *specific* land (*e.g.,* "a one-third interest in Blackacre") or goods (*e.g.,* "one-half ownership of my law library"). Similarly, an assignment of "40% of the funds in my savings account at National Bank" to another as trustee should be effective to create a trust of an undivided interest in the account as it exists on the date of the assignment.

b. Obligor as Trustee

As a general rule, an obligor does not, by agreement with the obligee calling for payment to a third person, become a trustee of what is simply his own debt. There is no identifiable trust res—no segregation of funds—as the debt remains merely a general claim against the obligor. [Rest. 3d § 40 cmt. b]

(1) Illustration—Insurance

An insurance company, while holding the proceeds of a matured policy and paying interest, is not the "trustee" of the funds. The beneficiary simply has a general, unliquidated claim against the company rather than a right to any particular asset or fund. This is true even where the proceeds are being held and paid pursuant to an "annuity option" or "pension payment plan" (or similar arrangement)—as long as no particular funds have been segregated and set apart by the company for this purpose.

(a) Note

If the company fails, the beneficiaries have no priority over other creditors because nothing is held in trust for them.

(2) Illustration—Bank Accounts

Bank deposits do not give rise to an identifiable trust property; there is no segregation and no inferred expectation of segregation by the bank of monies deposited, and there is but a general claim against it for the amount deposited (plus interest).

(a) Segregated Funds

A contrary result would follow if a trust were intended, where the bank *did* specially segregate the funds in question (*e.g.,* by having the specific funds on deposit placed in a separate vault or separately invested).

c. Obligee as Trustee

But note that a *depositor* may hold the deposit (the debt) as trustee for another. The deposit itself is clearly an identifiable res. The depositor, therefore, *can*, by declaration or assignment, name herself or constitute another as trustee of a bank account: *e.g.,* "I hereby declare myself trustee of Savings Account No. 123 at XYZ Bank, for the benefit of B."

(1) Totten Trusts

The usual problem presented by a deposit in one's own name "as trustee" for another, however, is whether the depositor really *intended* to create a trust and, if so, upon what terms. This is the so-called *Totten Trust* problem.

(2) "Special Deposits"

Problems may develop with "special deposits" where the depositor later becomes insolvent and creditors seek to reach the monies earmarked in the special account. For example, monies deposited in a special account to pay dividends to shareholders may be "trust" assets, belonging to the shareholders, and therefore not reachable by the depositing corporation's creditors.

5. Exception to the Res Requirement: Pourover Wills

The Uniform Testamentary Additions to Trusts Act (UTATA) addresses a common problem: a testator leaves property to a trust in her will, but fails to fund the trust during life. Under traditional trust law, this devise would fail because the trust, unfunded at the testator's death, does not exist. Because this happened often, defeating the testator's intent, the ULC drafted the UTATA, which is adopted in 44 states. The UTATA allows for a devise to a trust in a will to validly establish a trust as long as the trust is clearly identified and its terms are set forth in a separate trust instrument executed before, concurrently with, or after the execution of the testator's will. A will that funds a trust this way is called a "pourover will."

a. A pourover will can also validly devise property to a trust established in someone else's will

b. The fact that the trust is amendable or revocable does not affect the validity of the pourover provision.

e.g. **Example:** G executed a trust instrument benefitting B for life and remainder to D. A few years later, G amends to trust to benefit B for life, remainder to B's children, G does not fund the trust. At death, G's will devises property to the trust in a pourover will, The trust will be valid, and will go to B for life, with remainder to B's children.

WHAT CONSTITUTES SUFFICIENT TRUST RES	🔲 GILBERT
TRUST RES MAY BE:	**TRUST RES MAY *NOT* BE:**
• *Future interest*	• *Mere expectancy*
• Promise supported by *consideration*	• Unenforceable *gratuitous promise*
• *Equitable interest* (*e.g.,* beneficiary's interest in another trust)	• *Inalienable property* (*e.g.,* beneficiary's interest in a spendthrift trust)
• Fractional interest in *specific property*	• Fractional interest in *nonsegregated property*
• Debtor's *debt held by another*	• Debtor's *own debt*

D. Parties to the Trust

1. Settlor ("Trustor")

In general, a person who owns a property interest may create a trust with regard to it and become a settlor. The settlor may be called a trustor, grantor, or donor depending upon the context. [Rest. 3d § 3]

a. Capacity

A settlor's legal capacity to create a trust is measured by the same standards applied to similar nontrust conveyances. Thus, a settlor of a testamentary trust must have testamentary capacity, The settlor of a *revocable inter vivos trust* must have testamentary capacity (because such a trust is a will substitute), the settlor of an *irrevocable inter vivos trust* must have gift-making capacity and the settlor of a trust established as part of a commercial transaction must have contractual capacity. [Rest. 3d § 11 cmts. b, c]

(1) Voidability

Legal disabilities (*e.g.,* minority, mental incompetency) may render the settlor's act of creating the trust void or voidable, with the same consequences as any other void or voidable conveyance under appropriate local law. [Rest. 3d § 11 cmt. e] Under some circumstances, conservators or holders of durable powers of attorney may create (or amend) trusts on behalf of settlors under disability. [Rest. 3d § 11 cmt. f]

(2) Qualifications

In general, to have testamentary capacity, a settlor must: (i) be of legal age to make a will; (ii) suffer from no derangement (insane delusion) that affects the testamentary disposition; and (iii) be able to understand the nature and extent of her property, the natural objects of her bounty, the interrelationship of these, and to formulate and understand the disposition she is making. The settlor of an irrevocable inter vivos trust must meet the gift standard, which is probably the same as for wills with respect to mental sufficiency and freedom from derangement affecting the transfer. Capacity for an irrevocable inter vivos trust further requires the ability to understand the likely effects of such an irrevocable transfer upon the future financial security of the settlor and dependent family members.

b. Rights in Trust property After Creation of Trust

Once a trust is established, the settlor generally has only such rights or interests in the property as the terms of the trust grant to the settlor (*e.g.,* most commonly, a retained life estate or the expressed power to revoke and modify, or both). [Rest. 3d § 63] Hence, complete title vests in the trustee subject to equitable interests (beneficial rights and powers) conferred upon the beneficiaries (who may or may not include the settlor, depending on the trust's terms).

(1) Modern Trend—Revocability Presumed

Under the UTC and by statute in several non-UTC states (*e.g.,* California), inter vivos trusts are subject to revocation *unless expressly declared to be irrevocable* by the terms of the trust. [*See* UTC § 602(a)]

(2) Reversionary Interests

Even where no rights have been expressly reserved by the settlor, if the trust or some interest in it is invalid, the res is excessive for the trust purpose, or the equitable interests have not been completely disposed of, a *resulting trust* exists in favor of the settlor by operation of law. This just means that the trust property returns to the settlor—or the settlor's estate—as the settlor's property. This is an example of the use of the word "trust" for something that is not technically a trust: it just means that the property returns to the settlor in fee and there is no trust anymore.

(3) Mistake or Misconduct

A trust may be set aside or reformed for fraud, duress, undue influence, and other misconduct, or for mistake essentially upon the same grounds as other donative dispositions.

(4) No Right of Enforcement in Settlor as Such

Unless the settlor has retained beneficial interests in or powers over the trust (in which event she has the enforcement rights of a beneficiary), the general rule is that the settlor has no right to bring proceedings against a trustee or others for enforcement of the trust. This is because the settlor has no interest in the trust property.

c. Settlor's Creditors

If the trust is revocable, the settlor's creditors can reach all of the assets because the settlor herself still has access to them (i.e., the settlor can revoke the trust and regain fee title to the property). If the trust is irrevocable, whatever beneficial interests the settlor retains (*e.g.,* a right to income for life) can be reached by the settlor's creditors. Even if the trust provides that the settlor is entitled only to such income or principal as the trustee, in the settlor's discretion, deems appropriate, case law and numerous statutes indicate that the settlor's creditors can reach the *maximum* amount the trustee could permissibly distribute to the settlor.

(1) Exception—Asset Protection Trusts

A few states have enacted "asset protection" statutes that, in some circumstances, *deny* creditors access to settlor's assets even if the settlor retains a beneficial interest. One of the ways they achieve this is by setting a very short statute of limitations on applying fraudulent transfer law. [*See, e.g.,* Alaska Stat. § 34.40.110; Del. Code Ann. tit. 12, §§ 3570–3576]

(a) A recent case, however, cast uncertainty on the effectiveness of these arrangements. In 2008, a Washington real estate investor transferred his holdings to an Asset Protection Trust in Alaska, with an Alaska trust company and his son as trustees. The man, his son, and all the other beneficiaries were residents of the state of Washington. A bankruptcy court applied the Washington, not Alaska, statute of limitations for fraudulent transfers. The court noted that federal choice of law rules deferred to the settlor's choice of law unless that would violate an important policy of the state with which the trust had the most important relationship. [*In re* **Huber**, 493 B.R. 798 (2013).]

(2) Retained Powers

Creditors cannot reach the trust estate simply because the settlor reserved the power to direct the trustee regarding investments or distributions to others.

(3) Fraud

All states have Fraudulent Conveyance statutes with the effect that if a currently indebted settlor who transfers property to a trust the transfer will constitute fraud on creditors and will be voidable. In this case, creditors of the settlor can reach the trust estate.

2. Trustee

a. Qualifications

Any person or entity who has *capacity to acquire and hold property* for its own benefit *and has capacity to administer* the trust may be a trustee. Statutes limit the right of some persons or entities (*e.g.,* foreign corporations) to serve as a trustee.

(1) Capacity to Take and Hold Title

In the absence of statute, anyone who has capacity to acquire or hold title to the particular property for his own benefit also has capacity to receive the property as trustee thereof. [Rest. 3d § 32] Corporations and partnerships can hold title to property and can serve as trustees. [Rest. 3d § 33(2)]

(2) Capacity to Administer Trust

The capacity to take and hold property as a trustee is not the same as the capacity to administer the trust. Persons who have capacity to take and hold title to the property as trustee may not necessarily have capacity to *administer* the trust. Thus, a valid transfer may be made to such a person to create a trust, but that person will not be allowed to administer the trust (*i.e.,* to continue serving as the trustee). For example, minors or mentally disabled persons may validly receive property in trust, but because their contracts or acts are generally voidable and because such persons are not likely to possess the requisite skill and understanding to perform the trustee's duties, they lack capacity to administer an active trust, and will thus be removed by the court and replaced by another trustee. [Rest. 3d § 32 cmt. C]

(3) Corporations (Domestic and Foreign) as Trustees

Today *all* states authorize the use of corporate trustees (usually by statute). [Rest. 3d § 33(1)]

(a) Foreign Corporations

In several states today, *foreign* corporations (*i.e.,* those incorporated in other states) are *denied* the right to engage in trust administration or, as it is often provided by statute, "to carry on trust business" within the state.

(4) Co-Trustees

Where two or more persons or entities are named as trustees, each must have the requisite qualifications; if one does not, the right to act belongs only to the one or ones that do. Rest. 3d § 34 cmt. D] If the trust terms or purpose are construed as requiring a certain number of co-trustees for sound administration, the court will appoint an essential trustee to replace one who is disqualified or dies. [Rest. 3d § 34 cmt. E] (Co-trustees are generally deemed to hold the interest as joint tenants, with right of survivorship.)

b. Bonding

Although there was no automatic or presumptive bonding requirement at common law, statutes in many states require trustees of *testamentary* trusts to post a faithful-performance bond. More recent legislation tends to require a bond only if a court finds a need for it. [*See, e.g.,* UTC § 702(a)]

(1) Court May Order Bond to Protect Beneficiaries' Interests

Courts of equity (or probate or other appropriate court) generally have the power to compel the trustee of any type of trust to post a bond if there is a particular risk or if the trustee is involved in litigation with the beneficiaries in which there is a *personal attack* on the trustee (*e.g.,* for mismanagement of the trust, etc.).

(2) Court May Override Waiver of Bond

This equitable power applies even where the settlor has expressly provided that a bond is not necessary *if* there is a direct attack on the trustee's performance or a material change of circumstances; otherwise, the court probably will *not* order the trustee to post a bond where the settlor provided relief from bonding. A court generally may also relieve or reduce an otherwise applicable bonding requirement.

(3) Caution—Without Trustee an Intended Inter Vivos Trust May Fail for Lack of Delivery

Note, however, that the absence of a trustee may result in the failure of the attempted creation of an inter vivos trust because of the requirement of a present and effective transfer. In other words, if there is no trustee, there is no one to whom delivery can be made; without delivery, there is no transfer and thus no trust. Hence, the trust fails for *lack of a transfer*, not for want of a trustee.

(a) Attempted Transfer to Trustee to Be Named in Will

An attempted *inter vivos assignment* to the "trustee to be named in my will" fails for lack of delivery and for want of a trustee to pass the title to at the time of the purported conveyance. With no effective transfer, there is no trust.

(b) Trustee Disqualified

If there is an intended trustee to whom delivery (with requisite present intent) is made, but the transferee is technically disqualified by law from taking title (not merely disqualified from serving as trustee), it's not clear what happens. A court may salvage the trust (possibly as a declaration of trust or by appointing a trustee, especially for a natural object of the transferor's bounty). But supposedly "equity does not save defective gifts by treating them as declarations of trust." The question is unsettled, and the theoretical basis for a trust in such a situation is unclear.

(c) Testamentary Trusts

This problem does not arise in connection with *testamentary* trusts because no requirement of delivery exists. The transfer requirement is satisfied if there is a validly executed will and the testator dies; no more is required. If the trustee named in the bequest or devise is predeceased, lacks capacity, or disclaims, or even if no trustee has been named ("I leave my residuary estate in trust for L for life, remainder to R"), the trust is nevertheless good (unless personal to the named trustee), and a trustee will be appointed by the appropriate court.

EXAM TIP   **GILBERT**

If you encounter an exam question in which the named trustee dies, refuses to accept the trusteeship, or resigns, remember that the court will appoint a successor trustee **unless** it is clear that the settlor intended the trust to continue only so long as that particular trustee served. While a trust will not fail for want of a trustee, an attempted inter vivos trust that does not name a trustee **may fail** for lack of delivery.

---

c. Nature of Trustee's Interest

(1) Title to Trust Res

The trustee is said to have a "bare" legal title, meaning that it is devoid of beneficial ownership; *i.e.*, the trust property is held for and on behalf of the beneficiaries in accordance with the terms of the trust.

(a) Relation Back

The trustee's title in the res of a testamentary trust "relates back" to the settlor's death because the trust is treated as having been in existence from that date.

The relation back rule is important to remember because it is possible for a trustee, by accepting, to become **personally liable** on contract or tort claims arising **prior** to the time the trustee accepted.

(2) Trust Estate Not Liable for Personal Debts of Trustee

The trustee has only a "bare" legal title (no beneficial interest), and hence the **trustee's personal creditors cannot reach** or satisfy their claims from trust property. [Rest. 2d § 308; Rest. 3d § 42 cmt. c]

(3) Effect of Trustee's Death

(a) Death of Sole Trustee

Although the trustee has only a "bare" legal title, it is nevertheless title. On the trustee's death that title passes to the trustee's estate **subject to the trust**. Thus, the trustee's heirs take no beneficial interest; and the trustee's surviving spouse cannot claim an elective share in the trust property. Furthermore, the decedent's personal representative (i.e., executor or administrator) has no active administrative power over the property but probably has a duty to protect it and, if necessary, see to the appointment of a successor trustee. The court will direct the transfer of title to a successor, who then has the power to administer the trust. [Rest. 2d § 104]

(b) Death of One of Several Co-Trustees

Co-trustees are presumed to hold title as **joint tenants**, with the right of survivorship. Thus, on the death of a co-trustee, the title vests exclusively in the survivor(s). The law presumes, in the absence of circumstances indicating the contrary, that the settlor intended to have the survivor(s) discharge the burdens of the trusteeship. [Rest. 3d § 34 cmt. d] If the instrument provides otherwise or the court finds contrary intent, however, this presumption does not apply and a successor co-trustee will be appointed; this may also be done if the court concludes that this is administratively more efficient or prudent (*e.g.,* where the surviving trustee has a conflict of interest, often as a beneficiary).

d. Disclaimer or Resignation by Trustee

(1) Disclaimer

One cannot be forced to be a trustee. Thus, one who has not previously accepted a trusteeship or contracted in advance to do so can disclaim and refuse appointment as trustee for any reason (or for no reason) whatsoever. [Rest. 3d § 35(2)] The trustee cannot accept in part and disclaim in part; if he accepts at all, he is deemed to have accepted the entire trust. A trustee may, however, delegate certain duties to parties who are more qualified.

(2) Resignation

Once having accepted appointment as trustee, a person may resign only by complying with a method set out in the trust instrument, giving 30 days' notice to the qualified beneficiaries, the settlor, if living, and all co-trustees; or with the approval of the court. UTC § 705. Until the resignation is accepted and, if a court is involved, there is an appropriate order, the trustee must carry out and perform all the various trust duties, and the trustee remains personally liable for the consequences of any defaults in the meantime. [UTC § 707; Rest. 3d § 36]

(a) Effect of Unauthorized Reconveyance

The trustee cannot escape his responsibilities or defeat the trust by reconveying the trust property to the settlor after accepting the trusteeship. The purported reconveyance may be treated as a nullity, or at most the reconveyance may effectively return *legal* title to the settlor with the beneficial ownership remaining in the beneficiaries. The settlor would then hold title as *constructive* trustee for their benefit.

(b) When Resignation Becomes Effective

Even if the trust instrument permits the trustee to resign, the resignation usually is not effective until a successor is appointed. The common law notion of "no gap in succession" and the interest of sound, secure administration require that legal title and duties remain in the trustee until a successor trustee takes them on the trustee assumed this obligation in accepting appointment initially.

e. Removal of Trustees

Unless the settlor reserves the power to remove a trustee or confers that power on some named or described beneficiary(ies), or other person(s), only a court of competent jurisdiction may remove a trustee. [Rest. 3d § 37; UTC § 706]

(1) Grounds for Removal

Numerous grounds exist for removal of a trustee, but the basic criterion is whether the trustee's continuance in office would be detrimental to the interests of the beneficiaries. Among the various grounds for removal are as follows: legal or practical disability, serious or repeated breach of trust responsibilities, including the duty to cooperate with co-trustees and the duty to render accountings or reports, refusal to give a bond as required. commission of a crime involving dishonesty, and conflict of interest not contemplated by the settlor. [*In re* **Estate of Berthot,** 59 P.3d 1080 (Mont. 2002); UTC § 706]

(a) Insolvency

Insolvency of the trustee is generally not in itself a sufficient ground for removal, unless the court finds that the trustee's insolvency jeopardizes the welfare of the trust. But some state statutes do list insolvency as grounds for removal. [*E.g., In re* **Estate of Berthot,** 59 P.3d 1080 (Mont. 2002)]

Disagreement or tension between the trustee and one or more beneficiaries is not a ground for removal unless the animosity jeopardizes the sound administration of the trust.

(b) Settlor-Appointed Trustee

Generally, the courts are less inclined to remove a trustee named by the settlor than one appointed by the court. This is particularly true if the alleged ground for removal (*e.g.,* a conflict of interest) was one *known to or anticipated by the settlor*.

(2) Removal by Beneficiaries

If under the trust terms the beneficiaries have the power to modify the trust or to terminate it and compel the trustee to transfer the property to them, they have a power to remove the trustee directly, because it would be pointless to require them to change the terms of the trust or terminate it and immediately create a new trust upon the same terms with a new trustee. [UTC § 706(b)(4)]

GROUNDS FOR REMOVAL OF TRUSTEE	⬛GILBERT
SUFFICIENT GROUNDS FOR REMOVAL:	**INSUFFICIENT GROUNDS FOR REMOVAL:**
• Legal or practical *disability* • Serious or repeated *breach of trust responsibilities* (*e.g.*, failure to render accounting) • *Refusal to give bond* • Commission of *crime involving dishonesty* • *Conflict of interest* not contemplated by settlor	• *Generally, insolvency*, unless welfare of trust jeopardized • *Animosity* between trustee and beneficiaries, unless welfare of trust jeopardized

f. Merger of Title Where Sole Trustee Is Also Sole Beneficiary

Where the trustee (the holder of legal title) and the beneficiary (the holder of equitable title) are or become one and the same person, the legal and equitable titles merge, defeating the trust and creating a fee simple absolute in the trustee-beneficiary, who thus holds outright and free of trust. [Rest. 3d § 69]

(1) Merger and Living Trusts

In many revocable or living trusts, the settlor is often the only trustee and the only present beneficiary. Although this seems like a recipe for merger, merger does not apply as long as the future beneficiaries are different from the current settlor/beneficiary. Merger would apply only if the only future beneficiary was the settlor's estate. [UTC § 402(5)]

EXAMPLE	RESULT	RATIONALE
S TO A IN TRUST FOR A	Merger	Holder of legal title (A) and holder of equitable title (A) are **one and the same person** at outset
S TO A IN TRUST FOR B; B DIES, LEAVING A AS HER SOLE HEIR	Merger	Holder of legal title (A) **becomes** holder of equitable title upon B's death
S TO A IN TRUST FOR A FOR LIFE, THEN TO B; B TRANSFERS HER INTEREST TO A	Merger	Holder of legal title (A) **becomes** holder of equitable title upon B's transfer
S TO A IN TRUST FOR B; A DIES, LEAVING B AS HIS SOLE HEIR	Merger	Holder of equitable title (B) **becomes** holder of legal title upon A's death
S TO A IN TRUST FOR A AND B	No merger	Legal and equitable interests are **not identical**; A has entire legal interest and one-half equitable interest
S TO A AND B IN TRUST FOR A AND B FOR LIFE, THEN TO C	No merger	Legal and equitable interests are **not identical**; A and B hold legal interest in fee and life estate in equitable interest
S TO A AND B IN TRUST FOR A AND C	Merger	Although A has one-half legal interest and one-half equitable interest, A and B's **joint management** is required
S TO A AND B IN TRUST FOR A AND B	Merger	Although A and B seemingly have identical legal and equitable interests, **each holds for benefit of both**

(a) No Merger Where Several Trustees Are Also the Beneficiaries

"S to C and D upon trust for C and D" creates a valid trust (no merger). [Rest. 3d § 69 cmt.] S probably intended C and D to jointly manage the equitable interest of each—*i.e.,* each co-trustee to hold for the benefit of ***both***. Again, some authorities have disagreed, arguing that there should be a merger in this situation, the quantum and nature of the estate being identical.

(b) Comment

Controversy over whether a merger has taken place arises most frequently when a ***creditor*** is pursuing the beneficiary's assets. The creditor will argue for merger so that the creditor can satisfy the creditor's claim out of the "beneficiary's" merged share of the estate, which is usually more practical and effective than attempting to levy on a beneficiary's equitable interest.

3. Beneficiaries

a. Necessity of Beneficiaries

(1) Private Trusts

To create a private trust (as distinguished from a charitable trust or, if recognized, an honorary trust), the settlor must name or otherwise describe one or more beneficiaries (individuals or eligible legal entities) who can be identified with certainty, acquire a property interest and enforce duties on the trustee. Thus, "my friends" are not identifiable beneficiaries because views could differ about who they were. An intended trust will ***fail*** if the trust has no identifiable beneficiary. Without a beneficiary, there is no one capable of enforcing the trust (as there must be for a valid private trust), and it therefore fails. [Rest. 3d §§ 43–46]

EXAM TIP

Recall that a trust will ***not fail for lack of a trustee***. But it will fail for lack of an identifiable beneficiary. This is because, without a beneficiary, there is no one to enforce its terms on the trustee. Thus, a beneficiary is necessary to the validity of ***every*** trust ***except*** charitable and honorary trusts. If a trust fails for lack of a beneficiary, a ***resulting trust*** in favor of the settlor or the settlor's successors arises.

(a) What Satisfies the Identifiable Beneficiary Requirement?

To satisfy the requirement that there be at least one beneficiary if there is one or more of the following:

(i) Beneficiaries ***named*** by the trust terms;

(ii) Beneficiaries ***so described as to be presently identifiable*** from extrinsic facts, such as "my current employees" (evidence of extrinsic facts is admissible, *e.g.,* as a "fact of independent significance" in the case of a will—*see* Wills Summary); or

(iii) Beneficiaries ***to become ascertainable*** at a future time (*e.g.,* "for those of my issue living 20 years after the death of X") as long as they will become ascertainable, if at all, ***within the period of the appropriate Rule Against Perpetuities***. (Modest authority requires that there be at least one presently identifiable beneficiary.)

1) Unborn Beneficiaries

This requirement is satisfied even if some or (by the better view) all of the beneficiaries or classes of beneficiaries are presently unborn. [Rest. 3d § 44]

2) Beneficiaries to Be Selected by Trustee

It is even alright if the trustee may ascertain the beneficiaries by the exercise of the trustee's (or another's) discretion, as long as (under traditional doctrine) the class among which the selection is to be made is reasonably definite or will become so within the perpetuities period.

(b) Trustee's Awareness of Intended Beneficiary

The *trustee* need not actually know who the designated beneficiary is, as long as the beneficiary is capable of being identified when necessary (*e.g.*, where the trustee is handed a sealed envelope at the time the property is transferred to the trustee, who agrees to hold in trust for persons named therein).

(c) Effect of Lack of Beneficiary

Where a private trust fails for lack of a beneficiary (or for lack of properly ascertainable beneficiaries), there is a *resulting trust* in favor of the transferor, his heirs, or other successors in interest.

(d) Charitable Trusts

Identifiable beneficiaries are *not* required for charitable trusts; the Attorney General (or similar public official) enforces such trusts.

(2) Honorary Trusts

Jurisdictions that have adopted the UTC allow "purpose trusts" or "honorary trusts"—trusts that are *neither charitable nor private.* They are devices that allow the carrying out of certain objectives that are not private and that fall short of being charitable. The classic example is an intended trust for one's *pets*. Other honorary trust purposes have involved the *maintenance of graves* (now usually permitted by statute) or the *funding of masses* (now usually a religious charitable purpose).

Example: T bequeaths T's residuary estate "to B in trust to care for my dogs and cats." The trust is clearly *not charitable* because it is not broad enough to be charitable because it is only for T's pets. (Contrast a properly charitable trust for "stray" dogs and cats.) *Nor* is the purpose enforceable as a *private trust*, because there is no beneficiary capable of enforcing it; the "beneficiaries" are the pets.

(a) Pet Trusts

All fifty states now recognize pet trusts, either through the UTC or some other statute. [UTC § 408] A settlor can create these trusts for an animal or animals alive during the settlor's lifetime, and the trust will last until the death of the last animal alive. The settlor can designate a person to enforce the duties on the trustee, or a court may appoint someone to do so. If a court deems the amount in the trust to be more than necessary for the animal's care, a court may order that the excess be distributed to the settlor's successors in interest. This is exactly what happened in the case of the trust Leona Helmsley left for her dog, a Maltese named, apparently appropriately, Trouble. A judge declared the 12 million excessive for the dog's needs and ordered much of it distributed through her estate.

1) Effect—Transferee May Carry out Purpose

If and so far as the transferee voluntarily carries out the purpose, the transferee will be allowed to do so and no one can object. But if the transferee fails to do so, or after the transferee has carried out the purpose, the transferee holds the property (or what is left of it) on a *resulting trust* for the transferor or the transferor's successors in interest (*e.g.,* heirs).

 Example: Same facts as in the example above, except the jurisdiction applies the honorary trust doctrine. B is allowed to carry out T's purpose, and if B does, T's successors cannot complain, at least not for 21 years or until B has rejected or abandoned the purpose; but B cannot retain the property for B's own use.

(b) Distinguish

If *precatory* expressions (*e.g.,* "I hope," "wish," "request") are used and if no trust intent is shown, the transferee can disregard the suggestion and keep *the property* outright. In that case, if the transferee wishes, the transferee may carry out the transferor's suggestion, not as an honorary trust but because the transferee is free to do so as owner of the property.

---

b. Who May Be a Beneficiary of a Private Trust?

Broadly, any person, natural or artificial, who is capable of taking and holding title to property may be a beneficiary of a private trust. [Rest. 3d § 43]

(1) Minors, Incompetents

Minors and incompetents may be (and often are) beneficiaries because they have capacity to hold title.

(2) Unincorporated Associations (Partnerships, LLCs, etc.)

The trend today is to treat unincorporated associations as legal entities for at least some purposes (*e.g.,* to sue and be sued in the group name and to hold title to property). Accordingly, they now generally can be trust beneficiaries. [Rest. 3d § 43 cmt. d]

	CAPACITY REQUIRED	TYPE OF PERSON			
		ADULT	CORPORATION	PARTNERSHIP	MINOR OR INCOMPETENT
TRUSTEE	To take and hold title **and** to administer trust	Yes	Yes	Yes (modern view)	No
BENEFICIARY	To take and hold title	Yes	Yes	Yes (modern view)	Yes

c. Requirement That Beneficiaries Be Identified or Members of a Reasonably Definite Class

A valid private trust requires beneficiaries capable of enforcing the trust, and those beneficiaries must be ascertained or ascertainable when the trust is created or assuredly become ascertainable, if at all, within the period of the Rule Against Perpetuities (*see* Future Interests Summary). The purpose of this requirement of identifiable beneficiaries is, ostensibly at least, to assure that the trust is or will be enforceable, which in turn ostensibly requires or will require persons who are identifiable as beneficiaries or as members of a "reasonably definite and ascertainable class" of beneficiaries. [Rest. 3d §§ 44–46]

(1) Beneficiaries Unascertained When Trust Created

A beneficiary need not be identified or even identifiable at the date the trust is created. It is sufficient if the instrument gives a formula or description by which the beneficiary can be identified at the time when enjoyment of his interest is to begin. (That time, however, must be within the period of the applicable Rule Against Perpetuities; *i.e.,* under the traditional common law rule, it must be certain at the outset that the beneficiary will either be ascertainable, so that the interest will vest within the period, or that the interest will fail by that time. In either event there will assuredly be an ascertainable beneficiary, and an ability to enforce the trustee's duties, either via the expressed interest or by way of a resulting trust.)

e.g. **Example:** S's transfer "to T in trust for C for life, remainder to C's *"children"* is clearly valid. This is true even if C had no children at the date the trust was executed: Whatever "children" C later has will necessarily be ascertainable by the time enjoyment of their interest is to begin (on C's death). If there are no children, there will be a resulting trust for S or S's successors in interest.

(a) Note

The same also should be true for: (i) a trust executed for the settlor's "spouse" at a time when the settlor was still unmarried; (ii) a trust solely for afterborn children of the settlor; or even (iii) a trust for a *corporation* to be formed, *e.g.,* by the settlor or within 21 years.

(b) Status Until Beneficiaries Ascertained

If the as-yet-unascertained beneficiary or beneficiaries are the *sole* beneficiary or beneficiaries (*e.g.,* "S to T in trust for the children of B," when B has no children):

1) Majority—It's Still a Valid Trust

The more sound and usual view is that the trust is valid and enforceable [Rest. 3d § 44 cmt. c] A court might appoint a guardian ad litem to protect the interests of the unborn beneficiaries.

(c) Reference to Extrinsic Writing

Where a will does not identify the beneficiaries but involves reference to another document, that document must either satisfy the requirements of the applicable wills act or must satisfy the requirements of the doctrine of incorporation by reference. The doctrine, which allows an extrinsic document not present at the time the will was executed to be incorporated into the will, may be relied upon to complete the terms of the will.

(d) Reference to Acts of Independent Significance

Where unnamed beneficiaries of a testamentary trust are to be ascertained by a "formula" or description, that identification must be based on "acts of independent significance." Under this doctrine, a will may dispose of property by reference to acts or events that have significance apart from their effect on dispositions made by the will. (*See* Wills Summary.)

e.g. **Example:** A bequest "to Y in trust for such person as Y believes most deserving for having cared for me in my last illness" is enforceable. The beneficiary is ascertainable from circumstances outside the will that have an independent significance. In cases of doubt, the court can receive extrinsic evidence to determine the person entitled to take.

GILBERT

DETERMINING DEFINITENESS OF BENEFICIARIES UNDER PRIVATE TRUST

TO DETERMINE WHETHER THE DEFINITE BENEFICIARY REQUIREMENT IS SATISFIED, ASK YOURSELF THE FOLLOWING QUESTIONS:

- ☑ Are the beneficiaries *specifically named* in the trust terms?
- ☑ Are the beneficiaries *presently identifiable from extrinsic facts* (*e.g.,* incorporation by reference, acts of independent significance)?
- ☑ Will the beneficiaries be *ascertainable by the time their interests are to come into enjoyment* (and within the period of the Rule Against Perpetuities)?

(2) Gifts in Trust to a Class of Beneficiaries

A private trust may (and usually does, at least in part) benefit the members of a class of persons. These persons are trust beneficiaries and their interests are valid ***provided*** the trust describes them with sufficient certainty that its membership is or will become reasonably definite and ascertainable within the period of the Rule Against Perpetuities.

(a) Some Special Class Gift Questions

1) Was a Class Gift Intended?

Assume the settlor conveys "to Trustee in trust for the directors of the XYZ fraternal society." Is this gift to the directors as a class, or is it intended as a gift to the association? Cases of this type are generally resolved by extrinsic evidence of the settlor's probable intent. If the gift is construed as one to the association, this may raise the problem of whether an unincorporated group can be the beneficiary of a trust.

2) When Is the Class Determined?

Assuming a class gift was intended, did the settlor intend to benefit the ***present and/or future*** members of the class? This is merely a problem in construction of the trust instrument and comes up in gifts for a person's "family" (*see* below).

EXAM TIP **GILBERT**

If it appears that the settlor intended to benefit ***future class members***, the identity of the future beneficiaries must be ***ascertainable within the period of the Rule Against Perpetuities*** for the trust class gift to be valid. (*See* Future Interests Summary)

(b) Effect of Trustee or Other Person Having Power to Select Among Class Members

Trust interests for members of a class are normally uncomplicated where the class membership is limited and definite and where the class members receive the property or benefits in equal shares or in other fixed portions. Sometimes, however, a trustee has "discretion" to select, and to allocate or apportion trust benefits among, one or more members of a designated class. Trusts based on such powers are clearly valid [Rest. 3d § 45] if the class is sufficiently definite; but if the class is not sufficiently definite, a trustee's power of selection will normally not make the class definite or render the potential beneficiaries sufficiently ascertainable to sustain the trust in many American jurisdictions.

1) Amount of Gift Need Not Be Certain

The fact that the ***amount*** distributable to each member of the class is uncertain (*e.g.,* merely because the distributions are subject to the trustee's discretion, even "uncontrolled" discretion) does not impair the validity of the gift. As long as the class itself is sufficiently definite, the trust will be upheld.

a) Trustee's Discretion

If the trustee or third person is given the discretionary power to distribute among a class, the usual interpretation is that the trustee has the power to do so selectively—*i.e.,* can give all to one or more of the class and exclude everyone else. [Rest. 3d § 45 cmt. c] (There is, nevertheless, the possibility that a particular exercise will be found to be an abuse of discretion. [*See* Rest. 3d § 50])

b) Successor Trustee Appointed if Trustee Fails to Act

On the other hand, if the trustee fails (or refuses) to exercise the trustee's discretion as to which members of the class shall take, the court may appoint a successor trustee who may exercise the power provided the court finds that the settlor would so intend (*i.e.,* that the power is not personal to the original trustee and that the trustee's nonexercise was improper—not what the settlor had intended to permit); or the court may, if it deems necessary, direct distribution as a matter of construction, having all members of the class share equally (or perhaps according to some other principle, such as that of representation (or per stirpes) if the class is someone's "issue" or "descendants").

EXAM TIP

Remember that as long as the class is *reasonably definite*, the trust may authorize the trustee to *exercise the trustee's discretion in selecting members to be benefited*, or may provide that only those who meet certain requirements will benefit. Broad power to choose beneficiaries, however, may constitute a *power of appointment* rather than a trust.

(c) What Constitutes a Reasonably Definite Class?

For there to be a *trust* the class of beneficiaries must be definite enough that a court can determine: (i) by whom or on whose behalf the trust may be enforced (*any member of a definite class* of beneficiaries or of permissible discretionary beneficiaries may bring suit); and (ii) where the trustee has a power of selection, whether the selection is within the authorized class or, if no selection is made, to whom distribution is to be made by distribution to all or some members on some principle such as that of representation.

1) Definite

Most clearly, the following class gift terms describe a sufficiently *definite class* to serve as a class of trust beneficiaries (or as implied takers in default): "children," "brothers and sisters," "nieces and nephews," "heirs" or "next of kin," and "issue" or "descendants." "Cousins" is alright provided the court will determine the degree as a matter of construction (*e.g.,* meaning only "first cousins").

2) Indefinite

At the other extreme, the following references are *not sufficiently definite* to constitute a definite class: (i) "to such persons as my trustee may select"; (ii) "among such of my friends as the trustee shall determine"; and (iii) (in the absence of a formula or reasonably objective criteria) "to such persons as my trustee deems most appropriate."

3) Location

Location may be used to identify members of a class. "All those who resided or worked at the same address" as the settlor during the settlor's lifetime has been held to constitute a sufficiently definite class. (Remaining uncertainties can then be resolved by interpretation.)

4) "Family"

"Family" is not without potential difficulty, but it is generally so *construed* as to constitute a sufficiently definite class consisting of one's spouse and children and probably other persons living with the person whose family is designated in what is generally understood as a "family relationship" (thus leaving further room for interpretation, which courts are likely to be willing to undertake as necessary—*e.g.,* to determine specific questions about inclusion of stepchildren, etc.). [Rest. 3d § 45 cmt. e]

5) "Relatives," etc.

"Relatives," "relations," "kindred," and the like ("family" more broadly construed than above) present a more troublesome problem upon which the authorities differ, as the terms may be considered too vague. How many degrees of relationship are intended to be included? Second, third, or sixth cousins? First cousins twice removed? Aunts and uncles? Great-aunts and uncles? Grandnephews? Descendants (or collaterals) who have living ancestors between themselves and the transferor? A first step, again, is to decide whether to accept the class as *definite*; if a court decides to do so, it will undertake the task, inevitably involving guesswork, of clarifying the settlor's "definite" but carelessly vague class language.

a) Modern Construction—Next of Kin

Many and probably most courts today, however, will attempt to uphold the gift by interpreting "relatives" and the like to mean those who are the designated person's *next of kin* in existence at the relevant time (usually the time when the trust takes effect), and this would then constitute a sufficiently definite class of beneficiaries or discretionary beneficiaries to sustain a trust. [Rest. 3d § 45 cmt. d]

DEFINITE VS. INDEFINITE CLASS TERMS

GILBERT

| SUFFICIENTLY DEFINITE | | *NOT* SUFFICIENTLY DEFINITE |

← →

- "Children"
- "Issue" or "descendants"
- "Heirs" or "next of kin"
- "Brothers and sisters"
- "Nieces and nephews"
- "Cousins" (if only includes first cousins)
- "Such persons at [location]"

- "Family"
- "Relatives"
- "Kindred"

- "My friends"
- "Such persons as trustee may select"
- "Such persons as trustee deems appropriate"

PARTIES TO A TRUST—A REVIEW

GILBERT

	REQUIRED CAPACITY	RIGHTS IN TRUST RES	CAN CREDITORS REACH INTEREST?
SETTLOR	*Depends on type of trust:*	Expressly reserved rights (*e.g.,* life estate, power to modify or revoke) and reversionary rights (*e.g.,* resulting trust)	Yes
TESTAMENTARY TRUST	Must be of legal age and sound mind; know the nature of her act, extent of her property, and who are the natural objects of her bounty (*i.e.,* **testamentary capacity**)		
DONATIVE INTER VIVOS TRUST	Ability to understand **impact of transfer** upon financial security		

TRUSTEE	Must be able to (i) ***take and hold title*** and (ii) ***administer*** the trust (*Note:* Minors and disabled persons meet (i) but not (ii))	Legal title	No
BENEFICIARY(IES)	Must be able to ***take and hold title***	Equitable title	Yes, unless protected by a ***spendthrift provision***

(3) Extent of Interest

The beneficiary's equitable interest under the trust may be for years or for life; it may be an interest of infinite duration, or it may be a future interest. It may be contingent or vested, subject to a condition precedent or subsequent or determinable, and it may be possessory or nonpossessory. Furthermore, the settlor may make some beneficiaries primary or preferred and others only secondary. [Rest. 3d § 49 cmt. b]

(4) Form of Co-Tenancy

Whereas co-trustees are presumed to hold the interests as joint tenants with rights of survivorship, co-beneficiaries of an interest in the res are ***presumed*** to acquire and hold their interests as ***tenants in common*** unless the settlor has expressed another intent. Thus, on the beneficiary's death, any remaining interest she has in the trust passes to her testate or intestate successors; it does not belong to the other beneficiaries unless the trust expressly or impliedly so provides.

E. Trust Purposes

1. Requirement of Lawful and Appropriate Purpose

A trust may not have a purpose that is illegal or contrary to public policy. Statutes in some states provide that a trust may be created for any purposes for which a ***contract*** could be made, but it is not at all clear that these statutes alter the purposes allowed or prohibited by the general common law of trusts.

a. Private Trust

Usually, the objective of the settlor is to promote or secure the welfare of some person or limited number of people (spouse, children, siblings, etc.). This is, of course, a permissible "private" trust purpose. In fact, it is increasingly accepted that "a private trust, its terms, and its administration must be for the benefit of its beneficiaries." [Rest. 3d § 27(2); *and see* UTC § 404]

b. Charitable Trust

Where the settlor's objective is to promote the welfare of members of a large and indefinite group of individuals (*e.g.,* students at a particular school through a scholarship fund), or of the public at large, the trust purpose may be considered sufficiently important such that special rules apply to the trust as one having a "charitable" purpose.

c. Honorary and Mixed Trusts

Except for the special case of "purpose trusts" or "honorary trusts," a trust *must* either be private or charitable, or if the interests are separable, it may be partly each. [Rest. 3d § 28 cmt. e]

2. Impermissible Trust Purposes

Occasionally, a trust, or more often some provision therein, may be challenged as invalid if it appears that the settlor was attempting to accomplish an objective that is illegal, requires the commission of a criminal or tortious act by the trustee, or would otherwise be contrary to public policy. [Rest. 3d § 29]

a. Fraud on Creditors; Fraudulent Transfer

An example of an invalid trust purpose is where the owner of property transfers it to another in trust for the purpose of concealing the property to hinder or defraud the transferor's creditors.

(1) Effect

In this situation, the trust is regarded as a nullity, and the creditors of the settlor may reach the property as if the trust did not exist or set aside the transfer as fraudulent.

(2) Can Settlor Regain Property?

Suppose no creditors materialize or that the transferor was able or forced to pay the transferor's creditors out of other funds: Will the transferor be permitted to compel the transferee to return the property?

(a) The transferor's purpose may be considered to be so improper that he is not entitled to relief in equity ("unclean hands"). As "equity will leave wrongdoers where it finds them," the express trust will not be enforced and no constructive or resulting trust imposed; under such a rule, even a dishonest transferee may be allowed to retain the property.

(3) Distinguish—Protection of Beneficiary's Interest

While the settlor cannot employ the trust device to avoid the settlor's own creditors, the settlor *can* employ it to shelter the interest from the beneficiary's creditors.

b. Other Prohibited Trust Purposes

Other trust purposes or conditions that are invalid as being contrary to public policy include trusts or provisions for capricious purposes (*e.g.*, to destroy or waste valuable property) or that reward a person for committing an act that is immoral, illegal, or contrary to the perceived public interest. Significant examples of trust purposes that are against public policy are:

(1) Restraints on Marriage

Trusts that *unreasonably restrain* marriage by a beneficiary are invalid. "Reasonableness" turns on the duration and extent or breadth of the restraint. Thus, a gift in trust "for Daughter as long as she remains single, but if she ever marries, to Son" would be unreasonable, whereas a restraint on marriage until age 21 is likely to be upheld. A gift over on the remarriage of the settlor's surviving spouse (*e.g.*, "income for life to my spouse, W, but if W remarries, the trust shall terminate and be distributed to my issue") is, by nearly all cases and some statutes, not unreasonable, apparently because a settlor may provide for the settlor's spouse's widowhood.

(2) Encouragement of Divorce

Trusts that encourage a beneficiary to divorce are also invalid. However, in most states, if the gift merely attempts to provide for the beneficiary in the event of divorce, rather than induce divorce, it is valid. Parol evidence of the settlor's subjective motive is admissible to determine validity. Critics of this distinction point out the potential for manipulative drafting, the speculative or unreliable nature of such evidence, and that effect, not motive, should matter.

(a) Distinguish—Discouraging Divorce

Because public policy is said to favor marriage, courts have upheld conditions requiring that a beneficiary *not* divorce a spouse.

(b) Distinguish—Will Provisions

A bequest in a will that is conditioned on the beneficiary's being divorced or not having married *when the testator dies* is normally valid. This is because there is no continuing inducement as there would be if there were a trust. The testator is generally free to leave or not leave property to a beneficiary for whatever reasons the testator sees fit, but a person is not allowed to use a *trust* for all purposes that would have been permissible to that person during life or directly by will. Trusts, whether testamentary or irrevocable inter vivos, arguably impose an ongoing burden on others, and therefore must have "worthwhile" private or charitable purposes. Thus, reasonable regulation of "dead hand control" has long been allowed to limit freedom of testation; and similar principles apply to trusts.

EXAM TIP   GILBERT

If you encounter an exam question in which a beneficiary's interest is conditioned on the beneficiary's marital status, look at the settlor's *intent*. If the purpose of the restraint is to *penalize marriage or encourage divorce*, the restraint may be struck down. On the other hand, if the purpose is to *give support until marriage or during divorce*, the restraint is likely valid.

---

(3) Interference with Other Family Relationships

Cases have invalidated conditions that tend to disrupt other family relationships or to discourage resumption of family interaction.

Example: R devised R's residence to R's two children, J, and F, "so long as they want to live at the residence, provided their biological mother does not reside there also." If J's primary intent was to separate his two children from their biological, the provisions are violative of public policy. The condition would be removed.

(4) Religious Restrictions

Restrictions on religion come under close scrutiny but the case law on this matter is neither consistent nor clear; such conditions are sometimes upheld and sometimes not. Cases have consistently held, however, that a trust may condition benefits on the beneficiary's marrying someone of a particular religion. [*In re* Estate of **Feinberg**, 919 N.E.2d 888 (Ill. 2009).

(5) Effect of Invalid Provisions

The consequences depend on the settlor's probable intent, as expressed in the trust instrument or as otherwise apparent. The court's response is not a punitive one. Usually, courts will attempt to *excise* the illegal purpose or condition and enforce the trust without it, so long as this does not defeat the overall purpose of the settlor in creating the trust. [Rest. 3d § 29 cmt. i(1)]

e.g. **Example:** S bequeaths money to Trustee Bank in trust to pay the income to H "provided H divorces his wife, W." Because the condition appears to be aimed at procuring a divorce, it is invalid. H is therefore entitled to the income free of the condition, unless the circumstances indicate that Settlor would not otherwise have intended H to have the income at all—*i.e.,* either (based on the court's "interpretation") H receives the interest unconditionally at the outset or he does not receive it at all, regardless of the divorce.

(6) Rationale

Nothing can turn on the invalid condition, which is struck out. The choice the court makes depends on its assessment of probable intent, usually with a preference for allowing the benefit unconditionally. Courts sometimes suggest that it matters whether the intended condition is "precedent" or "subsequent," but this is dubious—and of little relevance anyway if probable intention is supposed to control.

3. Related Question of Permissible Duration

The law is concerned about the period of time during which the "dead hand" may keep property from vesting in the beneficiaries for them to make full use of—to use, sell, gift, etc. The trust is the principal device through which property is tied up in ways that affect this freedom, and the law has developed a variety of rules for dealing with problems of this general type—*i.e.,* for reconciling the competing values (*e.g.,* of free testation for the prior owner vs. free and efficient use by current owners) in this area. By virtue of these rules, private trusts (and sometimes partially charitable trusts) that are designed to last indefinitely, or that prevent beneficiaries' interests from being ascertainable (or more specifically from "vesting") for an unduly long time, will run afoul of various rules of property law.

a. Rule Against Perpetuities

The most famous of these rules is in most states today is the so-called common law Rule Against Perpetuities—a rule against excessive *remoteness of vesting*. The Rule was developed at common law and exists, usually in modified forms, in most states today, but many states have modified the Rule and some have abolished it entirely. Thus, in some states, trusts may last literally hundreds of years.

(1) Statement of Traditional Rule

For an interest to be valid, it *must* vest, if at all, no later than 21 years after some life in being at the creation of the interest. Stated conversely, an interest is void at the outset if, judged at that time, there is any *possibility* that the interest (as worded and without regard to the Rule) might vest later than the perpetuities period (of a life or lives in being at the time of the transfer, plus 21 years). [*See* Future Interests Summary; *and see* Rest. 3d § 29(b)]

(2) Explanation and Scope of Rule

The traditional Rule applies to nonvested future interests. At the moment of creation, the interest must be *absolutely certain either to vest or to fail* within the permitted period; otherwise the interest is destroyed. The Rule applies to both real and personal property and to equitable as well as legal interests. It invalidates offending beneficial interests in a trust even though the trustee has power in a fiduciary capacity to sell the trust assets.

(3) Requirements of Vesting and Certainty

The traditional Rule requires only that the future interests will certainly vest *in interest* (or fail) within the period—it need not entitle the owner to immediate possession or payments of trust income or principal. Traditionally, the common law rule insists upon absolute certainty at the moment the trust is created that the interest will vest or not within the perpetuities period with no wait-and-see opportunity. In 1983 the American Law Institute ("ALI"), adopted the wait-and-see approach. [Rest. 2d of Property § 1.4] Wait-and-see legislation also exists in a number of states. Alternatively. if the common law Rule is not satisfied, the Uniform Statutory Rule Against Perpetuities ("USRAP"), promulgated in 1986 by the National Conference of Commissioners on Uniform State Laws and enacted in a growing number of states. allows for a ninety-year waiting period. Over the past several years, many states have abolished traditional perpetuities rules altogether and adopted legislation allowing trusts to last hundreds, even thousands, of years without vesting.

Example: All interests are valid in a devise "to my children for life, remainder in equal shares to my grandchildren for their respective lives, and on the death of each, the remainder of his or her share to F." The trust may endure beyond the period, but that is all right because all interests will necessarily have *vested* and the amounts of their shares will be known by the death of the testator's last surviving child—who is necessarily "a life in being" at the testator's death, even if the child is in gestation (although modern reproductive techniques were not contemplated by the common law). At that time the grandchildren's secondary life estates will vest, while F's remainder (although not possessory) vested (*i.e.,* was in an ascertained person, free of conditions precedent) at the testator's death.

Example—Administrative Contingencies: Testator devises her estate "to my issue who are living when administration of my estate is complete." Under normal construction, the interest intended for the issue is invalid because it is possible (although barely conceivable) that estate administration will continue beyond the period of the Rule. Similarly, a trust "for my issue until my plan for development of Greenacre is completed, and then to be terminated with distribution to my then living issue," is invalid at common law. Thus, some instances of "excessive" delay in vesting involve innocent-looking interests or trusts that do not realistically involve dispositions of extended duration.

Compare: If in the above examples, respectively, the devise at completion of administration is "to my spouse H if then living, and if not then to my children in equal shares," and the trust is "for F" with distribution to F on the development project's completion, all interests are valid, despite the potentially "excessive" delays. In the latter situation, F's interest is "vested" at the outset. In the former, the interests of H and the children are all certain either to vest or to fail by the time of H's death (and furthermore, the children could serve as "lives in being" even if they had been expressly or (as would be unlikely) impliedly required to survive until administration ended).

(a) Interests Subject to Rule

The technical, formalistic nature of "vesting" traditionally requires one to distinguish between conditions precedent and conditions subsequent, and also between remainders and executory interests (as executory interests do not vest until they come into possession), but all possibilities of reverter and rights of entry are immune to the Rule. (*See* Property Summary.)

(b) Class Gifts

Also for technical reasons, in general (but subject to some exceptions) an entire class gift is void if the interest of any single class member may vest beyond the period; *i.e.,* all class members generally stand or fall together.

 Example: Grantor deeds to Grantee for life, remainder equally "to those of my grandchildren who attain age 50"; the remainder is void even with respect to the intended interests of grandchildren who are already alive at the time of the transfer and whose rights would, therefore, necessarily either vest or fail within their own lifetimes, because the *potential* interests of afterborn grandchildren upset everything.

1) Note

Under the Restatement rule, there would be no violation unless the interest of an *actual* afterborn grandchild *in fact* violates the perpetuities period. (Also *compare* USRAP's 90-year alternative.)

(4) Partial Exception for Charities

In general, the RAP does not apply to charitable trusts. A charitable trust may endure forever. But the RAP does apply to a possible shift from a private to a charitable purpose, or vice versa, and the interest that is to take effect in violation of the Rule fails.

The charity-to-charity exception to the Rule Against Perpetuities comes up occasionally on exams. The important point to remember is that the exception applies *only if* the gift shifts *from one charity to another*. If the gift shifts from a private to a charitable use or from a charitable to a private use, the Rule applies and you must consider whether the interest is valid.

(5) Perpetuities Period

The perpetuities period is "lives in being plus 21 years," measured from the time the interest is "created" (when the testator dies, if by will, or when an inter vivos trust becomes irrevocable).

(a) Gestation Period

The period is extended to encompass *actual* periods of gestation, so that a child conceived at the time of the transfer is a life in being, and one conceived at the end of the measuring lives is allowed the remaining gestation period plus 21 years for her interest to vest.

(b) Who Is a "Life in Being"?

One may serve as a measuring life without being either a beneficiary of the disposition or designated in the instrument (although designated measuring lives *must be* reasonable in number and difficulty of ascertainment). The period begins to run (and therefore the measuring life must be one who is "in being") at the date of the testator's death or at the date the inter vivos transfer becomes irrevocable. Although, strictly speaking, *any* life in being is technically eligible to serve, as a practical matter the only ones that are actually relevant (*i.e.,* useful) are those that bear some *causal relationship to* the eventual *vesting* of the interests in question. (Again, this traditional view is in contrast with the wait-and-see rule [Rest. 2d of Property § 1.4] and the 90-year alternative of USRAP.)

Example: Testator's bequest "to such of my grandchildren as attain age 21" is valid because Testator's children will necessarily be alive (or in gestation) at Testator's death and are relevant to vesting (and thus are useful as measuring lives) in that no grandchild's interest can possibly vest more than 21 years (and an actual gestation period) after the last surviving child's death.

Example: If the above remainder had been (i) by irrevocable *inter vivos* transfer *or* (ii) bequeathed to grandchildren who reach age *25*, under the traditional Rule, it would fail because in the first scenario all of the transferor's children are not necessarily "in being" (the critical last surviving child could be afterborn generally without regard to the transferor's age, sex, and physical condition), and in the second scenario an afterborn grandchild might be less than four years old when the last child dies (*i.e.,* the last relevant measuring life ends). Note that there would be no invalidity in (ii) if no child survived the testator, making the grandchildren themselves a class of lives in being.

Many students get confused about lives in being. Lives in being are merely people (not animals) alive at the time the interest is created. Obviously, many people are alive at the time an interest is created, but the only ones you care about are those who can **affect vesting**. To find a life that proves the interest is valid, look first to the people mentioned in the grant and weed out the ones that do not affect vesting (*i.e.,* the irrelevant lives). Then see if you can prove that the interest will vest within the life of any one of the remaining relevant persons, or within 21 years after one of those persons' death. For example, if S conveys "to T in trust for A for life, then to B's children whenever born," consider whether you can prove that the remainder will necessarily vest within the life of A or of B. It will vest within the life of B, because B's children will all be in being when B dies. So B is the measuring life. Sometimes the measuring life will **not be mentioned** in the instrument, but will be found in some person who can affect vesting of the future interest. Usually, this person or persons will be a parent or parents of the remaindermen. For example, if S conveys "to T in trust for such of my grandchildren as shall attain the age of 21," the measuring lives are S's children. You can prove the remainder will vest within 21 years after the death of S's children. Thus, the interest is valid.

(6) Effect of Remoteness

The Rule (in its traditional form) strikes down the offending interests; the trust and the other interests are carried out without it, unless under the doctrine of "infectious invalidity" to do so would defeat or unnecessarily distort the settlor's purposes. (A significant number of statutes, including those based on USRAP, and the current ALI view of the common law call for *reformation* to approximate the settlor's intentions within the perpetuities period, rather than destruction of the offending interest.

b. Trusts May Continue Beyond Perpetuities Period

Trusts are sometimes created to last beyond the period measured by a life or lives in being, or even potentially for an indefinite period of time. Thus, a testamentary trust to pay its income "to my children" and thereafter "to pay the income in equal shares to my grandchildren" indefinitely or forever (and thus, in effect, to the successors in interest of the respective grandchildren) is valid because all of the grandchildren will be *ascertained* and their *interests will vest* by the death of the last of the Testator's children (who are all lives in being).

CHARACTERISTICS	PRIVATE TRUST	CHARITABLE TRUST	HONORARY TRUST
ENFORCEABLE	Yes	Yes, by the Attorney General	No, but trustee may choose to perform
BENEFICIARIES	One or more identifiable beneficiaries ascertainable within the Rule Against Perpetuities, if applicable	Indefinite beneficiaries	No beneficiaries capable of enforcing
PURPOSE	Any legal purpose not against public policy	Charitable purpose only	Neither charitable nor private (*e.g.,* for care of a pet)
RULE AGAINST PERPETUITIES	Applies depending on the jurisdiction	Does not apply	Applies in absence of contrary legislation

Chapter Three
Creation of Express Trusts

CONTENTS	PAGE

Key Exam Issues 50

A.   Methods of Trust Creation 51

B.   Creation of Inter Vivos Trusts 52

C.   Creation of Testamentary Trusts 69

D.   Revocable Inter Vivos Trusts as Will Substitutes—Special Problems 73

Key Exam Issues

Exam questions often require you to consider whether the parties have in fact created a trust. Trusts may be created during the settlor's lifetime (inter vivos) or by will (testamentary). In either case, be sure to watch for the possible failure of the "trust" to meet formal requirements or to contain essential trust elements.

1. **Inter Vivos Trusts**

   For exam questions involving the creation of *inter vivos trusts*:

   a. Consider whether there was an *effective, present transfer* of property to the trustee (*e.g.,* watch for delivery issues) or an effective, present *declaration* of trust (*e.g.,* analyze the settlor's words and conduct).

   b. Remember that consideration is necessary not to create a trust *only to create* an enforceable *contract to create a trust* when the necessary present transfer or declaration is lacking.

   c. Consider whether the law requires the intended trust (especially for real property) to be expressed or declared *in writing.* If a writing is required, analyze carefully and in specific terms whether there is a potential violation of the Statute of Frauds: if so, analyze potential remedies to overcome it, such as a constructive trust (and, be sure to consider whether the remedy would accomplish the trust's intended purpose or merely restore the property to the transferor).

   d. Regardless of the Statute of Frauds, if there is a writing, consider possible *parol evidence* issues

   e. Consider whether a possible trust is *"illusory"* or a mere *"agency"* or totally something else. In bank account cases, be alert to the recognition, applicability, and consequences of the Totten trust doctrine.

   f. If the rights of a *spouse or creditor* are involved, consider whether the claimant of otherwise unreachable trust assets has special protection even if the trust is otherwise valid.

2. **Testamentary Trusts**

   For exam questions involving creation of *trusts by will*:

   a. Make sure that the *essential elements of a trust* (res, beneficiaries, and purpose) are *ascertainable* from the terms of the will.

   b. If the carrying out of an oral promise or an implied promise to hold assets in trust is problematic under the wills act, consider whether, under the circumstances, a *constructive trust* remedy is available for the enforcement of that promise, and watch for distinctions between *"secret"* and *"semi-secret"* trust situations. If a trust appears on the face of the will (a semi-secret trust) consider whether a constructive trust is appropriate.

   c. In *"pour-over" cases,* if the question does not involve statutory authorization of such trusts, consider the quite different doctrines of *incorporation by reference* (which tends to be rigid) and *independent significance* (potentially more flexible) and their possible applicability to the particular facts of the case.

A. Methods of Trust Creation

1. In General

The principal methods of creating a trust are by: declaration of trust during the settlor's lifetime or by will, transfer of property to the trust, exercise of a power of appointment, and contract. [UTC § 401]

2. Declaration

A trust may be created by a declaration by the owner of the property that the property owner holds the property in trust for another.

3. Transfer

A trust may also be created by a transfer of property by the owner or owners to another or others as trustee(s) for the benefit of the transferor(s) or third persons, or both

a. Testamentary

If the trust terms appear in a decedent's will, this means that the will creates the trust and the trust is a "testamentary" trust.

b. Inter Vivos

If the transfer is made (or contracted for) by the owner during the owner's lifetime, the trust is an "inter vivos" or "living" trust. Such trusts may be:

(1) *Revocable* (and amendable) in whole or in part; or

(2) *Irrevocable* (but even an irrevocable trust may be modified with the consent of the settlor and all of the beneficiaries).

4. Appointment

A trust may be created by the exercise of a power of appointment.

e.g. **Example:** T devised property to C for life with a "power to appoint the remainder among the children of D." C then makes an appointment to Trustee in trust for D's children until the youngest is 21 years old, and then to D's children in equal shares. This is a valid trust created by C's exercise of a power of appointment.

5. Contract

A valid inter vivos trust may be based on a promise enforceable under the law of contracts to create a trust (*e.g.,* for valuable consideration, A promises B that A will hold certain property in trust for B's children). It is not conceptually clear whether the promise creates a trust immediately or (with the promise serving as the trust property) or whether the later actual property transfer creates it. Be careful to distinguish this situation from a present assignment of another's enforceable promise, which *does* immediately create a trust (of a chose in action, the obligation, as property). For example, a settlor could create an insurance trust this way by transferring the *policy* to the trustee.

B. Creation of Inter Vivos Trusts

1. Requirement of Effective, Present Transfer or Declaration

To create a living or inter vivos trust, there must be an effective, present *transfer of the trust property*. This means either transfer to a trust or a declaration.

a. Present Versus Future Transfer

Because there must be an immediate, present transfer of the trust property to the trustee, a mere promise or expression of intent to hold or transfer property in trust in the future does *not* create a trust, at least in the absence of consideration. Compare these two examples:

Example: S writes, "I hereby promise to hold Blackacre in trust for C J." The normal interpretation of such language does not indicate an immediate, present transfer. The word "promise" seems to be a statement to hold in trust at potentially some point in the future, with no trust created.

Compare: Alternatively, S writes, "I hereby declare myself trustee of Blackacre for J." This language with the use of "declare" rather than "promise" is more likely to be interpreted to establish a present transfer. Accordingly, this language would be sufficient to create a valid trust.

b. Delivery to Trustee

A transfer requires adequate delivery of the trust property (i.e., res or corpus) to the trustee. This transfer can be accomplished by proper delivery in escrow or to the *trustee's* agent. The owner of the property must intend to transfer the property to the transferee *as trustee*—not merely *as agent* for the *owner*.

Example: A property owner's execution and delivery of a mere power of attorney (a written agency) which authorizes the agent to transfer the property to the trust, is not the equivalent of delivery of the property itself. The power of attorney could be revoked before title to the property is vested in the trustee.

(1) Personal Property

If chattels are involved, delivery means the *physical handing over* of possession of the chattel or of a deed (a writing stating the gift) to the trustee. If the nature of the property is such that the property cannot readily be physically transferred (*e.g.,* patent rights, bank accounts), *symbolic or constructive delivery* is sufficient. In such a case, the settlor will deliver a deed of gift or a bank passbook or other document to the trustee.

(2) Real Property

If real property is involved, the settlor must have made an effective *conveyance of title* to the real property involved—usually by delivering an appropriate deed. (As to what constitutes an adequate delivery of a deed to real property, *see* Property Summary.)

(3) Settlor as Trustee

(a) Segregation

Where the settlor *declares himself, herself, or themselves trustee*, the requirement of "delivery" is satisfied by the act of *segregating the trust assets* from the settlor's other property with the necessary trust intent, or the "deed" may take the form of a present declaration in writing (identifying the property, etc.).

(b) Real Property

Where real property is involved, the settlor-trustee's execution of a *writing declaring the trust* is generally legally sufficient. [Rest. 3d § 10 cmt. e] Further acts (*e.g.*, acknowledgment and recording) are *not required* (except in a few states), even when a standard deed form is used, but are desirable both to protect beneficiaries from third parties and to evidence the settlor's intent that a trust arise immediately with respect to the property.

(4) Effect of No Trustee

As noted previously, the existence of a competent trustee is an element of trust creation, but the existence of a competent trustee is not essential to the creation of a trust. *A trust will not fail for want of a trustee.* If a will fails to name a trustee for a trust, or if the named trustee is dead or incompetent or refuses to serve, and the instrument does not name a substitute or successor, the appropriate court will appoint a trustee, provided the transfer has been effective.

(a) Constructive Trustee

In an inter vivos trust, however, the absence of an initial trustee will raise a problem of delivery and hence of transfer. There is no transfer if the settlor has not delivered the property to someone as trustee. But even in such a case, if the requirements of an effective conveyance in trust are otherwise present and the only deficiency is that no trustee was named (or the named trustee is disqualified or dead, etc.), an *enforceable trust may result*. Title may be deemed held in the *settlor as constructive trustee* (or in the intended agent of the intended trustee), to be transferred to whomever the court appoints as trustee.

EXAM TIP

If you encounter an exam question in which the settlor of an intended *inter vivos trust* fails to name a trustee (or the named trustee dies or declines to serve), you should first state the rule that a trust *generally will not fail for lack of a trustee*. Then you should address the *delivery problem*—if there is no trustee, there is no one to whom delivery can be made; without delivery, there is no transfer and thus no trust. But don't end your analysis there. If all of the other requirements of a valid inter vivos trust are met (*i.e.*, intent, property, identifiable beneficiaries, valid trust purpose), you should note that the court may deem the settlor *constructive trustee* of the property, with the duty to transfer the property to a trustee appointed by the court.

---

c. Notice to and Acceptance by Trustee

If the settlor has made an effective transfer, a valid trust exists even if the trustee has not been made aware of the trust. Neither notice to nor acceptance by the trustee is essential to formation of the trust. [Rest. 3d § 14]

(1) Trustee Unaware

In many valid testamentary trusts, the trustee is unaware of the trust until the decedent dies. Of course, in most cases of living trusts, the requirement of delivery (above) assures that the trustee is made aware of the trust. Nevertheless, where this does not happen, a trust may be created without the knowledge of the trustee—as where there has been constructive delivery of the trust property or delivery to a third party (*e.g.,* in escrow). The fact that the settlor did not notify the trustee may, however, as an evidentiary matter, reflect on whether the settlor had the requisite intent presently to create an inter vivos trust if such a question arises. Alternatively, the court may conclude that a revocable trust was intended, or that the failure to inform the intended trustee had no significance and that an irrevocable trust was created.

(2) Acceptance

An individual cannot be forced to serve as trustee. The individual or entity with fiduciary powers may decline the trusteeship any time prior to accepting it. [Rest. 3d § 35; UTC § 701] Acceptance may be shown by substantial compliance with the method described in the trust, accepting the trust property, performing the duties of trusteeship, or otherwise indicating acceptance. [UTC § 701(a)]

(a) Declining

If there has been an effective transfer but the trustee declines to serve as trustee, the trust does not fail for lack of a trustee. Rather, unless a court holds that technical title vests in the trustee, the result may be that title remains in the settlor subject to the trust until a substitute trustee is appointed. Note that if the person designated as trustee does not accept the trusteeship within a reasonable time **after** knowing of the designation, the person is deemed to have declined. [UTC § 701(b)]

(b) Retraction

Once having declined, the trustee is usually not permitted to "retract" the decision to decline. Nevertheless, courts may permit a retraction where no harm or prejudice will result.

(3) Trustee's Obligations

Once having accepted the trusteeship, the trustee is bound by all of the fiduciary obligations imposed by law and by the terms of the trust, and can be held personally liable for neglect of those obligations. "Resignation" alone does not relieve the trustee of these duties and responsibilities. A trustee may resign (i) upon 30 days' notice to qualified beneficiaries, the settlor, if living, and all co-trustees or (ii) with the court's approval. [UTC § 705(a)] Ordinarily, the duties of one who has accepted a trust continue until a successor is in place. [Rest. 3d § 36]

(4) Acceptance Relates Back

The trustee's acceptance normally relates back to the time the trust came into being. Thus, acceptance by a testamentary trustee is effective from the date of the settlor's death.

(a) Duties Prior to Acceptance

Although for many purposes (*e.g.,* accrual of beneficiaries' rights to benefits) a trust becomes effective at the time it comes into existence, the trustee normally has no fiduciary duties until acceptance of the trusteeship, expressly or impliedly, occurs.

d. Notice to and Acceptance by the Beneficiary

Notice to the beneficiary that the settlor intends to create a trust, or has created one, is not necessary for a valid trust. Acceptance, approval, or consent by the beneficiary also is not essential to trust formation. [Rest. 3d § 14]

(1) Evidentiary Effect of Lack of Notice

But if the question arises, the fact that the settlor has not notified the beneficiary may, as an evidentiary matter, reflect on whether the settlor actually had the requisite intent presently to create a trust or was merely contemplating a future trust.

(2) Acceptance Presumed

Although the beneficiary's acceptance is not necessary to create the trust, acceptance by a beneficiary is normally *presumed* and will be *inferred* from the beneficiary's voluntary retention of any trust distribution with the knowledge of the trust terms. Upon acceptance, the beneficiary's rights are normally retroactive to the date the trust was created.

(a) Disclaimer

A trust cannot be forced upon a beneficiary. A person named as beneficiary has the right within a reasonable time after learning of the trust to disclaim (or "renounce") the beneficial interest, absent some act of expressed or implied acceptance. Upon disclaimer, depending on construction of the other trust provisions, other beneficial interests are adapted (*e.g.,* a remainder interest following a renounced life interest may accelerate) to carry out the trust as nearly as possible to achieve the settlor's purposes. If no such adaptation is appropriate, the trustee holds the disclaimed interest upon resulting trust for the settlor.

(b) Partial Acceptance

May a beneficiary accept or disclaim part of the beneficiary's rights under the trust?—In general, the answer is yes. The only exception is the rare case where the different interests of a beneficiary are inseparable or interdependent—for example, a trust conditions receipt of benefits on the beneficiary quitting smoking. The beneficiary can't disclaim the quitting smoking part and keep the benefits.

(c) Acceptance or Disclaimer Relates Back

Once a beneficiary accepts or disclaims a trust interest, the action is final and it relates back to the date of trust creation.

(d) Assignment of Interest

Despite an *acceptance*, of course, a beneficiary generally need not retain the beneficial interest because (unless inalienable): the beneficiary can assign or release the interest.

(e) Retraction

The law may even allow a beneficiary *withdraw a disclaimer*, where there has been no change of position by others in reliance on the renunciation that would render the result inequitable.

---

2. Registration of Trust (Uniform Probate Code)

In states that have adopted and retained the Uniform Probate Code ("UPC") as promulgated in 1969, the trustee of *either* an inter vivos or testamentary trust must register the trust with the probate court at the "principal place of administration" of the trust. [UPC §§ 7–101, 7–102] The registration must identify the trustee(s), the settlor, and the date of the trust instrument.

a. Effects of Failure to Register

Failure to register the trust *does not affect its validity*, but subjects the trustee to possible removal, denial of compensation, or surcharge by the court. Also, trust provisions purporting to excuse the trustee from registering are ineffective. [UPC § 7–104]

b. Distinguish—Other States

Non-UPC jurisdictions do not require registration of trusts. In these states, there is no attendant public disclosure to inhibit the creation of living trusts, but testamentary trusts are subject to the usual publicity of probate procedures and in some states to continuing jurisdiction of the probate court.

3. Role of Consideration

Consideration is not essential to the creation of a trust; indeed, most trusts are gratuitous. [Rest. 3d § 15] Nonetheless, the presence or absence of consideration may be important where an attempted trust would otherwise fail—*e.g.,* for lack of present transfer.

a. Promise to Create Future Trust

An unenforceable promise to hold or transfer property in trust in the future does not create a trust.

(1) Gratuitous Promise

If the promise is gratuitous, that is, without consideration, normally it is not enforceable—even if the promise is in writing. The promise is not enforceable even in equity, and damages will not be awarded for its breach (absent elements of promissory estoppel; *see* Contracts Summary).

(2) With Consideration

If consideration *was* given for the promise, however, it may be enforceable as a contract. Enforcement may be at law, and because trust obligations are unique, enforcement in equity is available including, by the general view, via specific performance.

(a) When Trust Arises

When the settlor makes an enforceable promise to create a trust sometime in the future (including one arising from a beneficiary designation, *e.g.*, under an insurance policy), a problem arises in determining at what point in time the trust actually arises. One view is that a trust arises at the time consideration is given, and the trust property is a chose in action—an enforceable promise. This was the preferred interpretation of the Second Restatement of Trusts, which opined that when such a trust arises is a matter of when the settlor *intended* fiduciary duties to arise. [Rest. 2d §§ 25, 30] The other view, preferred by the Third Restatement, is that, while there is an enforceable promise to make a conveyance at some later time, no trust arises until the conveyance is made, absent a manifestation of contrary intent. [Rest. 3d § 10 cmt. g] The question of when a trust arises may affect not only the point at which the trustee's fiduciary duties commence, but also when the perpetuities period begins to run.

e.g. **Example:** B promises E in writing that if E marries B, B will convey Blackacre in trust for E's parent. E marries B. Regardless of whether, conceptually, the trust arises at the marriage date or when B makes the conveyance, B's promise is enforceable in equity or at law.

b. Ineffective Trust Transfer

Where the settlor receives consideration for a promise to create a trust, a trust may be enforced even though the requisite transfer of property to the trust is somehow defective. This arises from the equitable principle that at least in litigation between the parties, equity is inclined to "treat as done that which ought to have been done," to protect the interests of a beneficiary who paid for the trust.

e.g. **Example:** K pays a large sum of money to P, in consideration for which P agrees to transfer Greenacre to P as trustee for K and K's family. The deed, however, is imperfectly executed and under the applicable law is not effective to transfer title. In litigation between K and P, specific performance would be ordered or a *constructive trust* in K's favor would be declared. (But K's equity—K's right to enforce the promised trust—would be cut off if P had in the meantime transferred legal title to an innocent purchaser.)

c. Promises Regarding After-Acquired Property

A purported declaration or transfer in trust of property that the settlor does not presently own fails for lack of a present transfer—there being no property to transfer and to become a trust res.

Example: G transfers to N in trust "the property I expect to receive as heir of my father's estate." If G's father had died *before* the assignment, the trust is good; assuming G's father was still alive, however, so that only an expectancy is involved, the question of whether there is a trust of the designated property when it is later acquired depends on whether G had received consideration in exchange for the promise.

(1) Gratuitous

If the promise was gratuitous, no trust arises unless the settlor (G in the above example) manifests an intention *after he acquires it*, to create a trust with respect to that property, in which case the trust becomes effective at that time.

(2) Consideration Present

If, however, the settlor received consideration, the settlor's promise is specifically enforceable and the trust thus arises immediately (or at least may be specifically enforced) upon her acquisition of the property, even without later expression of trust intent. [Rest. 2d § 86; Rest. 3d § 41 cmt. c]

EXAM TIP   **GILBERT**

Remember the difference between expectancies and future interests. A ***mere expectancy*** (*i.e.,* not yet in legal existence) ***does not*** constitute sufficient trust property, but a ***future interest*** (*i.e.,* a presently existing, legally protected right in property, although possession may be postponed until the future) ***does***. If, however, the settlor's promise to hold an expectancy in trust is supported by ***consideration***, a valid trust arises under the law of contracts when the settlor ***acquires the property***.

---

4. Requirement of a Writing—Statute of Frauds

Oral trusts of personal property are valid at common law, but in a few states statutes have changed this). On the other hand, trusts of land must be evidenced by some writing signed by a party empowered at the time to impress the trust upon the property. [English Statute of Frauds § 7]

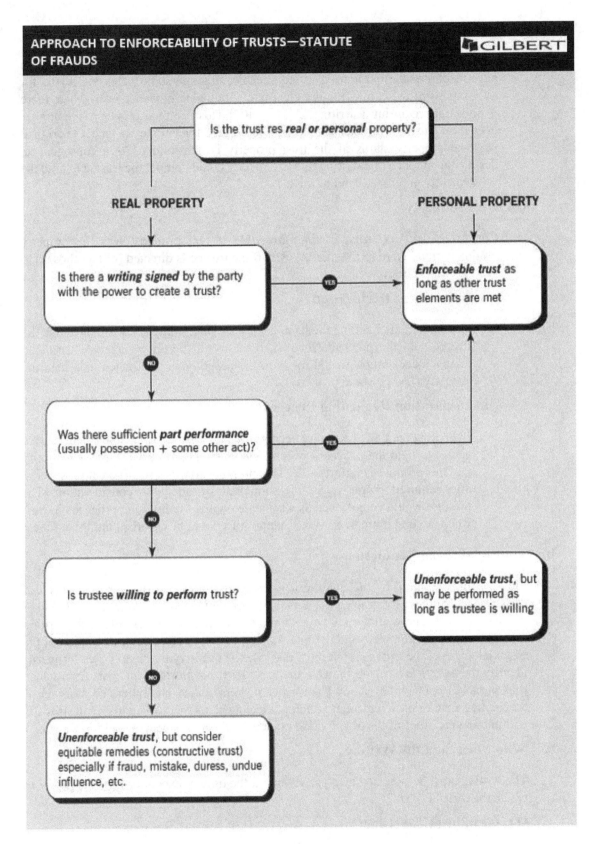

a. When Does the Statute of Frauds Apply to Trust Formation?

The Statute of Frauds applies to *any interest* in land, including, in most jurisdictions, leasehold estates.

(1) Personal Property

Absent a contrary statute, an oral trust of money (even of insurance proceeds the payee promises to hold in trust) is enforceable, although some states (especially for declarations of trust) may require clear and convincing evidence even where there is no statute requiring a writing. [UTC § 407] This personal property rule applies even if the trustee is directed (or has chosen) to invest the money in land; the original personal property status of the trust property is controlling. As a consequence, despite the absence of a writing, the beneficiary could compel the trustee to hold the subsequently purchased land in trust.

(2) Real Property

Conversely, an oral trust is *unenforceable* if real property was the property originally transferred to the trustee, even if the trustee is directed (or has chosen) to sell the real property.

(a) Subsequent Declaration

Note that if, after selling the land, the trustee *then* orally acknowledged that the trustee held the proceeds in trust, there would be an enforceable trust; the trustee's declaration would relate to the property as the trustee then held the property (*i.e.,* personal property).

(b) Declaration Regarding Proceeds

Even if, at the time the trustee accepts the oral trust of real property, the trustee agrees to hold the *proceeds* of any sale of the land in trust, there is authority that this promise is enforceable. This promise may be effective with respect to after-acquired property; *i.e.,* if supported by adequate consideration. The promise would be enforced as a separate contract to hold the proceeds in trust when, as, and if received. Note that no trust could be enforced until that time.

b. Type of Writing Required

The "writing" required by the Statute of Frauds need not be in the form of a deed of conveyance, and the writing need not even have been intended as a formal expression of the desired trust. The writing may be a simple memorandum. Nevertheless, the writing must be reasonably complete and definite. It must contain a reasonable indication of the essential terms of the trust—*i.e.,* it must disclose the property that is to be the *property*, identify the *beneficiaries*, and indicate the basic *trust purposes* or interests from which trust purposes can be inferred and from which powers, duties, and other necessary terms are implied. Once a sufficient memorandum is executed, its subsequent loss or destruction will not prevent proof of the trust by oral evidence of its contents. [Rest. 3d § 22]

c. Who Must Sign the Writing?

The writing must be executed by a party who (at the time of execution) has the *power* to create the trust.

(1) Grantor (aka Settlor)

Until there has been a transfer of title to the trustee, the property owner (the grantor) has the power to impress a trust upon the property, and hence, it would be sufficient (and usual) for the grantor's signature to appear on the writing. [Rest. 3d § 23]

(a) At or Before Conveyance

The grantor may evidence the trust terms either in the deed itself or in a collateral writing or memorandum, as long as the writing is sufficiently connected to the conveyance and was executed *at or before* the time the grantor conveyed title. If executed before title was conveyed, the writing must have been executed with reference to or have been adopted in the conveyance. [Rest. 3d § 23 cmt. b]

(b) After Conveyance

A writing executed by the grantor *after* delivery of the conveyance will not satisfy the Statute of Frauds or bind the grantee. Because title is no longer in the grantor, the grantor has no power to create a trust on the land; *i.e.,* the grantor subsequent declarations cannot affect title now held by another. [Rest. 3d § 23 cmt. c]

(2) Grantee

The trust is enforceable if the intended trustee, as the "party to be charged," has executed the writing (the trust instrument) *either before, at, or after* the time of the conveyance.

(a) Acknowledgment of Trust Sufficient

It is immaterial when the grantee's signature is actually affixed to the trust instrument; the grantee's acknowledgment of the trust is effective whether written *before, concurrently with,* or *after* the conveyance.

(3) Settlor and Trustee

Typically, both the settlor and trustee will sign a formal trust instrument.

(4) Beneficiary

Writings signed *only* by the beneficiary or beneficiaries are not sufficient to create an enforceable trust.

WHO HAS POWER TO IMPRESS A TRUST UPON REAL PROPERTY?		GILBERT
	AT OR BEFORE CONVEYANCE	**AFTER CONVEYANCE**
GRANTOR/SETTLOR	✓	
GRANTEE/TRUSTEE	✓	✓
BENEFICIARY		

d. Part Performance Doctrine

Acts of part performance by the parties that tend to prove the existence of a trust may be sufficient to take the matter out of the Statute of Frauds even when there has been no writing. [Rest. 3d § 24(1)] This is similar to the contracts doctrine of partial performance.

(1) What Constitutes Sufficient Part Performance?

Merely allowing the beneficiary to take *possession* of the property is sufficient part performance in many jurisdictions. In general, the trustee *must also perform some other act* (*e.g.,* repair, payment of taxes, erection of improvements, etc.).

(a) Beneficial Use

Allowing the beneficiary to have the beneficial use or otherwise distributing the fruits of the trust property may be sufficient part performance (*i.e.,* the trustee begins to perform aspects of the trust that specifically benefit the beneficiaries in a way that calls for an explanation and objectively suggests the existence of a trust).

(b) Trustee's Acknowledgment

In any event, under prevalent doctrine, the acts relied upon as part performance must involve the intended trustee, or have been approved by the intended trustee, to show the alleged trustee's (the title holder's) acknowledgment of the trust.

(2) Part Performance Can Cure Defective Conveyance

In certain cases, acts of part performance may perfect what would otherwise be an ineffective trust *transfer*.

e.g. **Example:** Grantor intends to transfer title to Grantee in trust for N. Grantor fails to make adequate delivery of the deed (no effective transfer), but N takes possession with the knowledge and consent of all parties. The transfer of possession may render the trust effective. (*See generally* Remedies Summary.)

e. Effect of Statute—Bar to Enforcement but Not to Formation of Trust

An oral trust of real property is not void; an oral trust of real property is merely *unenforceable* against the title holder. Thus, where lands are transferred upon an oral trust, in a significant sense a valid trust exists. The Statute of Frauds only prevents its enforcement—*i.e.*, against the will of the party to be charged (the trustee-transferee who refuses to perform the role of trustee).

(1) Trustee May Perform Oral Trust

If the trustee is *willing* to perform under the trust, *no one else has any right to object*. Thus, neither the settlor nor third parties (*e.g.*, under currently prevailing case law, grantee's creditors) can prevent performance of an oral trust by the trustee. If necessary, the trustee can prove the oral trust by parol evidence to uphold the performance of it. [Rest. 3d § 24(1)]

(2) Exception—Bona Fide Purchaser

If the trustee of an unenforceable trust sells the trust land to a bona fide purchaser, however, it is a valid transfer. A transfer to a bona fide purchaser *cuts off all latent equities*.

f. Unenforceable Oral Trust—Constructive Trust Remedy Against Trustee Who Fails to Perform

In cases where the trustee is *not* willing to perform and the Statute of Frauds renders the oral express trust unenforceable, the intended beneficiaries or the grantor may nevertheless have a remedy. The intended trustee is not necessarily entitled to keep the land.

(1) Conveyance Wrongfully Obtained

Where the transferee procured the conveyance through fraud, mistake, duress, undue influence, or in contemplation of the transferor's death, retention of the land is wrongful, and a remedial device, the *constructive trust*, will be imposed. The constructive trust requires the trustee to hold the property for the intended beneficiary and purpose. [Rest. 3d § 24(2)]. Remember, a constructive trust is not a trust. It is a remedy, in this case, for wrongfully obtained property.

(a) Rationale—Remedial Device

The *express* trust is not being enforced; rather, the transferee's wrongdoing justifies imposition of a constructive trust—a trust arising by operation of law as a remedial device. Traditionally, the Statute of Frauds does not apply to trusts arising by operation of law because they are equitable.

(b) Evidentiary and Remedial Aspects of Such Cases

1) Parol Evidence Admissible

Parol evidence is admissible to show both the oral trust agreement and the fraud, duress, undue influence, breach of confidence, mistake, or contemplation of death where such grounds are alleged in the petition. This is true even if the deed from the transferor to the transferee recites that the transferee takes the property "for his, her, or their own benefit." *Rationale*: The fraud, duress, etc., is a sufficient ground to *reform* the writing. (*See* Remedies Summary.)

2) For Whose Benefit Constructive Trust Imposed

Courts today generally impose the constructive trust in these types of cases in favor of the *intended beneficiary(ies)*. The transferor's intent to benefit the beneficiary is generally quite apparent, and the gift would have been effective but for the fraud, mistake, breach of confidence, etc. Therefore, the transferee's wrongful conduct in not performing may not frustrate the transferor's donative intent or the intended beneficiary's interest. Thus, not only will the transferee not benefit from the wrongful conduct, but despite the Statute of Frauds, the *intended* trust purposes will be implemented—*i.e.,* the remedy will "go forward with the trust," not just give restitution to the transferor in these special situations.

(2) Circumstances in Which Constructive Trust Imposed for Wrongful Conduct or Special Circumstances

(a) Fraud

Where the transferee procured the conveyance by affirmative misrepresentations to the settlor-transferor, a constructive trust is imposed.

1) Mere Breach of Promise Insufficient

The fact that the transferee later refuses to perform the oral promise that induced the transfer is not enough in itself for a fraud case. It must also be that, *at the time of the promise*, the transferee did not intend to perform, so that the promise was a misrepresentation of his state of mind that induced the conveyance—*i.e.,* "actual fraud."

2) Factors Court May Consider

In attempting to ascertain the transferee's state of mind at the time of the transferee's promise, courts are likely to emphasize: (i) the length of time between the making of the promise and its breach; and (ii) which party suggested the arrangement.

(b) Mistake, Duress, Undue Influence

A constructive trust may be imposed where there is mistake, duress, or undue influence.

Example—Mistake: Where Settlor executes a conveyance to County Bank in trust for Beneficiary, believing and intending that the conveyance is to State Bank, not County Bank, a constructive trust may be imposed if County Bank seeks to keep the property.

Example—Duress: G transfers property to R, telling R of G's plan to create a trust for R and R's sibling H. R threatens G, precluding G from executing a writing expressing the intended trust. A constructive trust may be imposed on R in favor of H.

Example—Undue Influence: F lives with D and has for years relied on D in making financial and other decisions. D is one of F's three children. F wishes to provide for all of F's children in trust, and D agrees to hold the property for herself and her brothers and sisters in trust for life, remainder to their issue. Even though D intends to perform the oral agreement,

D keeps the property for herself. A constructive trust may be imposed on D for the benefit of D's siblings and their issue.

(c) Abuse of Confidential Relation

Courts may impose constructive trusts where the transferor and transferee stand in a confidential relationship to each other and one of them makes an intended trust conveyance in reliance on that relationship. In such a case, the transferee's refusal to carry out an oral agreement to hold in trust is a breach of a confidential relationship. Thus, the same result would apply as when the transferee obtained the conveyance through the closely related conduct of fraud, duress, or undue influence: a constructive trust.

1) What Constitutes a Confidential Relationship

In many states, certain family relationships (especially spousal) are per se confidential relationships. Also, certain nonfamily relationships (*e.g.,* guardian-ward, lawyer-client, trustee-beneficiary, doctor-patient, spiritual advisor-member of congregation) are usually considered confidential relationships.

2) Other Confidential Relationships

A confidential relationship can arise outside of the list above. The scope of "confidential relationship" is rather broad. A confidential relationship may consist of actual habitual reliance and dependency by one person on another. Although many decisions say that a family relationship (*e.g.,* parent-child, brother-sister) alone is often *not sufficient* to constitute a confidential relationship, in such instances courts do not require much more to show an actual relationship of confidence.

(d) Contemplation of Death

A court will also probably impose a constructive trust when the transfer pursuant to an oral agreement was made in contemplation of death and as a substitute for a testamentary disposition.

e.g. **Example:** P, expecting P's imminent death, transfers Blackacre to P's child C, who orally agrees that on P's death that C will share the land equally with C's siblings. P dies. S holds Blackacre upon a constructive trust for P and P's siblings.

1) Rationale

The rationale comes from the vulnerable position of the transferor facing death, and in the fact that undoing the transaction would often be counterproductive when it is (usually) too late for the transferor to cure the transferor's error.

2) Note

This situation is also analogous to the "secret trust" cases (T devises or bequeaths property to B in reliance on B's oral promise to hold in trust for C).

(3) The Harder Cases—Where Wrongful Conduct or Special Circumstances Are Lacking

There is far less agreement in the cases where there was no wrongful conduct by the grantee and where no mistake or contemplation of death existed on the part of the grantor—*i.e.,* where the creation of the trust was likely valid, but the Statute of Frauds requires a writing. In such cases, the only justification for exposing a potentially good faith transferee to the risk of possibly unreliable oral testimony is that the transferee may be ***unjustly enriched***.

Example: Transferor transfers title to Transferee allegedly on Transferee's oral promise to hold the land in trust for Beneficiary. Transferee now refuses to perform the trust, but there is no evidence that he is guilty of fraud (*i.e.,* it appears that Transferee intended to perform when Transferee allegedly promised but ***subsequently*** changed the Transferee's mind). Should the court impose a constructive trust to avoid unjust enrichment if the allegations can be proved, or should the court rely on the Statute of Frauds and allow Transferee to retain the property outright? Or, if the trust was free of fraud, let the beneficiary sue the trustee/transferee or breach of fiduciary duty?

(a) Modern Trend

Most writers, the ALI, and the apparent trend of judicial decisions today would impose a constructive trust upon Transferee to prevent unjust enrichment in these cases. [Rest. 3d § 24(3)] But this trend so far appears largely confined to cases of oral trusts of land ***for the grantor*** (*e.g.,* Grantor to Grantee orally in trust for Grantor). he transferee may prevail or the remedy ("restitution") may return the property to the transferor when the intended trust is ***for third parties*** (*e.g.,* Grantor to Grantee orally for B1 and B2).

1) Criticism

To impose a constructive trust under this view for Grantor seems to enforce the very promise that is unenforceable under the Statute of Frauds—*i.e.,* to constitute an "end run" around the Statute of Frauds.

a) Response

The express trust is ***not*** being enforced. The trust that is being enforced arises by operation of law, and the Statute of Frauds does not apply to such trusts because the Statute should not act as a shield for wrongdoing. In addition, a higher burden of proof (clear and convincing evidence) is required.

b) Critics Reply

Realistically, courts often disregard the clear and convincing evidence requirement and the "constructive" trust point is purely semantics, even if restitution is made where the oral trust was to be for Grantor., if the trust is ***for B1 and B2***, to benefit them by constructive trust disregards the Statute, while restitution to Grantor (or Grantor's successors!) exposes Grantee (who might actually be innocent) to risks of litigation merely to offer a remedy that would still frustrate the trust intent (to benefit B1 and B2), if any ***did*** exist.

c) Result

Thus, despite the trend of case law, these situations (especially the oral trust for B1 and B2) have remained particularly troublesome for courts.

2) Intended Trust for Third Parties—for Whom Should Any Constructive Trust Be Imposed?

Where the settlor conveyed title to another upon an oral trust for the settlor, it is clear that, if a remedy is granted, the constructive trust will benefit the settlor. But what if the oral trust was intended for third parties (B1 and B2)?

a) For Intended Beneficiaries

One view is that, if there is to be relief, and if Grantee is forced to surrender the property, the constructive trust should benefit the intended beneficiary or beneficiaries—*i.e.,* that B1 and B2 can compel Grantee to transfer the property to them. The problem with this is that it disregards the Statute entirely. But this is not wholly true if the requirement that there be a higher than normal standard of proof courts actually do require in these cases.

b) For Transferor

Because of the above criticism, however, the traditional Restatement view was that the constructive trust should be imposed *in favor of the transferor* (Grantor) even here. [Rest. 2d § 45] This avoids unjust enrichment while leaving some "teeth" in the Statute. It also enables the transferor to make a new and valid disposition of the property.

c) For Intended Beneficiaries if Transferor Dies or Becomes Incompetent

As is so often the case when the issue arises, the grantor may be dead and the grantor's heirs are likely to be different from the persons and purposes the Grantor intended. Thus, this may still result in unjust enrichment; instead of Grantee, however, Grantor's successors would be unjustly enriched. The outcome is one that does justice to none of the people who "rightly" claim the property. Thus, to avoid unjust enrichment, if there is enough evidence to take the property from Grantee, the Third Restatement calls for a constructive trust for the *intended beneficiaries* (B1 and B2) *if* the transferor dies or becomes incompetent without having an opportunity to decide whether to retain the property or to create an effective trust for B1 and B2. [*See* Rest. 3d § 24(3); *and see* § 24(4)—on oral declarations of trust of land]

SUMMARY OF GROUNDS FOR IMPOSING A CONSTRUCTIVE TRUST	**GILBERT**
FRAUD	The transferee procures the conveyance by *misrepresentation* to the transferor.
MISTAKE	The transferee receives the conveyance through the transferor's *mistake* (*e.g.,* intended to convey to different trustee).
DURESS	The transferee performs or threatens to perform a *wrongful act* that *coerces* the transferor into conveying the property or *precludes* the transferor from executing a writing expressing the intended trust.
UNDUE INFLUENCE	The transferee exerts influence on the transferor that *overpowers the transferor's mind and free will*, resulting in a conveyance that would not have been made but for the influence.
ABUSE OF CONFIDENTIAL RELATIONSHIP	The transferee refuses to perform an oral trust agreement and at the time of the transfer stood in a *confidential relationship* with the transferor (*e.g.,* attorney-client, guardian-ward).
CONTEMPLATION OF DEATH	The transferee procures the conveyance pursuant to an oral agreement made in *contemplation of the transferor's death*.
UNJUST ENRICHMENT	Although the transferee did not procure the conveyance through wrongful conduct or special circumstances, allowing the transferee to retain the property would be *unjust*.

5. Where There Is a Writing—Parol Evidence Rule

Whenever there is a writing that purports to embody the terms of the transfer. [*See* Rest. 3d § 21], remember the Parol Evidence Rule excludes evidence of an oral agreement that purports to modify the terms of the writing.

a. Not Admissible to Vary or Contradict Writing

(1) Trust Specifically Excluded

Absent grounds for reformation or rescission (*e.g.,* fraud), evidence of an oral agreement to form a trust will *not* be admissible if the written conveyance expressly excludes a trust ("to Transferee, *for Transferee's own use and benefit*"), as it would vary or contradict the writing.

(2) Trust Clearly Stated

Nor is parol evidence admissible absent grounds for reformation or rescission, to vary or contradict a deed of gift or conveyance that states clearly that there is a trust. Thus, if the writing is clearly "to Transferee in trust for S," Transferee cannot show by parol that no trust was intended (*i.e.,* that Transferee was to take beneficially), nor can D show by parol that the trust was intended for D instead of S.

If you encounter an exam question in which the written conveyance *expressly excludes a trust* (*e.g.,* "to B for his own benefit") or *clearly expresses an intended trust* (*e.g.,* "to T in trust for B"), check to see whether the transferee procured the conveyance through *wrongful conduct* (*e.g.,* fraud, mistake, duress, undue influence, breach of confidence). Where such grounds are alleged, parol evidence *is admissible* to show both the oral trust agreement and the fraud, duress, etc., because these are sufficient grounds to *reform* the writing. In the *absence of wrongful conduct,* however, parol evidence is *not admissible* because the writing is unambiguous.

b. Parol Evidence Admissible to Clarify Ambiguity or Supplement Writing

If the instrument is ambiguous on the question of trust or no trust (or on the purposes and beneficiaries), parol evidence is admissible to clarify the matter.

(1) Silent as to Trust

If the instrument states simply that the transfer is to Transferee but contains no express indication one way or the other about the existence of a trust, is parol evidence of alleged trust intent admissible?

(a) Minority View

One view is that it is *not*—the instrument is not ambiguous, and so Transferee takes beneficially. To admit contrary evidence contradicts or varies this plain meaning.

(b) Majority View

The apparently prevailing (and Restatement) view, however, admits parol evidence because the writing says nothing on the point; thus, the parol neither varies nor contradicts but merely *supplements* and completes an otherwise incomplete writing. Such a case, would require, however, clear and convincing evidence.

1) Note

A recitation in a deed that the conveyance is "for valuable consideration received" does not "expressly exclude" a trust so as to exclude parol evidence under the majority rule.

C. Creation of Testamentary Trusts

1. Requirements of Wills Act and Supplementary Doctrines

A "testamentary trust" is one created by the decedent's valid will. This will and any codicils (plus other evidence that satisfies the Wills Act) must provide the essential elements of a trust; *i.e.,* the *trust property*, the *beneficiaries*, and the *trust purpose* must be ascertainable from the will or established in some other manner in compliance with Wills Act requirements and related doctrine. (The trust purposes, however, may be inferred from the ascertainable interests of the beneficiaries, and the court will supply a trustee if necessary.) A more modern view calls for the application of a rule of harmless error or substantial compliance in determining the validity of a will. Under the harmless error rule, a court may dispense with one or more statutory formalities, if they have not been followed, so long as the proponents of the document establish by clear and convincing evidence that the decedent intended that the writing constitute the decedent's will. [*See* Rest. 3d § 17 cmt. b; Rest. 3d of Property § 3.3; UPC § 2–503]

a. Sources

Thus, in addition to properly executed *wills* and *codicils*, facts of independent significance and documents that can be incorporated by reference may also provide missing trust terms (typically who beneficiaries are). (*See* Wills Summary)

e.g. **Example—Independent Significance:** C bequeaths to H "in trust for the person who, in Henry's opinion, has given me the best care in my declining years." Under this standard, objective evidence of acts or events that had significance apart from their effect on the will can serve to identify the beneficiary—even if the trustee fails to make a selection.

e.g. **Example—Incorporation:** On June 3, G executes a will bequeathing "to the Trust Co. in trust for the persons and purposes set out in the writing dated June 1 and kept in my safe." Assuming the writing conforms to the description in the will, did in fact exist when the will was executed, and otherwise meets the particular state's requirements for incorporation by reference (and assuming the doctrine is recognized in the state), the trust terms may be supplied by the described writing, even though that writing was not executed in accordance with the wills act formalities.

CREATION OF TRUSTS		GILBERT
	INTER VIVOS TRUSTS	**TESTAMENTARY TRUSTS**
WHEN CREATED?	During settlor's *life*	By settlor's *will*
REQUIREMENTS	Effective, present *transfer* (*i.e.,* delivery to trustee) of property or present *declaration* of trust	The essential elements of the trust • Property • Beneficiary(ies) • Purpose
	No notice to trustee or beneficiary required No writing required except for trust of real property	must be *ascertainable from will* or codicil or by other method allowed by wills act (*e.g.,* facts of independent significance, incorporation by reference)

2. Secret Trusts—Oral Trust or Outright Bequest or Devise

Sometimes a decedent makes a will leaving property to a particular beneficiary, relying upon that person's oral promise to hold the property in trust for others. Because the terms of the will do not include any references to a trust, the oral agreement is often referred to as a "secret trust." The oral agreement as such is clearly unenforceable under the wills act and related doctrines and amounts to an attempted testamentary disposition of the equitable interests (that is, an attempt to give the benefit of the property to someone other than the beneficiary listed in the will) without the required formalities if will execution.

e.g. **Example:** T devises Blackacre (outright so far as one can tell from the language of the will) to V, relying on an oral agreement with V that Blackacre will be held in trust for T's child.

a. May Be Voluntarily Performed

If the will beneficiary voluntarily *performs* as agreed, no one can complain.

b. Constructive Trust Remedy

If the will beneficiary *refuses to perform*, the oral agreement is not enforced directly as an express trust, but in most states, the law will not permit the will beneficiary to retain the property outright in breach of the oral promise to the testator. Consequently, courts will impose a *constructive trust* in favor of the person(s) for whom the property should have been held, in order to avoid unjust enrichment of the devisee. [Rest 3d § 18(1)] The rule applies to land as well as personal property. A minority of states would confine this remedy to instances of actual fraud, duress, undue influence, and abuse of confidential relationship. Also, under certain circumstances in a few states, "Dead Man Acts" (which prevent testimony to a personal transaction or communication with a deceased when offered against the representative or successors in interest of the deceased; *see* Evidence Summary) may present obstacles to enforcement.

(1) Rationale

Because the Statute of Wills does not apply to trusts created by operation of law, a constructive trust can be enforced even though the express trust cannot.

(2) No Requirement of "Fraud," etc.

The general view is that a constructive trust will be imposed in this situation for mere breach of promise, whether or not the will beneficiary was guilty of any fraud, breach of confidence, etc.

(a) Distinguish—Statute of Frauds Case

This general view (above) is different from the view of many states involving oral trust agreements that are unenforceable under the Statute of Frauds—*i.e.*, that no constructive trust will be imposed in the absence of fraud, mistake, breach of confidence, etc.

(3) No Requirement That Devisee "Induced" Gift

It is not necessary that (in the example above) Friend's promise or agreement actually induced the devise from Testator. It need only appear that Friend *knew* before Testator's death that it was Testator's intention that Friend hold in trust for another; Friend is deemed to have expressly or impliedly accepted the gift upon the intended trust. [Rest. 3d § 18(1) cmt. b] It is immaterial that Friend was notified of Testator's intent after execution of the will, as long as the knowledge was received before Testator's death; if Friend had refused, Testator could have revoked the bequest or devise to Friend and left the property to someone else who would agree to carry out the trust.

(4) For Whom Constructive Trust Imposed

As mentioned above, most courts grant a remedy in these cases, and most of these courts raise the constructive trust in favor of the *intended beneficiary*, rather than for the estate of the settlor (Testator). The rationale is that the injury flowing from the will beneficiary's breach of promise is primarily to the intended beneficiary rather than to the testator's estate. [Rest. 3d § 18] A few of the cases that grant a remedy, however, have held that the constructive trust should be in favor of the testator's estate; the property therefore goes to the testator's residuary devisees, or, if none, to the testator's intestate heirs. The court's reasoning is that enforcing the trust for the intended beneficiary's benefit would circumvent the Wills Act by rewriting a will.

EXAM TIP   🦅GILBERT

Keep in mind that a constructive trust will be imposed in the case of a secret trust even if the will beneficiary did not make the promise until *after* the will was executed. Furthermore, it does *not* matter whether the will beneficiary *intended to perform* the promise when the beneficiary made it; all that matters is that the testator *relied* on the promise in executing or not revoking the will.

---

c. Distinguish—"Semi-Secret Trusts"

Some courts impose a different remedy if the trust is semi-secret as opposed to fully secret. A semi-secret trust exists if the decedent's will devises property to someone *in trust*, but the trust is incomplete and thus defective because the will did not identify the beneficiary (*e.g.,* a devise "to Trustee in trust for persons and purposes agreed between us during my lifetime" or simply "to Trustee in trust"), the cases are split as to the result.

(1) Majority View—Resulting Trust

Many courts have held that the named trustee (Trustee) holds upon a *resulting* trust for the testator's heirs (or residuary beneficiaries), on the ground that this is simply an attempted testamentary trust the equitable interests in which have failed. Under this view, whether the trustee wishes to perform the trust is immaterial: The resulting trust is imposed even where Trustee acknowledges the oral trust and seeks to perform it! [**Olliffe v. Wells**, 130 Mass. 221 (1881)] And, because on the face of the will there is a trust that is defective, there is *no possibility of the transferee's being unjustly enriched* and thus no need to intervene with a constructive trust on that ground. This approach has received considerable criticism because it fails to carry out the testator's intent and benefit those the testator wished to benefit.

(2) Minority View—Constructive Trust

Accepting this criticism as valid, a number of courts have imposed a *constructive trust* for the *intended beneficiary* (also the preferred view of most commentators). *Rationale:* If a constructive trust can be imposed where *no* words of trust appear in the will, no logical reason exists as to why one cannot prove a part of the trust (*i.e.,* the names of the beneficiaries or terms of the trust) where the trust intent is expressed in the will and only the remaining part of the trust is missing. This is the Restatement position, emphasizing prevention of unjust enrichment of Testator's (other) successors in interest and that here there is not even the usual risk of spurious claims against a devisee who might have been intended to take beneficially. [Rest. 3d § 18 cmt. c]

d. Distinguish—Breach of Agreement by Intestate Heir

The "secret trust" principles also apply in cases where the decedent died *intestate*, forgoing the opportunity to make a will in reliance on a promise by an heir to hold the property in trust for another. [Rest. 3d § 18(2)] In this situation some courts require "compelling evidence" of the decedent's reliance on the heir's promise (or acquiescence), *inducing* the decedent *not* to make a will.

SECRET AND SEMI-SECRET TESTAMENTARY TRUSTS COMPARED	GILBERT
SECRET TRUST	**SEMI-SECRET TRUST**
Absolute gift in will (*i.e.,* no indication of trust) made *in reliance on the will beneficiary's promise* to hold the property in trust for another	Gift in will to a person "in trust," but *no trust beneficiary named*
Will beneficiary *may* perform trust if she chooses	Devisee or legatee *cannot* perform trust
If will beneficiary refuses to perform, *constructive trust* imposed in favor of *intended beneficiary*	*Majority view:* "Trustee" holds on *resulting trust* for *testator's residuary beneficiaries or heirs*. *Minority view: Constructive trust* imposed in favor of *intended beneficiaries*

D. Revocable Inter Vivos Trusts as Will Substitutes—Special Problems

1. Contemporary Approach

Under modern law, a settlor *can* validly create an effective, "nontestamentary" trust during life even if the settlor retains interests and extensive powers (including to revoke and amend). According to such modern case law (and the better view), the settlor can even (and often does) serve as trustee or co-trustee or hold administrative powers under such a trust. The real question therefore is *did* the purported settlor in fact create such a trust? *Was* the requisite intent present? In modern cases, most of the trusts that have failed involved oral and casual acts of alleged trust creation. The recognition of a valid present trust is not precluded by the fact that remainder beneficiaries—often the only beneficiaries other than the settlor, who usually has the exclusive right to income payments during life—are a class that is not ascertainable at the time the trust is created does not prevent the creators or (*e.g.,* "my issue living at my death" or "my heirs at law" even persons to be designated by the testator in the exercise of a power of appointment, in default of which the remainder goes to the settlor's "descendants" or the like). [Rest. 3d § 25(1)]

a. Property Requirement

There ***must***, however, be trust property, for no trust can exist without trust property. Thus, a trust of property to be subsequently designated or "to be received under my will" would not suffice to create a living trust, because of the absence of presently existing and presently identifiable trust property. On the other hand, as long as there is a present trust corpus, there is nothing wrong with the Settlor adding other properties subsequently during life or by will (*e.g.,* testamentary additions by pouring over). Thus, obviously, if anything interferes with the present transfer, there's no need to reach the question of whether the trust is testamentary,

b. Beneficiaries Other than Settlor

On its face, the trust must create some interests in some category of beneficiaries ***other than the settlor***, remember, but those can be purely future interests, and they can (at least according to proper analysis) exist in unascertained and even unborn persons. Also, the interests can be vested or contingent. Such interests can even be subject to change or selection or appointment by the settlor (and it should not be fatal that such a designation may come from the settlor's will, for there is no theoretical obstacle to the settlor's retention of a testamentary power of appointment).

2. Special Types of Revocable Trusts

a. Life insurance Trusts

(1) Irrevocable Life Insurance Trust

Normally, an irrevocable life insurance trust (called an ILIT) is created simply by the transfer (*i.e.,* assignment) of one or more life insurance policies to a trustee, much as any other item of property might be transferred to a trustee who thereby becomes its legal owner. In such a case, the life insurance policy itself becomes the trust property. Even though the trustee has little in the way of active duties until the insured dies and the proceeds are collected, the trust is not a passive one and its validity has not been a source of either practical or theoretical difficulty.

(2) Revocable Life Insurance Trusts

Case law has consistently ***upheld*** these trusts despite allegations that they are defectively "testamentary" in character or simply too insubstantial to constitute present trusts, ***unless*** there was some peculiar defect in the attempted creation of the trust [*see, e.g.,* purported transfer of policies was incomplete, there being no delivery for want of a presently identified trustee].

EXAM TIP   GILBERT

Be sure to remember that although a trust generally cannot exist without trust property, *life insurance trusts* have been *upheld* despite the absence of a significant res prior to the settlor's death.

(a) Creation of Revocable Life Insurance Trusts

There are two ways to create revocable life insurance trusts.

(i) No assignment: The owner of the life insurance policy may *designate the trustee as the payee* of the policy proceeds, normally designating the payee *"as trustee"* of the trust, and the settlor and trustee usually execute a written trust agreement. (In nearly all states, however, an oral promise by the payee to hold in trust or other oral manifestation of the trust terms will be effective if satisfactorily proven.) The trustee may have custody of the policy for convenience, but there is no formal assignment, and the policy ownership remains in the settlor-insured.

(ii) Assignment: A less common method is to *assign the insurance policies* themselves to the trustee pursuant to a trust agreement.

Whichever of these methods is used, the trust may be either *funded* (where there is a transfer to the trustee of other property, the income of which may be used to pay premiums) or *unfunded* (with no other transfer to the trust).

(b) Bases for Upholding Revocable Insurance Trusts

In the absence of special circumstances creating defects (such as lack of a trustee and thus lack of delivery, or the absence of properly ascertainable beneficiaries), courts have inevitably sustained revocable life insurance trusts.

1) Chose in Action Is Property

The trust may be upheld under the rationale that the trustee's right as the revocably designated beneficiary of the policy itself constitutes a property interest (not a bare expectancy but a chose in action in the form of a third-party beneficiary right under the contract—an interest that has been called vested subject to divestment) that serves as the trust property.

2) Proceeds Paid at Death Are Property

Under the more modern rationale, the trust arises at the insured's death by operation of contract—really by a pair of contracts, *one* between the insurance company and the settlor and the *other* between the settlor and the trustee. In other words, the insurance policy contractually requires the insurance company to make a transfer to the trustee, and that transfer creates a trust that the trustee must carry out in accordance with the terms of the trust agreement; under this view, the proceeds are readily recognizable as the res. According to this analysis, the transfer of the proceeds at the insured's death is no more invalid as an attempted "testamentary" disposition than any other payment of insurance proceeds at an insured's death where no trust is involved.

b. "Totten Trusts"—So-Called Tentative or Savings Deposit Trusts

People often make deposits rather casually with banks or savings and loan associations in their own names "in trust" for another person. These are Totten Trusts, but are they really intended to be trusts? If so, should they nevertheless fail as attempted "testamentary" dispositions? If it is a valid trust, what are its terms, who has rights, and when do they attach?

e.g. **Example:** Depositor deposits funds in Bank in Depositor's own name "as trustee for Child" or in the name of "Depositor in trust for Child." This example is the classic "Totten trust" situation.

cf. **Compare:** If Depositor deposits funds in Bank, not in Depositor's own name, but in the name of Friend "as trustee" or "in trust" for Child, this example is not a Totten trust. Nor is there a Totten trust if Grandparent had sent funds to Parent for Parent to deposit in the name of "Parent in trust for Child" (the common way a grandparent starts a trust account for a grandchild). In these cases the depositor was someone (or with funds from someone) *other* than the one designated as trustee. The account name presumptively means exactly what it says—that there is presently a regular trust—even though obviously in these examples the terms of the trusts are unspecified and subject to proof and clarification by other evidence. The focus of the present discussion, however, is upon deposits of the type in the first example above, in which the depositor (or source) *and* the nominal trustee are the *same person*.

(1) Question of Trust Intention

Such a deposit is not really clear on its face and does not by itself prove that the depositor intended presently to create an inter vivos trust. The depositor may have intended: (i) to create a trust upon her death, (ii) presently to create a trust that is revocable by her at any time prior to death, (iii) presently to create an irrevocable trust, or (iv) not to create no trust at all (the form of the deposit being merely to avoid certain restrictions or limitations on insurance protection or to set apart funds in case the depositor decides to create a trust in the future). The last of these has no trust intention at all. Although there is trust intention in the first, it is an intention to create a trust in the future and thus of no legal effect. The second and third intentions mentioned are permissible forms of trust *intention*, but the question is which of the possible intentions was at work? And, based on that, answer, is there a valid trust?

(2) Validity and Effect

Because of these uncertainties, courts have developed differing positions with respect to the validity, presumed intention, and effect to give to these bank deposit situations.

(a) Presumptively a Revocable Trust

Most cases hold that a deposit by one person of her own money in her own name as trustee for another presumptively creates a revocable trust. The depositor-trustee can and does, by inter vivos *withdrawals* (*e.g.,* simply by writing a check), revoke the trust in whole or in part during her lifetime; whatever remains at her death goes to the named beneficiary, if then living. [*In re* **Totten**, 179 N.Y. 112 (1904)] This is the "usual intention" attributed to the depositor, and the intention is implemented as just described. This presumption is rebuttable, and courts will receive evidence of contrary intention and will give recognition to other intent if discovered. [Rest. 3d § 26]

(b) During Depositor's Lifetime

During the settlor's lifetime, a Totten trust *differs* from other revocable trusts in several ways.

1) Depositor's Creditors May Reach the Assets in the Account

The depositor's creditors, in many states, can reach the deposit notwithstanding the "trust" name, even in jurisdictions in which this is not true of other revocable trusts. And if the depositor becomes incompetent, his guardian may have use and control of the funds without following procedures that might otherwise be necessary for property placed in a revocable trust.

2) Terminates if Beneficiary Predeceases Depositor

A Totten trust *terminates* automatically if the named beneficiary predeceases the depositor; *i.e.,* the beneficiary's will beneficiaries or heirs have no right to the deposit (not even what remains in the account at the depositor's death even though there has been no revocation by the depositor).

(c) Depositor's Death

On the depositor's death, a Totten trust is treated as a valid inter vivos transfer, so that the unrevoked balance in the account is *not* a part of the depositor's probate estate for most purposes, and testamentary formalities for its disposition are not required. [Rest. 3d § 26] Nevertheless, unlike other revocable trusts, which are generally not revocable or appointable by will unless the right to do so is expressly reserved, the depositor's *will may revoke* the rights of the named beneficiary under the Totten trust.

1) Express Revocation by Will

If the depositor leaves a will that expressly bequeaths the funds in the account to someone other than the named beneficiary of the bank deposit, the will effectively revokes the trust and leaves the funds to the will beneficiary. The mere execution of a will that would bequeath the deposit to another is probably not itself sufficient to revoke the tentative trust if that will is no longer in effect at the depositor's death.

2) Clear Intent to Revoke Required

The intention to revoke the tentative trust by will must be clear, and the intention to revoke must make apparent that the depositor intended the bank deposit to go to someone other than the beneficiary named in the account. Thus, generally, a mere direction that "all my property" or "all my money" go to another would not be sufficient. But some cases have held that the trust may be revoked in whole or in part by implication, such as where provisions of the will would fail and the will's contents would make no sense (as interpreted at the time of the will's execution) without drawing on the funds.

(3) Evidence of Intent

Evidence is admissible to show the Totten Trust depositor's intent. What evidence is admissible, and what is its effect?

(a) Statements and Conduct

Evidence of the depositor's statements or conduct at or near the time of the deposit, and often subsequent conduct, are relevant to show her intention or state of mind.

(b) Evidence of Intent to Create Irrevocable Trust

In many cases that have found the intent to create an irrevocable trust, particularly persuasive has been communication to the beneficiary about existence of the deposit, and especially persuasive has been the delivery of the savings account *passbook* to the beneficiary.

EXAM TIP

The important things to remember about Totten trusts (*e.g.,* a deposit by X "in trust for Y") are:

- The *depositor retains full control* of the money in the account during her lifetime.

- A Totten trust is revocable by: (i) the *withdrawal of funds*; (ii) any *lifetime act manifesting the intent to revoke*; and (iii) unlike other revocable trusts, a *contradictory provision in a will*.

- A Totten trust *does not protect* funds in the account from *creditors' claims*.

- A Totten trust *terminates if the beneficiary predeceases the depositor*.

---

3. Revocable Trusts and Substantive Policies

a. Elective Share of Surviving Spouse

Can a property owner transfer property into a revocable trust and thereby circumvent policies of the law of decedents' estates (or other policies) restricting testation or imposing obligations on a decedent's estate? This section addresses the use of a revocable trust to avoid the statutory *elective share* (aka *forced share*) of the transferor's surviving spouse.

Example: Under the law of the state involved, T's spouse S would be entitled to a one-third share of T's estate, and if T makes a will giving S less or something different (*e.g.,* a life estate in T's property), S has a right to elect against that will and to take S's one-third interest outright. During life, T transfers the bulk of T's property to a trust under which T retains a right to the income for life and a power of revocation. At T's death, T is survived by S, who elects against T's will in order to take S's elective share. Are the assets in that trust included in T's estate for purposes of determining the amount of S's elective share, and can S reach those assets to satisfy S's elective share?

(1) Majority View

Under the prevailing view in the absence of statute, the answer to these questions is *no*. This is also the position in the earlier Restatements. [Rest. 2d § 57 cmt. c] This result assumes (i) that the owner was free (as is generally the case) to defeat the spouse's elective share by giving away property outright during life, and (ii) that the revocable trust was valid rather than purely "illusory."

(2) Trust That Is Illusory or Mere Agency

It does appear, however, in some of the cases, that some courts have been more responsive to evidence suggesting that the trust was entirely illusory when the issue involves a spouse's elective rights.

(3) Other Views

(a) "Intent" Test

A few jurisdictions have employed an "intent" or "virtual fraud" test, asking whether the transferor's *subjective purpose* in creating the trust was to avoid the spouse's elective share. If such a purpose is found, in these states the spouse is allowed to have the assets treated as a part of the transferor's probate estate.

(b) Current Approach

Gradually increasing case law and a substantial and growing number of statutes have adopted the position that, even though the trust is otherwise valid and in no way defective as an "illusory" transfer or as a mere agency, the right of the surviving spouse *can be asserted* against the trust property. [*See, e.g.,* **Sullivan v. Burkin**, 460 N.E.2d 572 (Mass. 1984)—prospective change of law; **Moore v. Jones**, 261 S.E.2d 289 (N.C. 1980); UPC § 2–202] The details of this right and of its measurement vary from statute to statute, but the essence of these rules is that even though revocable trusts may and generally will pass challenges based on formal grounds ("testamentary" character and compliance with the wills act), revocable trusts may not be used to circumvent the serious substantive policy granting an elective share to a surviving spouse. The rationale is that rights under such a trust are so similar to complete ownership that it makes a farce of elective share legislation to allow the elective share to so readily be avoided. [Rest. 3d § 25(2)]

b. Other Situations—Taxation, Creditors, and Restrictions on Charitable Bequests

(1) Income and Estate Taxes

The federal Internal Revenue Code and the tax law of most states today make clear that a property owner who transfers property to a revocable trust achieves *no beneficial change in tax position*. For example, the income of the trust will continue to be taxable to the transferor [I.R.C. §§ 671–677] and the corpus of the trust will be included in his gross estate at death [I.R.C. §§ 2036–2038], not only when the trust is wholly revocable or freely amendable, but also when any of a broad variety of powers or beneficial interests have been retained.

(2) Creditors

The laws of the various states differ, but the property in a revocable trust may be reachable by creditors of the settlor. And once the debtor-settlor has died, the federal Bankruptcy Code is no longer available. Even in those states that do allow creditors of the settlor to reach revocable trust assets during life, these doctrines may not apply after the settlor's death (although there are exceptions). [*Compare* Rest. 3d § 25(2) cmt. e—revocable trust assets should be (as needed) subject to claims of settlor's creditors or creditors of his estate and should also be used to determine and satisfy shares of *pretermitted heirs*, adding further that *antilapse* and similar statutes should apply to revocable trusts]

(3) Charitable Bequests

The increasingly rare statutes restricting bequests and devises to charity are generally held not to invalidate inter vivos trusts for charitable purposes, despite the settlor's retention of a life interest and a power of revocation.

TESTS TO DETERMINE WHETHER PROPERTY IN A REVOCABLE TRUST IS SUBJECT TO SETTLOR'S SURVIVING SPOUSE'S ELECTIVE SHARE	GILBERT
MAJORITY VIEW	Transferred property is *not subject* to the elective share because an *owner is free to give away property during life*.
ILLUSORY TRANSFER DOCTRINE	Transferred property *is subject* to the elective share if the transferor *retained so much control over the property* to make the transfer illusory.
INTENT TEST	Transferred property *is subject* to the elective share if the transferor's *purpose was to defeat the surviving spouse's elective share*.
MODERN CASE LAW AND STATUTES	Transferred property *is subject* to the elective share because revocable trusts may not be used to circumvent the *policy* granting the surviving spouse such rights.

Chapter Four

Rights of the Beneficiary and the Beneficiary's Creditors in the Beneficiary's Interest

CONTENTS	PAGE
Key Exam Issues	82
A. Beneficiary's Rights in the Trust	82
B. Voluntary Transfers by the Beneficiary	83
C. Rights of Beneficiary's Creditors to Reach Beneficiary's Interest	84

Key Exam Issues

When answering questions concerning the *alienation of the beneficiary's interest*, consider generally the following:

1. When answering questions about the beneficiary's ability to reach the trust assets, consider the following:

   a. Is the language of the trust instrument mandatory or discretionary or a combination of both?

   b. Even if the trust language gives the trustee complete discretion, does the trust require the trustee to give the beneficiary a certain standard of living? Is the trustee unreasonably withholding distributions?

2. When answering whether the interest is *assignable* voluntarily or *reachable* by creditors remember that a beneficial interest is freely alienable unless there is a valid trust provision to the contrary.

3. What *effect* the assignment or attachment may have. Consider the exact nature of rights assigned or able to be reached. Be sure to consider priority questions.

Specifically, when *creditors* are involved, think about the following:

1. Whether creditors can reach a beneficial interest or assets subject to a power (*e.g.,* of revocation) depends upon whether the debtor is the *settlor* or merely a *beneficiary*. (This may also be relevant in determining the effect of a spendthrift restraint.)

2. Examine *spendthrift trusts* for (i) possible exceptions for *special claimants* and (ii) any *local statutory limits*.

A. Beneficiary's Rights in the Trust

1. Mandatory Trusts Versus Discretionary Trusts

a. If the trust language includes mandatory terms such as "shall," "will," "must," requiring the trustee to distribute certain amounts or at certain intervals, the beneficiary has a right to those distributions, and can have a court enforce that right. Language simply directing the trustee to make certain distributions can also be mandatory:

 Example: I give these assets to M in trust to distribute to R for life, and then to E for life.

b. If a trustee of a trust with mandatory distribution provisions fails to make those distributions, the beneficiary can likely successfully sue the trustee for breach of the trustee's duty. The court will direct the trustee to make the required distributions. In addition, the trustee may have additional liability for breach of the fiduciary obligations by failing to adhere to the trust provisions.

2. If, however, the trust terms use discretionary language, such as "may," "at trustee's sole discretion," then it does not require the trustee to distribute anything to the beneficiary, and the beneficiary has no right to force a distribution from the trust.

a.   Note that most trusts use both kinds of language to refer to different kinds of distributions or different types of beneficiaries.

Example: I give these assets to L to distribute the income at least monthly to my three children, A, B, and C. L may, at L's sole discretion, distribute as much of the principal in any amounts L considers necessary, in L's sole discretion, for their education and health.

Compare: I direct the trustee to make quarterly distributions of income to G with principal distributions to H in the trustee's absolute discretion as trustee determines appropriate.

b.   The more discretion the trustee has, the less likely the beneficiary will succeed at getting a court to force the trustee to make a distribution. This is because the more discretion the trustee has, the less "ascertainable" are what specific things the beneficiary has a right to. Here is a list of possible standards of distribution, from most to least e ascertainable:

1)   **Support and Maintenance:** Courts usually interpret this to mean the beneficiary's accustomed standard of living—thus, it's ascertainable. The beneficiary has a right to get what the beneficiary needs to maintain that standard.

2)   **Education:** Courts interpret this to cover tuition, room and board, and technical as well as four-year college, unless the trust instrument specifies otherwise. This is a fairly ascertainable standard.

3)   **Emergency:** This phrase refers to a real emergency that most people would agree was one—so not usually a personal emergency. Unless the trust gives some direction here, the trustee has a lot of discretion to determine what this means. Courts will usually defer to the trustee.

4)   **Welfare, Best Interests, Happiness, or similar terms:** These terms give the trustee very broad discretion, and it will be very hard for a beneficiary to challenge the trustee's exercise of that discretion. These terms are so general that what the beneficiary has a right to is hard to ascertain.

c.   Even with full discretion, however, the trustee must act in good faith and in the beneficiary's interest and in accordance with the terms of the trust. [UTC § 814]

EXAM TIP   GILBERT

When answering a question about a beneficiary's right to challenge a trustee's distributions, remember that a court will look at the trust instrument as a whole, not just the standard for distributions, for clues about the settlor's intent. Such clues might be a direction to the trustee to consider a beneficiary's other assets when making distributions, how many other beneficiaries the trust has, how much property is in the trust, etc.

B. Voluntary Transfers by the Beneficiary

1. Right to Transfer—in General

A beneficiary may alienate that person's interest in a trust *freely*, unless the trust contains a valid provision to the contrary, such as a spendthrift clause. Thus, a beneficiary can assign, pledge, or encumber the beneficiary's interest, or even transfer it in trust for another. Also, if the interest is not conditioned on the beneficiary's survival, it will pass by will or by intestate succession. [Rest. 3d § 51]

a. Rationale

The beneficiaries are equitable *owners* of the trust estate; their interests are property, and each therefore has power to transfer and convey her interest in the trust to the same extent that she could transfer her other property.

b. Transferee's Rights

A beneficiary can assign only such interest in the trust as is actually vested in the beneficiary. The transfer is *not a transfer of the trust res* itself, but only of the beneficiary's equitable interest in it. Whatever conditions or limitations attached to the beneficiary's interest prior to the assignment apply against the assignee.

e.g. **Example:** If B has a right to income for life and assigns it to F, F receives an interest for the life of B (not the life of F). If B dies, F's right to income ceases; if F predeceases B, F's successors inherit the remaining right to income for B's life.

2. Form and Manner of Voluntary Transfer

Generally, a beneficiary may transfer the beneficiary's equitable interests in the trust using the same methods and formalities required for nontrust interests in the same type of property.

a. Formalities

If the trust estate consists of *real property*, a writing is generally required by the Statute of Frauds to transfer the interest. Ordinarily no writing is required to transfer the beneficiary's present or future interest in a trust of personal property. [Rest. 3d § 53]

b. Consideration

No consideration is necessary to transfer an interest in a trust. As with other gifts, a gratuitous transfer is effective and (in the absence of statute) irrevocable. [Rest. 3d § 52(1)]

c. Delivery

In a few jurisdictions, even though the writing may not be required for Statute of Frauds purposes because the trust consists of personal property (*see* above), a writing or other symbol would still be needed for purposes of making delivery.

d. Notice

Notice to the trustee is not necessary for an effective assignment, unless required by the trust instrument. [Rest. 3d § 51 cmt. d]

C. Rights of Beneficiary's Creditors to Reach Beneficiary's Interest

The first question to ask in deciding whether and to what extent a beneficiary's creditors can reach the beneficiary's interest in the trust is whether the beneficiary is also the settlor or not.

1. Beneficiary Is Not Settlor

a. **Mandatory Distributions:** Because the beneficiary has a right to demand mandatory distributions, and the creditor stands in the beneficiary's shoes, the creditor in such a case can get a court order seizing these distributions. [UTC § 501]

b. **Discretionary Distributions:** Because a beneficiary has no right to demand discretionary distributions, the beneficiary's creditor generally has no access to them either. [UTC § 504]

   (1) This means that a creditor cannot get an order compelling a distribution. The most a creditor can do in this case is get a "Hamilton Drogo order," which allows the creditor to attach distributions once the trustee has made them.

   (2) **Exception creditors:** UTC § 504 establishes that a court may order a trustee to make distributions to a beneficiary's spouse, ex-spouse, or children, with a support order even if the trust is discretionary, if the creditor can show that the trustee "has not complied with a standard of distribution or has abused discretion." [UTC § 504(c)] Not all states that adopted the UTC, however, adopted this section.

c. **Trustee Liable for Misdelivery**

   Once notified of an assignment or attachment of the beneficiary's interest, the trustee will become personally liable to the assignee or creditor if the trustee distributes funds directly.

EXAM TIP

Remember that the creditor can reach only the beneficiary's interest in the trust, not the trust property itself (unless the debtor is the sole beneficiary).

---

2. Beneficiary Is Also the Settlor

a. **Revocable Trusts:** Because the settlor has retained the right to revoke the trust, the settlor has access to and control of all of the assets in it. Therefore, the creditor who stands in the beneficiary's shoes, has the same access to all of the assets in the trust. This is the case even if the trust has a spendthrift clause.

b. **Irrevocable Trusts:** In an irrevocable trust, the settlor has given up the right to revoke the trust, so the settlor has less control of, and access to, the assets. However, the settlor's creditors are able to attach whatever interest the settlor still has reserved in the trust for herself. For example, if the trust gives the settlor, "income for life," her creditors can attach that amount of the trust. Of course, the settlor can fully insulate the trust assets from creditors by creating an irrevocable trust in favor of a third party, giving up any interest in the trust property. But the downside to this arrangement is, obviously, that the settlor no longer has the assets.

3. Spendthrift Trusts

a. **In General**

   Almost all trusts today contain a spendthrift clause. These clauses prevent both voluntary and involuntary transfer of the beneficiary's interest. This means that the beneficiary cannot sell or give away the beneficiary's right to future income or capital, and the beneficiary's creditors are unable to collect or attach such rights. This type of trust is usually created to provide an interest for the beneficiary that will be secure against the beneficiary's own improvidence. [Rest. 3d § 58]

Example: A standard spendthrift clause looks like this: The interest of any Beneficiary of this Trust in the income and principal shall not be subject to claims of his or her creditors, or others, or be liable to attachment, execution, or other process or law and no Beneficiary shall have the right to encumber, hypothecate, or alienate his or her interest in any of the trust in any manner except as provided herein. Nor may a creditor compel a trustee to make a discretionary transfer to a beneficiary. Where the trustee is also a beneficiary, restraint on transfer is invalid against transferees or creditors of the Trustor. In no case shall a disclaimer by a beneficiary be considered a transfer to that Beneficiary.

b. Involuntary Transfers

Notice that, to be valid, a spendthrift clause must bar both voluntary and involuntary transfers.

(1) Validity of Spendthrift Restraints

Spendthrift provisions are valid in all American jurisdictions. [Rest. 3d § 58 cmt. a]

(a) Limiting Statutes

A few states (such as New York and California) have statutes that *limit* the effectiveness of spendthrift restraints. A few statutes provide that creditors can reach an arbitrary percentage (*e.g.,* 10%) of trust distributions or that creditors can reach income only (or some portion thereof). A more common restriction on spendthrift clauses allows only amounts needed for support to be insulated from creditors' claims. For example, creditors may be able to reach the beneficiary's interest if: (i) the right to payments exceeds the amounts needed for the beneficiary's support or education in the beneficiary's *accustomed standard of living*; and (ii) the trustee is *required* to make distributions (*i.e.,* the trust does not allow the trustee to accumulate the excess income).

(b) Bankruptcy Rule Follows State Law

The Bankruptcy Code has long respected the beneficiary-debtor's spendthrift protection as to interests that are validly inalienable both voluntarily and involuntarily under state law. [*See* 11 U.S.C. § 541(c)(2)]

(2) Effect of spendthrift Restraints

Spendthrift restraints prevent no *enforceable* transfers.

(a) Effect of Attempted Voluntary Transfer

Despite a valid spendthrift provision, if the beneficiary attempts to assign his trust interest to another, the *assignee cannot enforce* the assignment over the beneficiary's later objection—*i.e.,* a purported assignment is, in effect, *revocable*.

1) Trustee Authorized to Pay Assignee

The purported transfer, however, is *not void*; as long as the beneficiary or the trustee has not retracted it, it operates as a valid but revocable "authorization" for the trustee to pay and for the assignee to receive the payments to which the assignor (i.e., the beneficiary) would have been entitled. The trustee is protected if the trustee makes payment to the assignee in reliance on the purported assignment.

2) Beneficiary May Revoke Authorization

Once the beneficiary revokes the assignment, however, the trustee must pay the beneficiary alone. Failure to obey the beneficiary's direction to cease payments to the assignee will make the trustee liable. In this case, the assignee would have no rights at all against the trust or the beneficiary's interest (but if the assignee paid consideration for the assignment, he would be entitled to restitution, payable from the beneficiary's other assets).

It is important to remember that an attempted assignment in violation of a spendthrift provision is *not void*. Although the assignee *cannot compel the trustee to pay* because the assignee does not acquire the beneficial interest, the *trustee is authorized to pay* the assignee as long as the beneficiary does not revoke the trustee's authority. If the assignee *gave value* for the assignment and the beneficiary *revokes* the assignment (and the trustee's authority pursuant to it), the *beneficiary is liable* to the assignee. Although the assignee cannot reach the trust property, the claim can be satisfied from the beneficiary's other property or from trust funds *after they have been distributed* to the beneficiary.

(b) Creditor's Rights and Actions

If there is a valid spendthrift provision in effect, creditors are generally *barred from reaching* (*i.e.,* attaching) and selling or taking the beneficiary's interest in the trust.

1) Distributions from Trust Not Protected

As with discretionary trusts, once the monies are *paid* to the beneficiary from the trust, they are no longer protected. The beneficiary's creditors may attach and seize them, just as they could any other asset of the beneficiary.

2) Exceptions—Certain Creditors Can "Break Through" Spendthrift Restraints

Even where spendthrift restraints are otherwise valid, certain classes of creditors can "break through" and reach the beneficiary's interest in most states.

3) Classes of Creditors

The UTC and most states provide that the spendthrift restraint is not effective against the following types of creditors:

(i) The federal or state *government* (*e.g.,* tax claims) "to the extent provided by federal law or an applicable state statute";

(ii) A spouse (or ex-spouse) or child for *support*;

(iii) One who furnishes *necessaries of life* to the beneficiary; and

(iv) One who in some way *"preserves the interest"* of the beneficiary (*e.g.,* legal counsel).

4) Split of Authority

Cases generally support ***most*** of the exceptions above in ***most*** states, but the case authority is in conflict on other than governmental claims.

a) Spouse

A number of states have held that the spouse (or ex-spouse) and a few have held that children of the beneficiary of a spendthrift trust ***cannot*** reach his interest for the satisfaction of their support judgments.

b) Necessaries

There are also cases holding that claims for "necessaries" furnished to the beneficiary cannot be enforced against the beneficiary's interest in the spendthrift trust. Recovery is more likely if the ***state*** is the party seeking reimbursement for, *e.g.,* institutional care of the beneficiary. The UTC does not recognize an exception for "necessaries," although it does include services to protect a beneficiary's interest in its list of exceptions. [UTC § 503]

c) Tort Claims

A few states may allow tort creditors to reach a beneficiary's interest in a spendthrift trust, especially where the beneficiary's acts were ***intentional or grossly negligent***. [*See* Ga. Code Ann. § 53–12–28] But these states are in the minority on this issue.

SPECIAL CLASSES OF CREDITORS EXEMPT FROM SPENDTHRIFT PROTECTION	

IN MOST STATES, A BENEFICIARY'S INTEREST IN A SPENDTHRIFT TRUST *CAN* BE REACHED IN SATISFACTION OF A CLAIM AGAINST THE BENEFICIARY:

- ☑ By the federal or state ***government***, to the extent provided by law.
- ☑ For ***support*** of a child, spouse, or ex-spouse.
- ☑ For services or supplies provided for ***necessaries***.
- ☑ For services or supplies provided for the ***protection of the beneficiary's interest*** in the trust.

EXAM TIP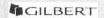

Watch out for fact patterns that try to hide the fact that the settlor is trying to protect the settlor's assets with a spendthrift trust. The settlor may be disguised as a beneficiary. When you are trying to determine whether a beneficiary is the settlor, ask who supplied the property for the creation of the trust. If a person furnishes the consideration, the person is likely the settlor even though another person technically created the trust.

---

4. Arguments for and Against Spendthrift Trusts

(a) Arguments Against

There are two basic arguments against spendthrift trusts:

(1) Symmetry of Estates

Equitable estates should not be treated differently from legal estates. Because the beneficiary's interest is generally conceded to be an equitable ownership of the trust property, any restraint on ownership should therefore be deemed to be "repugnant to the interest created."

(2) Social Policy

People should pay their debts. A creditor should be able to reach the assets of the debtor on the same basis and with the same exceptions, whether the assets are held in trust for him or not. Hence, there is no social justification for upholding a spendthrift provision—allowing the creditor to go wanting while the debtor enjoys the benefits of wealth without need of financially responsible behavior. Statutes specify the exemptions allowable for insolvent debtors; settlors should not be able to create additional, private exemptions for their trust beneficiaries.

(b) Argument for

The only real argument to support spendthrift trusts is based on a settlor's freedom of disposition: The donee (and thus the donee's creditor) has no *right* to the property, which the settlor was free to withhold; therefore, with respect to interests he chooses to give to the donee, the wishes of the donor settlor should control. It does not "violate any principles of sound public policy to permit a testator to give to the object of his bounty such a qualified interest in the income of a trust fund, and thus provide against the improvidence or misfortune of the beneficiary." [**Broadway National Bank v. Adams**, 133 Mass. 170 (1882)]

(c) Circumventing Limitations on Spendthrift Protection

The discretionary trust is a much-used device, not only in jurisdictions that do not recognize or significantly restrict spendthrift trusts, but also to avoid mandatory payments that creditors could reach after distribution.

EXAM TIP   **GILBERT**

If you encounter a discretionary trust on your exam, remember that *before* the trustee exercises the trustee's discretion to make payments to the beneficiary, the beneficiary's interest *cannot be reached by the beneficiary's creditors* (although a more precise common law analysis might allow creditors to compel proper exercise of the discretionary power if the trustee has abused the discretion). But *after* the trustee exercises his discretion and elects to make payments to the beneficiary, the trustee must make those payments not to the beneficiary but *directly to the beneficiary's creditors if the trustee has notice of an assignment or attachment* by the creditors, *unless* the beneficiary's interest is protected by a *spendthrift restraint*.

---

5. Special Needs Trusts

a. Special Needs Trusts (SNTs)

SNTs allow disabled people receiving state assistance to have more assets than these means-tested benefits normally allow. There are two kinds of SNTs:

(1) Third Party SNTs

Third Party SNTs are funded by someone other than the beneficiary with that person's assets. They must contain wording making clear that the funds they provide for the beneficiary do not pay for the same benefits that the government aid covers. These trusts are appealing for parents of disabled children in particular, because Medicaid and SSI leave many of the needs of disabled people uncovered, SNTs can be drafted to pay for these services, and yet allow the beneficiary to receive state aid.

(2) Self-Settled SNTs

Self-settled SNTs are trusts funded by the beneficiary, often from damage awards after an accident. They provide the same benefits as Third Party SNTs. The only difference is that, at the beneficiary's death, any remaining funds must go to the state.

6. Asset Protection Trusts (APTs)

a. In General

Under traditional trust law, a settlor could not create a spendthrift trust for herself—that is, one that would prevent the settlor's creditors from reaching the settlor's assets. The quest for such a form of asset protection led, however, several countries to start offering asset protection trusts in so-called "offshore" jurisdictions like the Cook Islands, the Caymans, and other Caribbean Islands. These trusts offered settlors a way to benefit from their assets while keeping them out of the reach of creditors.

b. Growth

Over the past two decades or so, some states in the U.S., hoping to garner some of this lucrative business, have created so-called Asset Protection Trusts. The first state to legislate this kind of trust was Alaska, and several other states, including Delaware, Hawaii, Mississippi, Missouri, Nevada, New Hampshire, Ohio, Oklahoma, Rhode Island, South Dakota, Tennessee, Utah, Virginia, and Wyoming, have followed. These trusts essentially allow a settlor to do what we have so far said a settlor cannot put her own assets in a trust to protect the assets from her own creditors, often including ex-spouses and children with support orders. It is not clear how these trusts will fare in U.S. jurisdictions, and that story is still unfolding.

(1) Conflict of Laws

Conflict of law rules state that a state need not apply another state's law if that law conflicts with the state's public policy. So, if a Massachusetts resident sets up an Alaska DAPT, and is sued by a creditor in Massachusetts, a Massachusetts court might refuse to apply the Alaska law if it determined that Alaska DAPTs violated Massachusetts public policy. One case has tested this issue in the context of bankruptcy: [*In re* **Huber**, 493 B.R. 798 (Bankr. W.D. Wash. 2013).] Here, a Washington resident transferred several real estate holdings and some personal assets into an Alaska DAPT. Almost all of the assets transferred were in Washington, and the settlor resided there as well. When the settlor declared bankruptcy, the court held that Washington, not Alaska law, applied, because Washington had a strong public policy against asset protection trusts. A federal bankruptcy judge issued a similar ruling in 2011, applying the federal statute of limitations, rather than the shorter Alaska, when applying fraudulent transfer law to assets transferred to an Alaska DAPT. Finally, in 2007, the Alaska Supreme Court ruled that Alaska could not limit the ability of another state to render judgments against the settlor of an APT when it has an independent basis for jurisdiction. As such, the other state's judgments finding a fraudulent conveyance were valid and enforceable. [**Toni 1 Trust v. Wacker**, 2018 WL 1125033.]

COMPARISON OF TRUSTS LIMITING TRANSFERABILITY OF BENEFICIARIES' INTERESTS		GILBERT
	DESCRIPTION	**EXAMPLE**
SPENDTHRIFT	Beneficiary *cannot transfer interest* in trust voluntarily *nor can creditors reach* it. Does not protect settlor's retained interest.	S to T in trust for B for life, income to be paid personally and to no other whether claiming by B's authority or otherwise.
DISCRETIONARY	Trustee has *discretion to make (or withhold) distributions* of income or principal or both, to or for one or more beneficiaries.	S to T in trust for B for life, distributions to be made according to T's discretion.
SPECIAL NEEDS TRUST	Beneficiary may get distributions from the trust without losing eligibility for state support.	S to T in trust to pay or apply such amounts as T deems appropriate for the support of B.
SPRAY AND SPRINKLE TRUSTS	Trustee may distribute to any member *of a group at her sole discretion*.	S to T in trust to distribute income or principal to any one or more of a group consisting of B and her spouse and issue.

Chapter Five
Charitable Trusts

CONTENTS	PAGE

Key Exam Issues 94

A. General Nature and Treatment of Charitable Trusts 95

B. Requirement of Public, Not Private, Benefit 97

C. Charitable Purpose Defined 99

D. Limitations on Charitable Trusts 109

E. Modification of Charitable Trusts—the Cy Pres Doctrine 112

Key Exam Issues

A charitable trust is a type of express trust. When an exam question set forth a trust with an apparently charitable purpose, do not immediately assume that you have a charitable trust. It is important for you to make a determination of whether the trust is in fact legally defined as charitable. This determination may be important because the correct answer to your question may turn on the special privileges accorded only to charitable trusts. Alternatively, the trust's validity may depend upon its purpose being classified as charitable. Take each step of the analysis in turn to fully respond to the question.

Your initial task then is to determine that the trust meets the requirements of a charitable trust, with focus on whether the trust has:

(i) A *public benefit*; and

(ii) A *charitable purpose* as defined by law.

Charitable trusts receive favorable treatment in the law because they benefit members of the public.

1. Public Benefit

There must be an *indefinite number of potential beneficiaries*. If there are inseparable private benefits, such as benefits passing to a named individual, the trust may fail as a charitable trust.

2. Charitable Purpose

First, assess whether the purpose falls within one of the generally accepted categories of charity (*i.e., relief of poverty, advancement of education or religion, promotion of health*, or *governmental or municipal purposes*). Second, if the objectives of the trust do not fall into a specific charitable category, consider whether the purpose is sufficiently *of interest or beneficial to the community* to justify permitting the property to be dedicated to its accomplishment. Note that an established category (*e.g.,* "educational" purposes) has a fair amount of stretch, and broader purposes (*e.g.,* public interest) are fairly open-ended.

Remember, even if a trust purpose seems to be charitable, watch for some particular basis for disqualification (*e.g., private benefits*).

3. Cy Pres

If a trust seems to have outlived its original charitable purpose, analyze whether it can be modified under the doctrine of cy pres. Courts use three steps to determine whether to apply the cy pres doctrine:

a. *Has the specific purpose been accomplished or become illegal or impracticable,* or are the trust funds *excessive* for the specified purpose (so that adhering solely to that purpose would fail to utilize the funds or would be objectionably wasteful under cy pres standards)? Remember that under standard doctrine it is not enough to convince a court that the funds would better serve another charitable purpose.

b. *Did the settlor have a "general charitable intent"* meaning did the settlor want the funds to be used for charity even if the charitable purpose changes (or did the settlor intend for the fund or excess to revert by resulting trust to the settlor or her successors in interest if the specified purpose was accomplished or became impossible)? The mere fact that the settlor directed the funds to be used "only" or "exclusively" for the specified purpose is not determinative.

c. *If the preceding are established* and the cy pres doctrine applies, now the court considers *what altered purpose or modification* it should allow to reflect the underlying intent and circumstances of the gift.

A. General Nature and Treatment of Charitable Trusts

1. Creation and Purpose of Trust

A settlor creates a charitable trust in the same manner (by will, inter vivos transfer, or declaration) as a private trust, but for a purpose the law regards as charitable. It is a trust the performance of which will, in the view of the law as interpreted by the courts (rather than merely in the opinion of the settlor), confer appropriate benefits upon *the public* or upon some *reasonably broad and appropriate segment thereof*. [Rest. 3d § 28]

2. Charitable Purposes

The Third Restatement lists the following purposes as charitable:

(i)   The *relief of poverty*;

(ii) The *advancement of knowledge or education*;

(iii) The *advancement of religion*;

(iv) The *promotion of health*;

(v)   *Governmental or municipal purposes*; and

(vi) *Other purposes* that are *beneficial to the community*. [Rest. 3d § 28; *and see* UTC § 405(a)]

3. Favored by the Law

The law gives charitable trusts special privileges that are not given to private trusts. Charitable trusts are generally construed in a manner that serves to uphold and preserve them (*i.e.,* to limit the purposes to those that qualify as charitable), and they are exempted from some of the restrictions applicable to private trusts.

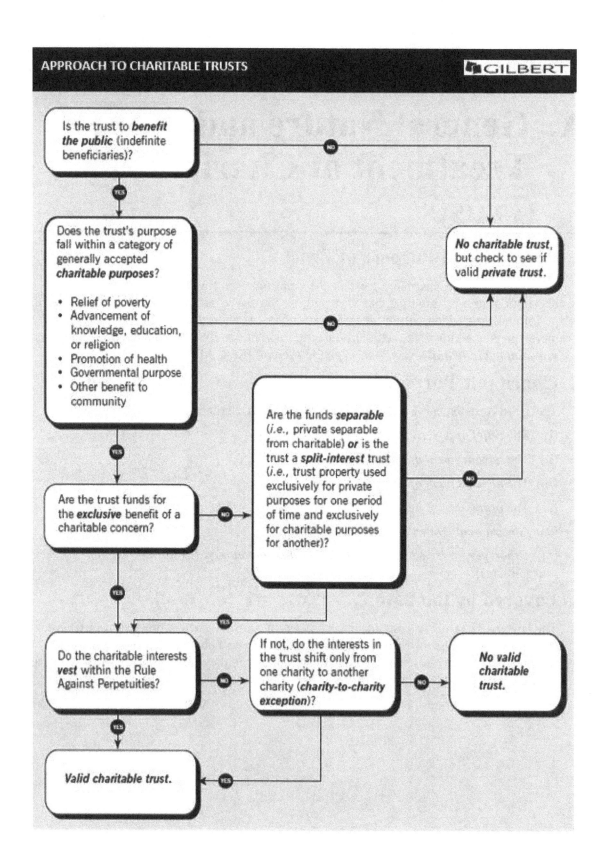

B. Requirement of Public, Not Private, Benefit

1. Indefinite Beneficiaries and the Public Benefit Requirement

A charitable trust must benefit society or a sufficiently broad segment thereof such that the trust's performance is of interest to the community as a whole.

a. Indefinite Number of Potential Beneficiaries

A charitable trust must be for the public benefit generally or for the benefit of some members of a class of the public that is *indefinite in number*.

(1) Distinguish—Private Trust

Unlike a private trust, a charitable trust is valid precisely because of the lack of definite, designated beneficiaries.

(2) Enforcement of Charitable Trust

Because there need not be specific beneficiaries capable of enforcing the trust, a system for enforcing charitable trusts is needed. The state attorney general (or other public official) is authorized to enforce such trusts on behalf of the community. A co-trustee or successor trustee also has standing to sue another trustee or predecessor trustee to prevent or redress a breach of trust or otherwise enforce the trust, as in most states does a person having a "special interest" in the performance of the trust. Accordingly, where a particular individual or charitable institution is sufficiently identifiable as eligible to benefit from the charitable trust, that individual or institution may enforce the trust. Under the traditional view of most of the states that have no contrary statute, a settlor, as such, does *not* have such a special interest. [*But see* UTC § 405(c)—"The settlor of a charitable trust, among others, *may* maintain a proceeding to enforce the trust."] The state attorney general must normally be made a party to proceedings initiated by a trustee or person with a "special interest."

WHO HAS STANDING TO ENFORCE A CHARITABLE TRUST?	GILBERT	
	TRADITIONAL VIEW	UTC VIEW
ATTORNEY GENERAL	✓	✓
TRUSTEE	✓	✓
PERSON WITH "SPECIAL INTEREST"	✓	✓
BENEFICIARY		✓
SETTLOR		

b. Effect of Limited Number of Direct Beneficiaries

Problems arise where the trust requires the selection of a limited number of actual recipients or where the eligible group of potential recipients is limited. Does the fact that definite beneficiaries will be designated disqualify the trust as charitable?

(1) General View

Generally, a large number or indefiniteness of *direct* recipients is *not* essential to a charitable trust. The fact that one or more individuals will become ascertainable as the person(s) to receive benefits directly from the trust does not make the trust a private one if: (i) the recipient(s) will be selected from an *indefinite group* (*i.e.,* if entry into the limited class of recipients or potential recipients is sufficiently open); and (ii) the benefit would be *sufficiently in the general public interest* that the community as a whole could arguable be the ultimate beneficiary of the trust. [Rest. 3d § 28 cmt. a(1)]

> **e.g.** **Example:** A trust for the education of "a fine [child,] preferably one who is handicapped" has been upheld as a charitable purpose. [*In re* **Chapman's Estate,** 39 Pa. D. & C.2d 701 (1966)]

> **e.g.** **Example:** A trust "to aid victims of California wildfires" qualifies as charitable even though the number of actual recipients will be limited by the description of who would be eligible to receive the trust funds.

> **e.g.** **Example:** A trust to provide educational opportunity (or medical care) for two needy persons from the settlor's town selected each year by the trustees is a trust both for the relief of poverty and for the promotion of education (or health).

> **cf.** **Compare:** A trust for the education of worthy, needy *descendants* of the settlor is *private*, not charitable.

(2) How Direct Must the Benefit to the Community Be?

The following three groups potentially stand to benefit from a charitable trust: (i) the community at large; (ii) the direct recipients of the trust funds expended; and (iii) the somewhat larger group from which the direct recipients are to be selected. The group of actual recipients may be small—it could even be one individual—provided the category of individuals from which the recipient or recipients are chosen is *substantial in size* and *indefinite in membership*. It has occasionally been said that the benefit to the community at large must be "substantial," and where only a few persons actually benefit, the benefit to the community is not "substantial." Criticisms of this view suggest that it might mean that a wealthy person creates a large trust that would qualify as charitable because such a trust can make a "substantial" contribution to the community, while a small trust created by a person of lesser means might not qualify for its inability to make a "substantial" contribution. Properly, the substantiality of the contribution to the community should be relative to the size of the fund.

2. Effect of Trust Having Noncharitable Co-Beneficiaries

If a trust has *both* charitable and noncharitable purposes (*e.g.,* "payments to be made in the trustee's discretion to and for the benefit of any one or more of my son, my daughter, or University"), *or* has a purpose that (as construed) includes but is *broader* than charitable, the trust *does not qualify* as a charitable trust. In other words, a trust cannot have combined charitable and private purposes and still receive "charitable" trust treatment. In that instance, the trust must stand or fall as a *private trust*.

a. Distinguish—Separate or Successive Shares

But if the trust is so divided by its terms such that it may be treated as if the trust was instead two separate trusts or as two separate funds within the trust, or as funds devoted exclusively to a charitable purpose for one period and thereafter to a private purpose (a "charitable lead trust") or vice versa (a "charitable remainder trust"), the amount or interest designated for the charitable purpose (University in the above example) can qualify as a charitable trust, and the other portion and purpose must stand or fall as a private trust, governed by the more restrictive rules applicable thereto.

Example: Settlor devised property "to Trustee in trust to pay one-half of the income forever to Charity A, with the other one-half to be applied as reasonably appropriate to the support and care of Settlor's Brother; upon Brother's death, the one-half principal share from which Brother had been receiving the income shall be distributed to Brother's then living issue per stirpes." Here, the independent share that is dedicated to Charity A will be treated as, and eventually will become, a separate charitable trust.

C. Charitable Purpose Defined

1. Meaning of "Purpose" and "Charitable" in Requirement

A charitable trust must have as its trust "purpose" some activity of such general public interest and benefit as to come within the meaning of the term "charitable.". As stated above, the qualifying trust purpose or purposes must be *exclusively charitable*; the charitable *purpose* cannot be mixed with private or other noncharitable *objectives*. But remember, a trust could have terms that effectively divert into separate trusts. [Rest. 3d § 28]

a. Distinguish—Motive and Purpose

A "motive" is the reason the particular settlor acted; *i.e.,* it is subjectively what influenced the settlor to establish the trust. The trust "purpose" is the objective the trust was created to accomplish. It is not the settlor's motive that determines whether the trust is charitable or not. A court does not care why the settlor did what the settlor did, even though an understanding of motive may be helpful in construing the trust terms and even in determining its purpose. Mere benevolence is insufficient to establish a charitable purpose. The *trust purpose alone determines the validity* and charitable—or noncharitable—character of the trust. Thus, if a trust is actually for the relief of the poor, the advancement of religion, or some other recognized "charitable purpose" as described below, it is immaterial *why* the settlor established the trust. For example, the settlor may have been motivated to create the trust to spite loved ones and keep property away from relatives, to minimize tax liability, to salve a guilty conscience, or to gain public approval. These motivations are not relevant when evaluating the charitable purpose.

EXAM TIP   **GILBERT**

Remember that the *effect of the gift to the public* or a portion thereof, *not the settlor's motive*, controls. Do not be fooled by a fact situation on your exam where a school, park, scholarship, etc., created through a trust is required to be named after the donor (*e.g.,* Sarah Smith School). Even though the naming may have influenced the settlor's decision to create the trust, the trust is still a charitable trust. Likewise, if the settlor establishes a trust to build public tennis courts on land adjacent to the settlor's home, it is irrelevant that her motive was to use them herself.

b. What Does "Charitable" Mean?

The word "charitable" is a term of art and encompasses more than relief of poverty but does not encompass everything that a person (or even many people) may think of as good and worthwhile. As we have seen, in addition to the relief of poverty, trusts for the promotion of religion, health, and education, as well as purposes that are governmental or "beneficial to the community," are all charitable according to the Restatement, UTC, and other traditionally accepted definitions. Other authorities have, of course, used different or additional terminology—*e.g.,* "the advancement of the arts and sciences."

(1) Limitation

Legitimately, "charitable" is a purpose that society would deem desirable and beneficially enough that the trust merits true special treatment of charitable trusts. Remember, admirable goals are not sufficient to establish a charitable purpose.

(2) Subjective Aspect

Basically, the label "charitable" is a *conclusion* meaning that a court would deem it—in the inevitably subjective views of courts—sufficiently desirable and of such benefit to the general public that the dedication of property to that purpose, selected and restricted by one who no longer owns the property, is desirable.

(3) Purpose Must Not Be Illegal, Immoral, Irrational, or Otherwise Contrary to Public Policy

Like private trusts, the purposes of charitable trusts must not be unlawful or contrary to public policy. A trust, for example, to promote a cause that is illegal, immoral, or irrational will not be upheld as a charitable trust (but the question of what is "irrational" is obviously highly subjective). The Third Restatement also states that a purpose involving *"invidious discrimination,"* which it attempts briefly to describe, is noncharitable and against the policy of trust law, even without a finding of state action. [Rest. 3d § 28 cmt. f]

c. Certainty of Purposes

The trust purpose must be sufficiently certain that the court can (i) tell what the settlor intended and (ii) thereby ascertain whether that purpose is exclusively charitable. This does not mean that the purpose must be narrow or any more defined or certain than the legal concept of "charitable" itself. The charitable purposes of a trust may be very broad and general. In fact, the narrower and less general the purpose, the greater the risk of its being found noncharitable.

(1) "For Charity"

As a consequence, a trust simply "for charity" ordinarily will be and often has been upheld as charitable. The language is sufficiently definite (i) to be implemented (as there is no need to determine what specific charitable purposes are not included), and (ii) to make clear that the property is to be applied to purposes that are "charitable" under the law.

(a) Particular Charitable Purpose Need Not Be Specified When Charitable Intent Clear

A settlor may authorize a designated trustee to select one or more charitable purposes. If necessary, the court will appoint a trustee and either authorize the trustee to select specific charitable application(s) or determine or frame the specific charitable activity or activities to be undertaken by the trustee. [Rest. 3d § 28 cmt. a] In fact, bequests "to charity" have been construed to mean *in trust* for charity, with a trustee to be appointed.

(2) "For Benevolent Purposes"

Trusts for "benevolent" or "philanthropic" purposes may raise some questions and uncertainty because the dictionary meaning of these terms, while including charity, is generally said to be somewhat broader.

e.g. **Example:** References to "benevolent objects," "objects of benevolence and liberality," and the like have been held objectionably broad because purposes that are benevolent are not necessarily charitable.

(a) Modern View

Today, such "benevolence" language would probably be interpreted and limited as to qualify as charitable, at least in most states, even if the court also recognizes a broader "dictionary meaning" of the word "benevolence."

(b) Court May Construe Trust Language as Charitable

A trust "for the benefit of humankind" has been held charitable, and although a few critics have felt that the expression was either too indefinite or too broad, the varieties of wording that have been upheld show the willingness of courts to construe instruments so as to confine purposes to "charitable" when needed. This result, however, depends on the interpretation of the instrument and is not a broadening of the definition of charity for purposes of eligibility as a charitable trust.

e.g. **Example:** A trust for "benevolent" purposes would almost certainly fail if the settlor were to say that the term "includes but is not to be confined to charitable purposes." The fact that an instrument has provided for "charitable *or* benevolent" purposes does not preclude a court from interpreting the words as limiting the purposes to those that are both "charitable *and* benevolent," even though this violates the usual judicial admonition that "each word is to be given meaning" rather than to attribute redundancy to a testator or donor—better that than to attribute an intention to "create" a failed trust!

GENERALLY ACCEPTED CHARITABLE PURPOSES   **■GILBERT**

TO DETERMINE IF A TRUST PURPOSE IS CHARITABLE, CONSIDER WHETHER THE PURPOSE INVOLVES:

☑ The *relief of poverty*

☑ The *advancement of knowledge or education*

☑ The *advancement of religion*

☑ The ***promotion of health***

☑ The support of ***governmental or municipal purposes***

☑ ***Other purposes*** that are ***beneficial to the community***

2. Particular Charitable Purposes

a. Relief of Poverty

The relief of poverty is a charitable purpose per se because the community has a substantial interest in preventing want and suffering. [Rest. 3d § 28 cmt. g] Trusts to provide food, clothing, shelter, and other necessities of life to those in need clearly fall under this heading. Even when the term "necessities" is used, the term is not used in a narrow sense, nor does it exclude comforts that others enjoy.

(1) Where Nonindigents May Benefit as Well

A trust created ***primarily*** to aid indigents (or potential indigents) will likely qualify as "charitable" even though it may benefit indefinite nonindigents as well. In this context, the result is not a matter of accepting (or retracting the prohibition against) a mixture of charitable and noncharitable purposes; it is a matter of defining what constitutes a charitable purpose.

(a) Rationale

The public as a whole benefits from such a trust, which, without being burdened with selectivity, has a tendency to and will have the effect of alleviating poverty within the overall class. A court that is unwilling to accept this rationale might find it necessary to construe the language (as courts have done in some analogous situations) as limited to, for example, "those in need because they are children in a single parent household."

b. Education

A trust to improve the minds of indefinite members of the public is charitable (whereas a trust to educate one's own children is private and does not qualify for the favorable treatment given to charitable trusts). This is so whether it involves the support of formal education or of generating or spreading knowledge, information, and culture. Support of education includes providing for the establishment or support of schools, colleges, universities, libraries, art galleries, museums, or similar institutions. It includes aiding students, teachers, or research activities (within or outside educational institutions, as long as in the latter case the purposes are the advancement of knowledge rather than increasing the profits of a particular concern). Support of education also includes the publication and distribution of books, but some questions may arise if the publications are limited to the support and promotion of particular views or particular objectives. [Rest. 3d § 28 cmts. h, *l*] The discussion below considers purposes involving policies and changes in the law.

(1) Need Not Benefit the Poor

An educational trust need not involve relief of poverty to be charitable because the acquisition and spread of knowledge per se is beneficial to society. Generally, however, funds cannot be granted to profit-making institutions in an unrestricted fashion that is calculated to increase profits. Such institutions may, however, hold or receive funds that are restricted to use for charitable purposes within the sphere of their activities.

(2) Profit-Making Institutions

A trust created simply "for purposes of education" has been held noncharitable because the purpose was not limited to nonprofit educational institutions (the profitmaking purposes not being charitable, as discussed in more detail below).

(a) Court May Construe Trust Language as Benefiting Only Nonprofit Institutions

Courts have been willing to construe such dispositions so as to avoid the "profit" defect by *implying* that only nonprofit institutions can benefit.

(b) Tuition Must Not Be Used to Make a Profit

The fact that a trust benefiting an educational institution charges tuition does not prevent the trust from being charitable. The education need not be free, but the fees charged must not be for the purpose of making a profit (*i.e.,* must not be for the purpose of earning dividends for investors as opposed to merely meeting expenses of or improving the institution's operations).

(c) Profit Makers as Incidental Beneficiaries

Nor would it affect the charitable character and validity of a trust for education or scholarships if the trustee were to send the persons to be educated under the trust to a private school (probably even a profitmaking school) or even if the trustee were to hire private tutors. The cost of private schooling or tutors would merely be expenses of the trust and its administration—the incidental beneficiaries not being encompassed within the "purposes" of the trust and having no status to enforce it.

(3) Politics and Change of Law

Trusts to disseminate particular political views or beliefs have not always been upheld as charitable, but in most jurisdictions today these probably would be upheld as charitable, under the heading of "educational." It is not relevant whether the views are popular ones, as long as some substantial group of persons is interested in the views and ideas, as distinguished from views that are irrational or virtually unique to the particular would-be settlor. A "charitable" public interest appears to be recognized not only in the protection of dissident views and beliefs, but also in stimulating the "marketplace of ideas." [Rest. 3d § 28 cmts. h, *l*]

(a) Political Views

Although the questions of whether, to what extent, and in what instances support of particular political views or beliefs will be upheld as charitable has no doubt varied from place to place and from time to time. For example, a trust to promote women's suffrage was not considered to be a charitable purpose by a case in the early twentieth century. Today, the trend appears to be to *uphold* such activities as charitable.

(b) Particular Political Party

An important distinction exists between a political belief and a political party . A trust to promote a particular political party is not considered to be charitable, however, because "there is no public interest in subsidizing one political group over any other." [Rest. 3d § 28 cmt. *l*]

(c) Change in Law

Clearly a trust for the *general improvement* of the law (*e.g.,* "to support the work of the State X Law Revision Commission") is charitable, but trusts to bring about a *particular change* in the law may or may not be.

> **e.g.** **Example:** Trusts to bring about changes in the law or form of government through *legal* means (sometimes including lobbying) have been upheld as charitable.

c. Religion

A trust for the maintenance and support of religion by providing for religious services, places of worship, salaries and maintenance of religious workers, religious education of youth, and other similar objectives is generally held to have a valid charitable purpose per se. Even a trust created simply "for religious purposes chosen by my trustees" should qualify as a valid charitable purpose. [Rest. 3d § 28 cmt. i]

(1) Masses

(a) Majority View

In most states, trusts to support masses for the soul of the settlor or others are upheld today as valid charitable trusts because they are deemed to benefit indefinite interested members of the public through religious exercises.

(b) Minority View

A few decisions hold such trusts are intended only to promote the memory or "benefit" of a particular decedent, and hence lack sufficient public or religious benefit.

(c) Trust May Be Honorary if Not Charitable

Even if such a trust were invalid as a charitable trust, its purpose might be allowed to be carried out through an "honorary trust" or, if the named recipient of such a bequest were willing, as a mere precatory request as to its disposition.

(2) What Constitutes Religion?

The usual problem in the limited number of "religious" charitable trust cases is that of what constitutes a "religion" or a "religious" purpose. A trust for any religious doctrine or group is likely to be upheld if there is *any substantial interest* in it at all (and not essentially peculiar to the particular settlor), there being a public interest in religious freedom and tolerance, with practically any doctrine having some followers throughout the community being recognized.

(a) Irrationality

Some cases have caused difficulty when trusts are established to support beliefs that are deemed so "irrational" or "inconsequential" as to be of no community interest. Line drawing can be difficult, as it has been in cases involving spiritualism, emerging religions, or religions that may be considered "nonconventional."

(b) Illegality and Immorality

Sects advocating or engaging in illegal or immoral practices have been held not to qualify.

(c) Atheism

Courts have frequently attempted to define religion as a belief having some recognition of a Supreme Being. Thus, a trust to promote atheism might not be recognized as a "religious" charitable trust, although it could well be sustainable as one for "education" in that such beliefs add to the marketplace of ideas.

d. Health

The cure of disease and promotion of health, including relief from pain, are charitable objects per se. [Rest. 3d § 28 cmt. j]

e.g. **Examples:** Trusts to maintain hospitals, encourage medical research, provide care and treatment of individuals with health issues, and promote public understanding of health issues are charitable.

(1) Nonindigents May Benefit, but No Profit Purpose Allowed

As noted in connection with education, the trust need not be for the benefit of impoverished persons who are unable to provide their own medical care; but, again, funds that are provided to hospital institutions and the like must not be for the purpose of enhancing profitmaking.

e. Purposes That Are "Governmental" or "Beneficial to the Community"

A trust for governmental or municipal purposes will be considered as having a charitable purpose because of the general community interest in having a functioning government. The beneficiary of such a trust is the *public* through the governmental body (*e.g.,* city, county, state, etc.). Similarly, a trust for the promotion of other purposes that are beneficial (or of widespread interest) to the community is charitable. [Rest. 3d § 28 cmts. k, *l*]

e.g. **Example:** The following have been held to be charitable purposes: relieving taxpayers from the burden of supporting government; constructing and maintaining public improvements, buildings, and institutions; providing parks and playgrounds; and even encouraging patriotism. The promotion of arts and culture within the community also is charitable, which may be considered the support of education and the beneficial to the community.

(1) Animals

To prevent suffering and want on the part of indefinite groups of domestic or wild animals is a charitable purpose. So too is the prevention of cruelty to animals. Gifts for the care of particular animals (*e.g.,* "my dog, Rover") are not charitable. Nor do they qualify under the typical rules for private express trusts because pets are not ascertainable beneficiaries. Today, statutory purpose trusts may be created for the care of a pet. Statutory purpose trusts are a particular type of private trusts. Charitable trusts to provide for stray animals or to support a local humane society could as well fit under "health," but they are generally sustained as of benefit or interest to broad segments of the "community," and as a relief to "governmental" resources. Such trusts fit somewhere within the charitable categories, and it is worth noting through this example that purposes listed as charitable are not always precise, nor are they mutually exclusive.

(2) Political Changes

A trust to bring about improvements in government through orderly constitutional or statutory change has a charitable purpose. But, as noted previously, a particular, specified change believed in by the settlor may in some jurisdictions raise difficulties, and certainly the advancement of a particular political party is generally rejected as a charitable purpose.

3. Other Charitable and Noncharitable Purposes

According to the Third Restatement, dicta in cases, and observations of commentators, charitable trusts may also exist for other objectives that are difficult to define precisely—*e.g.,* as mentioned, other purposes, the accomplishment of which is "beneficial to the community," and other specific purposes that have not been mentioned and may be difficult to categorize. Clearly, however, not every kindly purpose is "charitable."

a. Subjectivity

A settlor may believe the settlor is leaving the settlor's property to a worthwhile cause that the settlor deems to be "charitable," but the settlor is not the final judge of what is of *benefit* or *interest* to the community. The charitable purpose must be one designated as such by law—but, apart from legislation, this must be decided by a human being or panel of human beings who make up a court. The judges may obtain aid from the testimony of experts and the like, but ultimately what is of benefit or interest to the community depends on a process that will make precise definition a difficult matter in marginal cases.

b. General Standard

The standard, nevertheless, remains one of *benefit to the public or indefinite members thereof*. If the purpose of the trust at its creation is not a charitable one within this definition, a trustee's promise to limit herself to "charitable purposes" does not save the gift.

c. Some Examples of Other Purposes

(1) Care of Graves

Trusts for the perpetual care of graves, although once in substantial doubt, are now generally upheld as charitable. Care of graves in public cemeteries should be upheld as beneficial to an attractive community.

(a) Statutes

Even if the trust is for the maintenance of a particular set of graves, such as a family plot, such trusts are often expressly permitted by statute. This is similar to the recognition of pet trusts as a special set of recognized trusts.

(b) "Religious"

Even if not qualifying as "beneficial to the community," even many nonpublic cemeteries may be upheld as religious in nature, so that a trust for the erection and care of graves might qualify in the "religious" category.

(c) Honorary Trusts

Finally, in some jurisdictions such gifts may be carried out for a limited time by willing trustees as "honorary trusts." (*See* Chapter 2 of this outline for a discussion of honorary trusts.)

(2) Senior Citizens

In contrast, trusts "for older people" or "for the elderly" (not necessarily indigent) may be kind and well-meant but have occasionally been held *not* to fit under any of the specific categories previously mentioned and not of sufficient benefit to the community as a whole to qualify under the more general charitable characterization.

(a) "Health" or "Relief of Poverty"

Other cases, however, are clearly contra. Such a trust can also be sustained as one to promote "health" (particularly if it is to house or "take care of" elderly persons), or as one for relief of poverty (either by construing the trust as confined to or by concluding that it is *primarily* for those in need—*see* the "children of single parent household" example *supra*). [*See also* Rest. 3d § 28 cmt. j]

(3) Other Noncharitable Purposes

The following have also been held to be noncharitable purposes: aid to private social clubs or lodges (but some fraternal and like organizations may serve primarily charitable functions); and providing for the care of inanimate personal property, for homes or estates, for the preservation and display of the settlor's collections or creations, or for the erection of statues or monuments—or the like—*where there is no real public interest* in the particular person's life or activities or in the perpetuation of that person's memory.

(a) Distinguish—Historical or Artistic Merit

On the other hand, collections or homes can be of public interest for historical reasons or because of peculiar qualities. Trusts to collect, maintain, and display, *e.g.,* the artwork of a particular individual may be charitable if the artwork has substantial artistic merit or if it is the work of an important historical figure, such that in either event there would be a public interest in it and thus a public benefit exhibiting it. The mere fact that an individual is prepared to fund such activities does not mean that a charitable trust can operate to display the "art" collected or produced by that would-be settlor (on the merits of which expert testimony is admissible).

d. Qualification as a Private Trust

If a particular trust purpose fails as a "charitable" purpose, the trust may nevertheless qualify as a private trust. As such, it is subject to ordinary trust requirements of definiteness of beneficiaries, and of the Rule Against Perpetuities and related doctrines.

(1) Note

If the trust likewise fails as a private trust, and is not an honorary trust, it will be held upon resulting trust for the settlor or the settlor's successors in interest.

Keep in mind that the categories of charitable purposes are **not mutually exclusive**. A specific trust purpose may fit under multiple charitable categories. For example, a trust for the promotion of temperance in the use of alcohol or other addictive substances may involve education, promote health, support governmental services, and contribute to the general quality of life within the community. Identifying a charitable purpose is critical but try not to focus too much on identifying every possible charitable purpose. As long as the trust purpose meets the standards of **at least one of the charitable categories**, the purpose will be upheld as charitable.

4. Mixing Charitable and Noncharitable

a. Trust Administration

The trustee of a charitable trust may be, and often is, a profit-making concern (*e.g.*, a bank or trust company) or an individual. As noted in connection with specific charitable purposes above, however, the trust *purposes* must not be to benefit a profit-making organization even if that organization functions within one of the areas normally associated with charitable activities (*e.g.*, education, health). And in particular, because profit-making organizations can administer charitable trusts in connection with their own operations, the funds must not be used exclusively for a charitable purpose. What is crucial is that the trustee must be absolutely limited to expending the trust funds exclusively for nonprofit, charitable purposes.

b. Segregation of Trust Funds

If there is any possibility that the trust funds may validly be used for profit-making purposes, for the personal gain (other than proper compensation for services) of the trustee, or for any other *private* purpose, the trust cannot qualify as charitable—unless the funds that may be so used (*i.e.*, those that do not qualify as charitable) are separated by portion or by time (*see infra*) from those that are solely and exclusively permitted to be devoted to charitable purposes. And, again, remember that the trustee cannot save a trust with a purpose that is overly broad by promising to dedicate the funds strictly to charitable purposes; the failed disposition causes a *resulting trust*, so that the trustee cannot "declare" a new trust.

c. "Split-Interest" Trusts

Just as a trust can be divided in quantum (*i.e.*, by share or portion) between charitable and profit-making or private purposes, a trust does not have an objectionable mixing of purposes where property is to be devoted exclusively to private purposes for one period of time and exclusively to charitable purposes for another; these "split-interest" trusts are common today in the form of *charitable remainder trusts* (*e.g.*, to T in trust "to pay $30,000 per year to L for life, and on L's death to University") or *charitable lead trusts* (*e.g.*, "to pay $30,000 annually to University for 20 years, principal then to X or X's issue").

d. Incidental Benefits

Despite these strict rules, a trust may be charitable despite an incidental benefit that may accrue to the trustee, such as invitations to an annual event hosted by a charity.

5. Conditional Gifts to Charity

If conditions attached to the charitable interest require that the property also be devoted to a noncharitable purpose (*e.g.,* "provided the trust employs the settlor as an advisor at $25,000 per annum"), the trust is not charitable under trust law.

a. Settlor's Name

A condition that the fund, endowment, or activity, etc., created and supported by the trust be named after the settlor (*e.g.,* "The Jayne Doe Foundation") does *not* detract from the charitable status of the trust; any such "benefit" would be incidental.

b. Conditional Amount

Nor does it preclude a charitable purpose that the *amount* of the gift is conditional, such as where matching funds from other donors are required (*e.g.,* a trust to pay $1,000 to University for every $1,000 it raises from other sources).

D. Limitations on Charitable Trusts

1. Mortmain Acts

Few, if any, states still have legislation invalidating or restricting amounts that may be left by will to charity. These statutes, sometimes imprecisely referred to as "Mortmain Acts" (after the early legislation in England restricting ownership of land out of concern for the power of the church to overpower the wishes of the testator), invalidate or limit gifts by will to charity in various ways. (*See* Wills Summary.)

a. Types of Limitations

Such a statute may simply limit the total amount that can be left to charity (*e.g.,* one-third of the decedent's probate estate), especially if the decedent is survived by certain close relatives who would otherwise inherit, or may provide that bequests and devises to charity in wills executed within a brief period of time prior to the testator's death (*e.g.,* 30 days or three months) are entirely void. A statute might also contain some combination of these approaches.

b. Relevance

These statutes are noted here because although such statutes would unlikely be revived, such statutes share a reminder that charitable trusts have not always received special treatment.

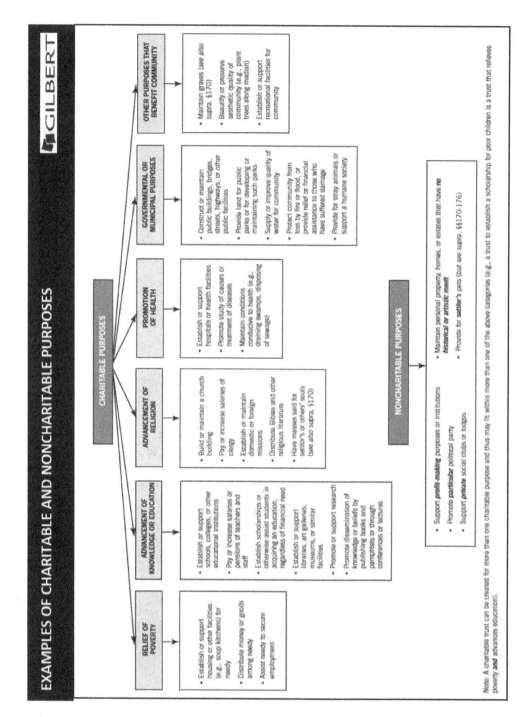

EXAMPLES OF CHARITABLE AND NONCHARITABLE PURPOSES

Note: A charitable trust can be created for more than one charitable purpose and thus may fit within more than one of the above categories (e.g., a trust to establish a scholarship for poor children is a trust that relieves poverty *and* advances education).

2. Charities and the Rule Against Perpetuities

a. Duration

A charitable trust may continue perpetually, whether because no durational limitation is provided or the durational limitation is expressly in perpetuity. The common law Rule Against Perpetuities *does not apply* to the *duration* of charitable trusts. [Rest. 3d § 29 cmt. g(2)] Note that a charitable trust may be created for a specific duration. In the absence of a specified duration, the trust will be considered to continue perpetually.

b. Vesting of Gift

The Rule does apply, however, to the *vesting* of a charitable gift later than lives in being plus 21 years. Similarly, a shift from a charitable purpose to a private purpose that may vest later than the period allowed by the Rule is also invalid (although the prior interest to charity would be unaffected).

c. Change of Charitable Beneficiary or Purpose

The interests in or benefits of a charitable trust can shift from one charity *to another charity* at any time, even after the period of the Rule Against Perpetuities has expired; thus, it is sometimes said that the interest need only *vest in charity* within the period, but it does not matter that the particular charitable beneficiaries or purposes shift thereafter.

EXAM TIP

One of the key differences between private trusts and charitable trusts is that, unlike private trusts, **charitable trusts may be perpetual** (*i.e.,* can last forever). There is no objection to shifting the benefits of trust property from charity to charity through time (*e.g.,* "to T in trust for A Charity for 100 years, then to B Charity for 100 years, then to C Charity for 100 years, etc."); this is known as the **charity-to-charity exception** to the Rule Against Perpetuities. Thus, if your exam question involves shifting among only charitable purposes, you need not consider the Rule. You are more likely, however, to encounter a fact pattern where the gift shifts from a **private use to a charitable use** or from a **charitable use to a private use**. When analyzing those facts, you must think about the Rule.

---

3. Constitutional Limitations on Charitable Purposes

Constitutional limitations on state action may also affect charitable trusts in certain situations. For example, state action may not require or further racial discrimination. Accordingly, to the extent a trust involves state action, racially discriminatory provisions are unenforceable under the Equal Protection Clause of the Fourteenth Amendment to the United States Constitution. The troublesome question is when in this context is state action involved.

a. State Agency as Trustee

A state agency may not serve as the trustee of a trust that involves racial or other prohibited discrimination.

b. State as Prior Trustee

A trust may become so tainted with state action as to render such discriminatory provisions unconstitutional—*e.g.,* a trust once publicly administered but thereafter administered by a private trustee, as a result of the facts and history, had become so intertwined with the state as to render its administration a continued form of state action.

c. No Public Trustee

Where a public agency does not and has not served as a trustee so as to provide state action in that manner, it remains *uncertain* whether state action is so inherently a characteristic of all charitable trusts today (via the state Attorney General's duty and power of enforcement, state and federal tax immunities, and various other special privileges not available to private trusts) that a charitable trust is by its very nature a form of state action precluding discriminatory provisions and their enforcement. Regardless of state action, public policy under state trust law may invalidate trusts or trust provisions that involve "invidious" discrimination.

An easy way to distinguish private trusts, charitable trusts, and honorary trusts is to assess the *beneficiaries* and *trust purpose*. A *private trust* (other than a statutory purpose trust) must be for the benefit of one or more *identifiable beneficiaries* ascertainable within the Rule Against Perpetuities and for *any purpose not against public policy*. *Charitable trusts* must benefit *indefinite beneficiaries* and *only charitable purposes*. An *honorary trust* has *no beneficiaries* capable of enforcing the trust and *no charitable purpose*.

E. Modification of Charitable Trusts—the Cy Pres Doctrine

1. Nature and Requirements of Cy Pres

Because a charitable trust can last indefinitely, a charitable trust may outlive or outgrow its original purpose. A court may then use the doctrine of cy pre to modify the trust—*i.e.,* to apply the trust funds in a manner "as near as may be" to the settlor's original plan. Accordingly, the cy pres doctrine is the law's basis for deviating from the trust's original purpose or purposes and *modifying* them to fit current circumstances, if the court finds that permissible, rather than having the property revert by resulting trust to the settlor or the settlor's heirs.

a. Requirements

To invoke cy pres, the court must find the following:

(1) Designated Purpose Fulfilled or Frustrated

First, the particular charitable purposes specified by the settlor must either be fully accomplished without exhausting the trust estate, or have become illegal, impossible or impracticable to carry out. Note that cy pres is not applicable merely because some other purpose might be *preferable*. [Rest. 3d § 67, UTC § 413]

(a) Illegal, also called unlawful, purpose would be purpose that requires unlawful discrimination or violates public policy.

(b) Impossible purpose occurs when the charitable cause no longer exists, such as the case when the trust was created to eradicate a disease and the disease has been eradicated. Impossibility can also arise when the charitable organization that the trust was to support is no longer in existence. A trust to support an educational institution that has been closed is an example of impossibility.

(c) Impracticability arises when the trust funds are no longer sufficient to support the trust purpose.

(d) Waste is the most recent ground for applying cy pres. Waste arises when the trust property so exceeds what is necessary to support the purpose that such use is wasteful.

(2) Settlor Had "General" (and Not Restricted) Charitable Intent

Second, it must appear that the settlor had what is usually called a "general charitable intention." This means there is evidence that the settlor would have wanted the trust to support a similar or related purpose if the original one became impossible or impracticable. This is not the case if evidence shows that the settlor intended to limit the gift, absolutely and regardless of unanticipated circumstances, to the specified charitable purpose or purposes. Cy pres is an intent-effectuating doctrine that has the potential to apply unless the trust terms *expressly* provide otherwise, under the Third Restatement and the UTC. [Rest. 3d § 67; UTC § 413]

b. Result—Apply Funds to Similar Purpose

Where the above are found to exist, the court, exercising its general equity power of cy pres, will direct application of the trust estate (or excess portion thereof) to some charitable purpose that is as similar to the designated purpose as circumstances allow and as would be consistent with the settlor's probable intentions (or "that reasonably approximates the designated purpose"). [Rest. 3d § 67 cmt. d]

2. When Cy Pres Is Not Applicable

It is not sufficient to find that, as circumstances have developed, a better purpose for the trust funds can be found. There are situations in which cy pres is not applicable.

a. Where Trust Would Otherwise Terminate

Even though the circumstances would otherwise justify or cause a termination of the trust (with a resulting trust arising, *see infra*), the courts may intervene under this doctrine to modify the trust so as to continue it in effect as long as this is consistent with an underlying general charitable intent of the settlor.

b. Expressed Gift over if Purpose Fails

Where the settlor has provided a valid express gift over in the event the designated trust purpose fails or the funds become excessive for that purpose, cy pres is not applicable. In other words, if there is an effective gift over to another charity, the trust's "designated" purpose does not fail.

(1) Rule Against Perpetuities

This, of course, assumes that the gift over is valid and effective—*e.g.,* not precluded by the Rule Against Perpetuities (as a private purpose would be if the interest, as created, could vest later than the period of the Rule). But a remote gift over *to another charity* is valid without concern for the Rule.

(2) Resulting Trust

If cy pres is not applicable and the gift over fails because of the Rule Against Perpetuities or otherwise, a resulting trust arises for the settlor or the settlor's successors in interest.

c. Restricted Charitable Purpose

Cy pres does not apply where the settlor apparently intended only to benefit a particular charity or charitable purpose and that charity has ceased to exist or the charitable purpose is now impossible.

(1) Tendency to Construe Trust Purpose as Nonrestrictive

Courts are usually reluctant to find the settlor's intention so restrictive, especially if the trust has been in operation for a long time. If the charitable trust fails, the resulting trust might be considered a windfall to those who would take under it. Hence, as indicated earlier, even a statement in the trust that the settlor intended the benefits to flow to charity "and to no other purpose" often means so long as practicable and does not prevent application of the doctrine.

(2) Where Trust Fails

It may appear (or be expressed, as required by the Third Restatement view) that the settlor had only a limited charitable purpose in mind and would have preferred the whole trust to fail if that purpose can no longer be carried out. In such cases, cy pres does not apply (in the absence of contrary legislation requiring a valid express gift over for a charitable trust to fail), and the trust must terminate and the property will revert.

e.g. **Example:** Settlor bequeathed property in trust for the operation of a park for white persons only. The court held that the trust failed because the purpose was illegal. Many of the terms of the will, including the trust, included discriminatory provisions. Settlor had been vocal during Settlor's lifetime about racial restrictions. As a result, the court held that cy pres was inapplicable because Settlor was so opposed to integration that to apply cy pres to operate the park without the racial restriction would have violated Settlor's intentions.

cf. **Compare:** On the other hand, a devise in trust to establish a home for "aged white men" was modified to delete the term "white" where continued racial discrimination would be unconstitutional and the court believed, based upon the language of the instrument and external circumstances known about the settlor, that the settlor was more interested in helping aged men than helping white men only.

d. Frustration of Purpose

Courts are reluctant to find a failure of the trust's original charitable purpose. The usual test of cy pres is a severe one—as noted before—requiring more than inconvenience or a preferable purpose. Courts may, for example, broadly interpret the specified purpose; and certainly a mere breach or failure by the trustee to carry out the designated purpose is not enough if the purpose could be carried out by a more willing and determined trustee.

e. Nearest Purpose

Once a court has determined cy pres is appropriate, the court must modify the trust in such a way as to approximate, some might still say *as nearly as reasonably possible*, the original purpose or the settlor's probable intention. Cases suggest it is proper to consider (as a settlor probably would) the degree of community benefit along with the degree of proximity. Just be careful not to narrow the purpose too much. Consider a broad range of alternatives.

e.g. **Example:** Thirty years ago, T properly executed a will that included a testamentary trust "to build and maintain a hospital in the county for individuals suffering from tuberculosis." When T died, the number of individuals with tuberculosis was low, hospitals exclusively for tuberculosis patients were no longer common, and the funds in the trust were insufficient to construct a hospital. The purpose should be considered impossible, impractical, or both. Assuming general charitable intent, a cy pres proceeding may be filed to present alternatives, such as a mobile vaccine unit that will travel throughout the county, hiring a school nurse at the public elementary school in the county, or the purchase of medical supplies (such as masks and respirators) for the publicly funded hospital. None of these programs have the exact purpose that T intended, but all could provide medical benefit to the community.

(1) Comment

Sometimes it is possible only to speculate about the best modification when a number of reasonable and close alternatives are available. Extrinsic evidence may or may not be illuminating.

(2) Applicable Only to Charitable Trusts

Cy pres is a doctrine that applies only to charitable trusts. Charitable trusts receive favorable treatment under the law. Cy pres provides the ability to "fix" charitable trusts that have outlived or outgrown their original charitable purposes. Cy pres does not apply to private trusts.

EXAM TIP   █GILBERT

A common theme throughout this chapter has been that the law favors charities. As a consequence, if you encounter a *charitable trust* on your exam that appears to have outlived or outgrown its original purpose, remember the *cy pres doctrine*. First you must determine whether the charitable purposes have been *fully accomplished* or have become *illegal, impossible, impracticable, or wasteful* to carry out. If *some* valid purpose remains, even if an arguably better purpose exists, the trustee must continue to carry out the original purpose. Second, consider the settlor's intent. If the settlor has provided an alternative, cy pres will not apply. If no alternative is provided by the settlor and the settlor had a *general charitable intent*, a court will direct that the trust property be applied to *another charitable purpose that approximates the settlor's probable intent*. Today, courts will presume a general charitable intent. The party opposing cy pres (who are often the individuals who will receive the property via the resulting trust) have the burden of establishing the settlor's specific intent.

SUMMARY OF CY PRES DOCTRINE	█GILBERT
DEFINITION	Doctrine permitting modification of charitable trust in which trust estate is applied to some charitable purpose *as near as may be to* settlor's designated purpose.
REQUIREMENTS	• Designated charitable *purpose fulfilled or frustrated*, and • Settlor had *general charitable intention* (traditional view).
WHEN NOT APPLICABLE	• Where settlor has provided a *valid express gift over* upon failure of designated purpose. The gift over will be given effect, so cy pres is unnecessary. • Where settlor only intended to benefit a *particular charity or charitable purpose* that has failed. A *resulting trust* will be implied in favor of settlor or settlor's successors in interest.

Chapter Six
Duties, Powers and Liability of the Trustee

CONTENTS	PAGE
Key Exam Issues	118
A. General Responsibilities and Authority of Trustees	119
B. Trustee Duties	120
C. Powers of the Trustee	126
D. Trustee's Liabilities and Beneficiaries' Remedies	137
E. Trustee's Liability to Third Parties	142
F. Duties and Liabilities of Beneficiaries	144
G. Liabilities of Third Parties	146

Key Exam Issues

Questions involving trust administration generally require an analysis of the trustee's powers and duties. As you make your analysis, always keep in mind the terms and objectives of the trust.

1. **Does the Trustee Have the Power The Trustee is Trying to Exercise?**

   When considering issues related to the trustee's powers, under the traditional view you should first identify the source of the power the trustee seeks to exercise:

   (i) Do the terms of the trust grant the trustee this power? Be sure to consider not only the *express terms* but also powers that construction of the trust terms may be *implied.*

   (ii) If neither the express terms, nor a reasonable construction of them, do not grant the power, is there a statute that grants the power?

   (iii) If neither the express nor the implied terms of the trust, nor a statute grants the trustee the power, is it arguably *implied* by law as being *"necessary or appropriate"* (or something even less strict) to carrying out the trust purposes?

   (iv) If none of the above, have all the possible beneficiaries unanimously agreed to grant the power?

   Remember that, when in doubt, a trustee may petition for court instructions for rulings on law or interpretation of the trust, but not for decisions based on the trustee's business judgment.

2. **Has the Power Been Properly Exercised?**

   Once you have determined that the trustee has the power, consider whether the trustee:

   (i) Exercised the power in accordance with *trust terms and purposes; and*

   (ii) Exercised the power in accordance with *general fiduciary standards* (*i.e.,* acting with care, skill and caution (each of which has a different meaning but together add up to prudence, loyalty, and impartiality).

   (iii) In cases of trustee distributions, w made the distribution in compliance with the distribution standard. Here, look for whether the standard is mandatory or discretionary (and remember, this might be different for income distributions and principal distributions). Also, look for the specific instructions in the standard, if there are any, for what kind of distributions the trustee is allowed to make, and for what purpose(s).

   In particular and in addition, consider the following:

   a. Look for violations of the strict duty of *loyalty* (*e.g.,* watch for self-dealing or potential conflicts of interest), but keep in mind that the current UTC requires only that a self-interested transaction, with a few exceptions, just must be in the best interest of the trust and the beneficiaries. Also, watch for a violation of the duty of *impartiality* (*e.g.,* inappropriately favoring income beneficiaries over remainder beneficiaries, or one beneficiary over another). But remember that the duty of impartiality does not mean that the trustee must treat all beneficiaries equally. Look to the other terms of the trust to determine whether there has been a breach of this duty.

   b. Also look for *improper delegation of duties* (consider, *e.g.,* whether and how a reasonably prudent person would delegate) and for *failure to segregate or earmark* trust property.

c.   In considering the duty to invest and make the trust property productive, do not overlook the duties to *diversify* and to consider a *suitable risk-reward level* (replacing the traditional view to avoid even careful "speculation" and "excessive" risk taking).

d.   If you decide that the trustee did improperly exercise a power, check to see if the trust has an *exculpatory clause* (within the permissible limits of those clauses) that may protect the trustee. And remember to look for possible *estoppel* of the objections of one or more of the beneficiaries based on their expressed or implied consent.

3.   What Is the Trustee's Liability?

If the trustee has acted improperly, think about the *remedies the beneficiaries* may have (consider other relief as well as damages) and the amount or extent of the trustee's liability in surcharge cases, especially when multiple breaches are involved. Other liability issues may concern the following:

a.   **Trustee's Liability to Third Parties**—UTC and most current statutes limit the trustee's personal liability to situations where the trustee committed a breach by entering into the transaction. This limitation on the trustee's liability cannot be waived by the settlor because it affects third party rights. The modern view is that, in the absence of fault, suit and liability are against the trustee in a *fiduciary* (or representative) capacity—*i.e.,* the trust estate, not the trustee personally, is liable.

b.   **Liability of Beneficiary and Third Party**—There is also the possibility of beneficiary liability to the trustee or other beneficiaries (of the trust) and third-party liability, especially in the absence of bona fide purchaser status.

A. General Responsibilities and Authority of Trustees

1. Introduction

This chapter deals with the trustee's management of the trust over time under the settlor's plan.

a. Powers, Duties, and Rights

The actions of trustees and beneficiaries are subject to the legal rules discussed in this chapter, and the powers, duties, and rights of these parties are based on these rules. In the UTC, trustee duties and rights appear in Article 8.

FUNCTIONS OF A TRUSTEE   **GILBERT**

THE PRIMARY DUTIES OF A TRUSTEE ARE TO:

- ☑ Be loyal to the beneficiaries: collect, segregate, *reserve and manage trust property in their best interest*

- ☑ **Prudently** invest and manage funds in accordance with the Uniform Prudent Investor Act

- ☑ *Act impartially* by taking into account the interests and needs of current and future beneficiaries as the trust terms instruct

---

2. Sources of Trustee's Duties, Powers, and Liability

A trustee's powers and responsibilities are derived primarily from the *trust instrument* and the *applicable law*.

a. Trust Instrument

A most important and flexible source of a trustee's powers is the trust instrument or other admissible evidence of settlor intentions. [*See* Rest. 3d § 4—defining "terms of the trust"] (Of course, all trusts need not be in writing, and not all extrinsic evidence is admissible.) The powers thus created are not only those that the trust instrument expressly states, but also those that are imposed *by law* or *found by implication through construction* of the trust provisions.

b. Law

Another important source of the trust terms and the trustee's powers is trust law itself. Trust powers under the common law generally include those powers that are "*necessary or appropriate* to carry out the purposes of the trust" and *not forbidden* by its terms. [*See* Rest. 2d § 186] Today, the law allows the trustee *almost unlimited authority* subject to the trustee's fiduciary duties. [*See* Rest. 3d § 85] The UTC gives the trustee "general" and "specific" powers in sections 815 and 816. These powers include: the power a competent unmarried adult has over her own property and the power to buy, sell, exchange, deposit, borrow as necessary to manage the trust. The trust instrument can limit or expand these powers.

c. Court Instructions

A trustee may ask a court for a determination of trustee duties and powers (both those derived from the instrument and those derived from law).

d. Beneficiaries' Ability to Determine Trustee's Actions

Under appropriate circumstances and when acting with unanimity, the beneficiaries may possess and exercise the power to amend and terminate the trust and may thus alter the terms of the trust.

SOURCES OF TRUSTEE'S POWERS   **GILBERT**

A TRUSTEE'S POWERS AND RESPONSIBILITIES ARE DERIVED FROM:

- ☑ Express or implied provisions of the *trust instrument*
- ☑ Applicable *trust law* (*i.e.,* powers "necessary or appropriate" to carry out trust purposes)
- ☑ *Court instructions* (but generally not as to matters resting within the sound discretion or business judgment of the trustee)
- ☑ *Beneficiaries' actions* (*e.g.,* through modification of trust terms)

B. Trustee Duties

The first three duties discussed below, the duty to administer the trust in good faith, the duty of loyalty, and the duty of impartiality, are the broad, overarching duties: the trustee must perform all the other duties in compliance with these three.

1. Duty to Administer the Trust

A trustee has a duty to administer the trust in accordance with the trust's terms, in good faith, in the best interest of the beneficiaries and in accordance with the applicable law.

a. Duty to Inquire

Even a trustee whose power is discretionary has a duty to inquire into the financial situation of the beneficiary to ascertain the beneficiary's needs [**Marsman v. Nasca**, 573 N.E.2d 1025 (Mass. Ct. App. 1991).]

b. Changed Circumstances

It may happen that the terms and purposes of a trust may at some point come into conflict due to unforeseen circumstances. For example, a trust instrument may call for the distribution of the principal to a child or grandchild at a certain age. If a child or grandchild of the settlor is later born or becomes disabled and needs government aid receiving the money outright might disqualify her from those government programs. In such a case, the trustee may petition a court under Section 412 to modify or terminate the trust. Such a petition may or may not succeed. [*See In re* **Trust under Will of Stuchell**, 801 P.2d 852 (Or. Ct. App. 1990).]

c. A trustee is not required to obey trust terms that are illegal, impossible, or against public policy.

d. Reasonable Costs

A trustee may incur reasonable costs in connection with trust administration. [UTC § 805]

e. Special Skills

A trustee who has special skills concerning trust management, or was named trustee because of those skills, must use the skills in administering the trust. [UTC § 806]

f. Delegate

A trustee may delegate aspects of trust management to suitable agents, but the trustee must exercise reasonable care, skill and caution in choosing an agent, setting the scope of the agent's responsibilities in light of the terms of the trust, and monitoring the agent's performance. If the trustee exercises proper due diligence in choosing and monitoring the agent, the trustee will not be liable for improper actions of the agent. [UTC § 807]

g. Settlor's direction

A trustee of a revocable trust has the power to comply with a direction of the settlor that is contrary to the terms of the trust. [UTC § 808] This is because the settlor of a revocable trust retains the power over the trust and can change its terms or terminate it at any time. Compare this to an irrevocable trust, where the settlor has relinquished all power over the trust. Note that a settlor can delegate the settlor's power to direct to third parties, such as trust advisors and trust protectors. A trustee generally must comply with the direction of these third parties if the trust instrument so instructs, unless doing so would constitute a breach of fiduciary duty or a serious violation of the terms of the trust.

2. Duty of Loyalty

A trustee must administer the trust solely in the interest of the beneficiaries. [UTC § 802]

a. Traditional Approach: No Further Inquiry Rule

This traditional approach meant that **any** transaction that benefited the trustee was a breach of the duty of loyalty, even if the transaction also benefits the trust and/or the beneficiaries. These transactions were called "self-dealing," and the law forced the trustee to "disgorge" (return) any profits. Once it was determined that the trustee had benefitted from a transaction, the law asked no further questions. This was called the "No Further Inquiry Rule."

b. Modern rule

Today, the consensus is that such a strict rule is out of keeping with the nature of the modern, often professionally managed trust, and the most recent UTC rule is more flexible. UTC § 802(b) continues the No Further Inquiry Rule to some degree. It states that transactions the trustee enters into that benefit him personally are automatically voidable by a beneficiary affected by the transaction, unless any of the following exceptions apply:

1. the terms of the trust authorize such a transaction;

2. a court approved the transaction;

3. the beneficiary did not start a judicial proceeding within the time allowed by Section 1005, *see infra*;

4. the beneficiary consented to the transaction, ratified the transaction, or released the trustee in compliance with Section 1009; or

5. the transaction involves a contract entered into or claim acquired by the trustee before the person became or contemplated becoming trustee—but note that the trustee still has to carry out the contract so as to avoid conflict between personal and fiduciary interests.

c. Under 802, a transaction is also presumed to be self-dealing and presumptively voidable when it is entered into with certain relatives of the trustee or entities that have a connection with the trustee:

1. the trustee's spouse;

2. the trustee's descendants, siblings, parents, or their spouses;

3. an agent or attorney of the trustee; or

4. a corporation or other person or enterprise in which the trustee as an interest.

d. The difference between section (b) and section (c) transactions is that section (b) transactions are voidable by a beneficiary without evidence, In the case of section (c) transactions, the trustee has an opportunity to rebut the presumption and show that the transaction was not affected by a conflict between her fiduciary and personal interests. Evidence that will tend to prove this lack of conflict is usually a showing of a fair price, and similarity to other, arms-length transactions in the relevant market.

e. A presumption of abuse arises when a trustee contracts with a beneficiary during the life of the trust in a transaction not involving trust property. Even though there is no trust property at issue, the presumption is that the trustee exploited a confidential relationship with the beneficiary. But the trustee can rebut the presumption by showing that the benefit the trustee received was the same as would have been received in an arms-length transaction. And if the trust has terminated, the beneficiary has the burden of proving that the trustee's influence has nonetheless continued.

f. The duty of loyalty does not preclude the following:

1. an agreement between a trustee and a beneficiary relating to the appointment or compensation of the trustee;

2. payment of reasonable compensation to the trustee;

3.   a transaction between a trust and another trust, decedent's estate, or conservatorship of which the trustee is a fiduciary or in which a beneficiary has an interest;

4.   a deposit of trust money in a regulated financial-service institution operated by the trustee; or

5.   an advance by the trustee of money for the protection of the trust.

6.   This section does not prevent aa trustee who is also a beneficiary from making distributions for his own benefit.

g.   Even if no presumption arises, a beneficiary may establish self-dealing if the beneficiary can prove that there was a conflict between the trustee's fiduciary and personal interests. A transaction the trustee enters into with trust property for the trustee's own benefit is voidable by a beneficiary.

h.   A trustee may not take for herself an opportunity for investment or some other beneficial transaction available to the trust.

i.   No presumed conflict arises when the trustee also receives compensation for managing trust funds though a financial institution. This refers to a trustee who manages mutual funds in which the trust has an interest and receives compensation from the institution for doing so.

j.   If the trustee votes stock as a trustee, that is, in a corporation in which the trust owns stock—the trustee must vote in a way that furthers the best interest of the fiduciaries.

k.   The duty of loyalty does not preclude the following transactions as long as they are fair to the beneficiaries:

1.   An agreement between a trustee and a beneficiary relating to the appointment or compensation of the trustee;

2.   payment of reasonable compensation to the trustee;

3.   a transaction between a trust and another trust, decedent's estate, or conservatorship of which the trustee is a fiduciary or in which a beneficiary has an interest;

4.   a deposit of trust money in a regulated financial-service institution operated by the trustee; or

5.   an advance by the trustee of money for the protection of the trust.

EXAM TIP   🛑GILBERT

Conflicts often arise when a trustee is also a beneficiary, especially when the other beneficiaries are all future or remainder beneficiaries. The court may require the trustee to deliver an accounting to the other beneficiaries in such a case.

---

3. Duty of Impartiality

Closely associated with the duty of loyalty is the "duty of impartiality," which is an obligation to *each* of the beneficiaries. The duty of impartiality also requires fair treatment of the interests of present and future, or remainder, beneficiaries. Trust administration, however, involves virtually unavoidable forms of conflict within the trustee's fiduciary obligations, because the interests of beneficiaries are almost inherently diverse and economically conflicting (*e.g.,* certain investments will inevitably favor income beneficiaries over remainder beneficiaries or vice versa). The duty of impartiality attempts to reconcile these conflicting obligations. This, however, is not a duty to treat, or weigh the interests of, all beneficiaries equally; it requires a balancing that reflects the terms, purposes, and priorities of the particular trust—as distinct from bias or favoritism injected by the trustee personally.

a. Trust Terms

A trustee's duty of impartiality is subject to the specific terms of the trust. For example, if a trust does not require the trustee to consider other resources of a beneficiary when making distributions to a that beneficiary, even if not doing so may cause distributions to deplete the principal for the remainder beneficiaries. [**Howard v. Howard**, 156 P.3d 89 (Or. Ct. App. 2007).]

EXAM TIP   🔖 GILBERT

Remember that **"impartiality" does not mean "treat equally"**—i.e., don't assume that the interests of all beneficiaries have the same priority and weight in the trustee's balancing of those interests. Rather, the trustee must consider the ***terms, purposes, and priorities of the particular trust*** in balancing the beneficiaries' differing interests.

EXAM TIP   🔖 GILBERT

Keep in mind that the trust instrument may actually instruct the trustee to favor one or some beneficiaries over others. In this case, the trustee must follow the trust terms.

---

4. Duty of Prudent Administration—Standards of Care, Skill, and Caution

Trust law requires that a trustee exercise the care and skill of a reasonable person in the performance of trust functions. This means considering the purposes, terms, distributional requirements, and other circumstances of the trust. In fulfilling this duty, the trustee shall exercise reasonable care, skill, and caution. In addition, the trustee must act with a degree of caution appropriate to the particular trust and the skills of the trustee. These terms, although regularly used together, are not redundant. [UTC § 804]

5. Uniform Prudent Investor Act

The most recent version of the Uniform Trust Code was drafted to conform to the Uniform Prudent Investor Act (UPIA). Instead of physically incorporating the UPIA into the UTC, the drafters encouraged states to adopt it as Article 9 of their versions of the UTC. The UPIA is consistent with and Sections 802, 803, 805, 806, and 807 of the UTC. The standards set out in the UPIA are now the criteria for a trustee's management of trust assets.

a. Prudent Investor Rule

The central tenets of the Prudent Investor Rule are as follows:

1. I trustee must make investment decisions "in the context of the trust portfolio as a whole and as a part of an overall investment strategy having risk and return objectives reasonably suited to the trust."

2. The factors that the trustee should consider when making investment decisions include:

    a) Consideration of each investment as part of the portfolio as a whole. That is, no investment is too risky on its own, but must be evaluated in terms of the trust portfolio as a whole and the trust goals. A "speculative" investment could still be a prudent investment if other assets in the portfolio were more conservative and balanced out the risk.

    b) Investing according to the risk tolerance of the beneficiaries and the purposes of the trust. For example, a trust meant to support an elderly widow would have a lower risk tolerance than one designed to grow over several decades for a settlor's very young grandchildren.

    c) The central tenet of the UPIA, and Modern Portfolio Theory on which it is based: the need to diversify assets in the trust. [Section 3]

    d) the only exception to the duty to diversify is a situation where lack of diversification is consistent with the role of the trust: for example, if taxes are a big concern.

6. Duty to Control and Protect Trust Property

This generally means that a trustee must take physical possession of all trust property, and collect any money or other property belonging to the trust, such as debts, rents, etc. [UTC § 809]

7. Duty to Record and Identify

A trustee must keep records of trust property and transactions with it, and segregate it from her own property, or property held in separate trusts (*i.e.,* the duty to earmark). If the assets of the trust are liquid, a record of the trust must also appear in the records of a third party, such as a bank. This does not mean that a trustee may not invest the assets of two or more trusts together if that is more economically beneficial; as long as a third party has the trust records, there is little risk of comingling. [UTC § 810]

8. Duty to Enforce Claims of the Trust Against Third Parties, and to Defend the Trust Against Claims Third Parties Bring Against It

This includes the duty to compel someone holding trust property—a former trustee or a third party—to deliver the property. But remember, it might not always be "reasonable" to do this— it might not be cost effective to do so. The trustee must make this decision in the best interests of the trust and the beneficiaries. [UTC § 811]

9. Duty to Inform and Report

a. General Rule

This is one of the central duties of the trustee. A trustee must provide basic information to the qualified beneficiaries including the material facts they need to protect their interests in the trust. [UTC § 813] This section requires the trustee to deliver certain information to the beneficiaries whether they request it or not, and requires the trustee to respond promptly to a beneficiary's request for additional information.

b. Qualified Beneficiaries

Qualified beneficiaries are: current beneficiaries, those who would become beneficiaries if a current beneficiary's interest ended, and those who would become beneficiaries if the trust terminated.

c. Types of Information

A trustee is required to inform the qualified beneficiaries about the following:

1. Acceptance of the trusteeship and of the trustee's name, address and phone number.

2. The existence of creation of an irrevocable trust (remember that a revocable trust can become irrevocable due to the settlor's death or its own terms), their right to receive a copy of the trust instrument and a trustee's report of the trust property, liabilities, receipts, and disbursements.

3. At least annually, the qualified beneficiaries and any others who request it, must receive the trustee's report above.

4. Upon request, the trustee shall give any beneficiary a copy of the complete trust instrument. This is true despite any expressed intent of the settlor that the trust or aspects of the trust remain concealed from the beneficiaries. [**Fletcher v. Fletcher**, 480 S.E.2d 488 (Va. Ct. App. 1997)]

10. Duty upon Termination of the Trust

Upon the termination of the trust according to the trust instrument, the trustee must distribute the property as the trust terms instruct.

11. Duty of Prudent Administration

Trust law requires that a trustee act as a reasonable person in the performance of trust functions. This means considering the purposes, terms, distributional requirements, and other circumstances of the trust. In fulfilling this duty, the trustee shall exercise reasonable care, skill, and caution. [UTC § 804]

C. Powers of the Trustee

1. Meaning and Nature of Trustee "Powers"

The term "power" in this context refers to authority expressly or impliedly conferred upon the trustee by trust provisions or by law—*i.e.,* the acts the trustee may perform. Note that a trustee may *have* power to perform a particular act but nevertheless violate a duty in so doing, such as by acting negligently, unreasonably, or arbitrarily.

2. What Powers Will Be Deemed "Appropriate"?

In addition to those powers specified in the trust terms or by statute, appropriate powers will be inferred if not otherwise forbidden. [Rest. 2d § 186] In general, implied powers are those clearly necessary to fulfill the trustee's role and are the same as the power a competent unmarried adult owner would have over his own property. They include the following: buying. selling and mortgaging trust property, depositing trust assets in banks or other financial institutions, partitioning or otherwise changing the nature of trust property, vote stock, borrow money, lend money or other trust property, abandoning or declining to administer unprofitable property." [UTC § 815–815, Rest. 3d §§ 70, 85]

3. "Mandatory" vs. "Discretionary" Powers

Most trust powers are permissive or *"discretionary"* in that the trustee is *expected to use judgment* as to whether and in what manner to exercise any particular power. If, however, the trustee is *required* to perform a particular act (*e.g.,* "the trustee is directed to distribute the sum of $1,000 monthly to X" or "the trustee shall, within one year after B's death, sell that land of the trust estate used by B as her residence"), the power is said to be *"mandatory"* or *"imperative"*—*i.e.,* the trustee *must* (in the absence of grounds for deviation) exercise the power, the only discretion being with respect to the reasonable and proper manner of performing the power, to the extent that is not also prescribed.

a. Mandatory Powers

(1) Identification of Mandatory Powers

Whether a power is mandatory depends on the wording of the trust. If the language is unclear, a court will try to determine the settlor's purpose or intention in creating the power.

(2) Enforcement of Mandatory Powers

Whenever a trust power is imperative and the trustee fails or refuses to perform, a court of equity will, upon petition of an interested beneficiary, order the trustee to exercise the power in the manner required by the trust instrument (in addition to the possibility of surcharge for harm done).

b. Discretionary Powers—Limited Judicial Review

Even where a trust power is "discretionary," a court may review the exercise (or non-exercise) of the power to ascertain whether the trustee has abused the trustee's discretion in deciding whether and how to exercise that power. [**Ventura County Department of Child Support Services v. Brown**, 117 Cal. App. 4th 144 (2004).]

(1) Trustee's Discretion, Not Court's Discretion

In the absence of abuse, a court will not substitute its judgment for that of the trustee, nor will it direct the trustee whether or how to exercise the trustee's discretion.

(a) Trustee's Petition for Instruction

Also, unless there is uncertainty as to the *terms* of the power (*e.g.,* meaning of stated guidelines or the relevance of a beneficiary's other resources; courts generally refuse to grant instructions to a trustee with respect to *judgment aspects* of the exercise of a discretionary power.

(b) Review of Trustee's Action

Where a trustee has already acted, courts refuse to "second guess" the trustee's actions in the absence of *abuse*—*i.e.,* unless the power is shown to have been exercised *unreasonably*, *in bad faith*, or in a manner *inconsistent with the terms or purposes* of the discretion. The mere fact that the court would have decided the question differently is immaterial.

(2) Grant of "Absolute Discretion"—Effect

Despite language granting a trustee "absolute" or "sole and uncontrolled" discretion, however, discretion is never absolute. A trustee must exercise discretion in good faith, and a court of equity will still intervene if the trustee has acted in bad faith or with a motive or state of mind "not contemplated by the settlor." Also, a trustee holding such a power may not arbitrarily refuse to make a decision; a court will compel *some* exercise of judgment. [UTC § 814]

(3) Discretionary Powers over Distributions

A trust often gives the trustee discretionary power to invade the trust corpus for a beneficiary or to make discretionary distributions of income or principal. In the absence of careful drafting, these provisions present certain recurring construction issues. In general, a court will not second guess a trustee's exercise of discretion in making distributions unless there is evidence of dishonesty (accepting bribes to make distributions), improper motive (distributing to a beneficiary for something the trust assets were not meant to pay for), or distributing without inquiring into the surrounding circumstances or the beneficiary's situation (unless the trust makes such inquiries unnecessary).

(a) Standards to Be Applied

If no standard for the exercise of such a power is stated, a court is likely to impose simply "a general requirement of reasonableness." The standard of "support" is generally means the amount necessary to maintain the standard of living to which the beneficiary was accustomed at the time the trust was created, and thus usually is held to include the support of persons residing with the beneficiary. Language such as "general welfare" and "happiness" implies even broader distributive powers. [Rest. 3d § 50]

(b) Consideration of Other Resources

Another frequently litigated issue in connection with such powers is whether a trustee, in applying a standard, should take into account the *other* resources available to the beneficiary (and if so, merely other income, or other forms of support, like scholarships, for example?). In other words, is a trustee's refusal to invade based on the availability of other assets an abuse of discretion? Courts are split on this continuously troublesome issue. The Third Restatement provides that the inference is that the trustee "is to consider the [beneficiary's] other resources but has some discretion in the matter." [Rest. 3d § 50 cmt. e]

EXAM TIP

If an exam question tells you a trustee *fails or refuses to exercise a power*, look to see whether the power in question is mandatory or discretionary. If the power is mandatory, a court will *order the trustee to exercise the power* in accordance with the terms of the trust. On the other hand, a *discretionary* power is subject to judicial review *only for abuse of discretion* (*e.g.*, if the trustee *arbitrarily or in bad faith* fails to exercise the discretion, a court will likely intervene and compel some exercise of the power).

---

4. Who May Exercise Trust Powers

a. Co-Trustees

Where a private trust has several trustees serving together, they hold all trust powers *jointly* unless the instrument provides otherwise. In the absence of a statute or trust provision to the contrary, co-trustees may exercise jointly held powers may by majority vote, if they cannot achieve unanimity. [UTC § 703(a); Rest. (Third) § 39]

(1) Sale or Transfer

An attempted sale or transfer of trust property with the consent of fewer than the required number of trustees passes no title, even to a bona fide purchaser.

(2) Duty of Care

Each trustee is liable to the beneficiaries for any losses resulting from his improper or negligent acts, including by failure to prevent or redress another's breach of trust, or by reason of improper delegation of duties to a co-trustee. A co-trustee may not delegate to another co-trustee functions the settlor reasonably expected the trustees to perform jointly. [UTC § 703(e)]

(3) Court Order—Trustees Deadlocked

If the trustees are deadlocked on an action with respect to which a decision is needed, a court may direct the trustees (or appoint a trustee ad litem) with respect to the matter. If the problem becomes chronic, a change of one or more trustees (or the addition of a trustee) may be appropriate.

---

b. Delegation of Powers to Third Persons (Agents)

Not every act of trust administration has to be performed by the trustee personally. The trustee has power to employ agents and servants to perform various acts and exercise various of the powers conferred upon the trustee.

(1) Care in Delegation

A trustee may delegate to others where a reasonably prudent trustee would do so. As long as the trustee exercises reasonable care, skill, and caution in choosing and monitoring the agent, the trustee is not liable to the beneficiaries or to the trust for an action of the agent. [UTC § 807(c)]

c. Successor Trustees and "Personal" Powers

Unless the instrument or circumstances clearly indicate otherwise, powers granted to a trustee attach to the office and are **not personal** to the trustee originally named. [Rest. 3d § 85(2)] Hence, the powers conferred upon a trustee or trustees originally named may be exercised by successor or substitute trustees.

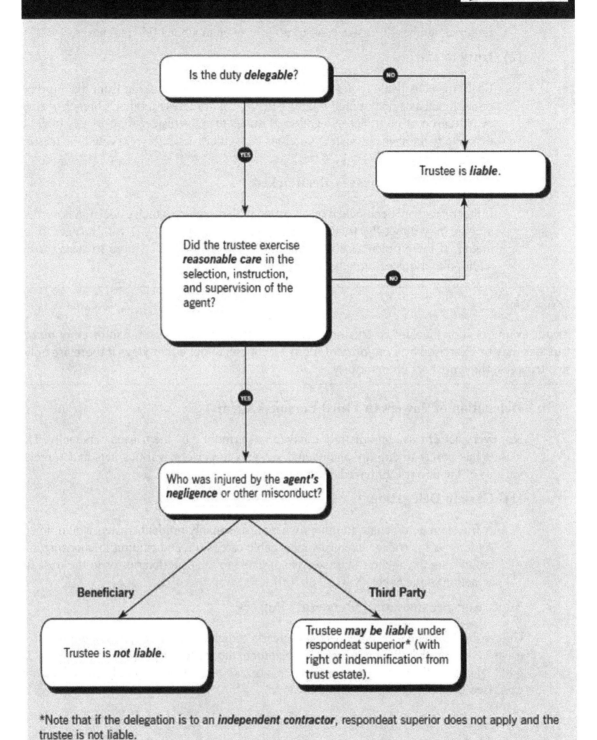

*Note that if the delegation is to an *independent contractor*, respondeat superior does not apply and the trustee is not liable.

(1) Liability for Losses Caused by Acts of Agents

(a) Proper Delegation—Not Liable

If the duty *is* delegable and the trustee used *reasonable care* in deciding to make the delegation and in selecting, instructing, and supervising (or monitoring) the agent, but a loss nevertheless results because of the agent's acts of negligence, dishonesty, or other misconduct (for which, incidentally, the agent would be liable), the trustee is *not liable* to the beneficiaries. [Rest. 2d § 225; Rest. 3d § 80 cmt. g; UPI § 9(c); UPI § 807(c)]

1) Distinguish—Liability to Third Parties

If, under the same circumstances (delegable duty and reasonable care in delegating), an injury *to a third person* is caused by the *agent's negligence*, in most states the trustee is ordinarily liable to the injured party for the resulting loss according to traditional doctrine under the doctrine of *respondeat superior*. [Rest. 2d § 264] Under the modern view and most statutes today, the liability is not personal (absent personal fault) but in the trustee's *representative capacity*. Even where personally liable, without breach of duty, the trustee is entitled to *indemnification* from the trust estate, if it is sufficient (otherwise the loss will fall on the trustee individually).

2) Independent Contractors

Respondeat superior applies when the delegatee is an employee subject to the trustee's supervision and control. If the person is an *independent contractor*, respondeat superior does not apply; thus, an independent contractor's negligence would not ordinarily render the trustee personally liable unless she, too, had been negligent in the matter.

d. Duty with Respect to Other Trustees

(1) Co-Trustees

Where there are two or more co-trustees, each ordinarily is responsible for all functions in the administration of the entire trust, and each must use reasonable care to prevent a co-trustee from committing a breach of trust (and even must use reasonable care to recover any damages if the other does breach his duty). [Rest. 3d § 81(2)]

(a) Duty to Actively Participate in Administration

It is a breach of trust for a co-trustee to fail to exercise reasonable care with respect to the actions of another co-trustee in the management of the trust estate. Each trustee has a duty (and a right) to check the trust records and accounts and to be familiar with trust affairs and activities in order to guard against any improper acts or mismanagement by a co-trustee, as well as to discharge her own duty to participate in administration. [Rest. 3d § 81 cmt. c]

(b) When Delegation to Other Co-Trustees Permitted

It is also a breach of trust for one co-trustee to abandon to another the exercise of any major trust power. That is, except in cases of necessity, emergency, or other special circumstances, delegation to a co-trustee is permissible only to the extent expressly or impliedly authorized by the terms of the trust.

(c) Liability for Breach of Trust by Co-Trustees

A trustee is not an insurer of the honesty and performance of her co-trustees; liability requires some showing that the former was negligent or otherwise at fault in failing to prevent, discover, or remedy the co-trustee's breach of trust.

(2) Predecessor Trustees

For various reasons, the beneficiaries or a court may appoint a successor trustee. The question then is: what is a successor trustee's duty with respect to the acts of a prior trustee? A trustee is *not* liable for the predecessor trustee's breaches of trust *unless*:

(i) *The new trustee knew or should have known* of the breach and failed to take proper steps to compel redress of that prior breach; or

(ii) *The new trustee negligently failed* to determine the amount of property that should have been turned over to her or otherwise neglected to obtain an accounting for and delivery of the full trust estate from her predecessor.

e. Trustees with Special Skills

Although the minimum standard is not lowered for a particular individual who lacks the requisite degree of skill, generally if a trustee possesses (or holds herself out as possessing) *superior or special* skills or knowledge, the trustee is under a duty (*i.e.,* "care" requires her) to exercise such superior skills or ability.

(1) Professional Fiduciary Trustee

A professional fiduciary (*e.g.,* a bank or trust company) is generally held to a higher standard than a lay trustee. It must apply the skills, knowledge, and facilities ordinarily possessed by *those engaged in the trust business*.

COMPARISON OF TRUSTEE'S STANDARDS OF SKILL	GILBERT
MINIMUM STANDARD	Trustee must exercise skill of an *ordinarily intelligent individual*
TRUSTEE WITH SPECIAL SKILLS	Trustee must exercise *superior or special skill she possesses or holds herself out as possessing*
PROFESSIONAL FIDUCIARY TRUSTEE	Trustee must exercise skill *ordinarily possessed by those engaged in the trust business*

f. Effect of Compensation

The duty of prudence applies (and other fiduciary duties apply) whether the trustee serves gratuitously or for compensation. Generally, the same standard of care applies in either event.

SPECIFIC SELF-DEALING RULES

PURSUANT TO THE DUTY OF LOYALTY, A TRUSTEE GENERALLY *CANNOT*:

☑ *Buy trust assets or sell her personal assets to the trust*, even if the price is fair

☑ *Lend her personal funds to the trust*, except for advances in urgent, short-term situations to *protect the trust*

☑ *Borrow trust funds* for her own use, even if she agrees to pay interest

☑ *Personally gain* through her position as trustee (*i.e.,* cannot, with few exceptions, accept any bonus, commission, or other benefit from a third person)

☑ *Employ herself, family members, or some company in which she is financially interested*, except that a trustee who renders *additional services* to the trust may be entitled to extra compensation

☑ *(In the case of an institutional trustee) Purchase or retain its own stock* as a trust investment, unless *authorized* by the settlor, the court, or the beneficiaries

g. Duty to Insure Trust Res

The trustee has a duty to obtain insurance on trust assets, including liability insurance whenever and to the extent a prudent person with like responsibilities would do so. Generally, the insurance premiums may be paid from trust funds, even though liability insurance has the effect of protecting the trustee personally as well as the trust estate.

ELEMENTS OF TRUSTEE'S DUTY TO COLLECT AND SAFEGUARD

A TRUSTEE'S DUTY TO COLLECT AND SAFEGUARD THE TRUST ESTATE INCLUDES THE DUTIES TO:

☑ *Take possession* of the trust estate as soon as reasonably possible after accepting the trusteeship

☑ *Act as a reasonably prudent person* would in keeping the trust assets *safe from loss, deterioration, or waste*

☑ *Defend actions* (including those by the settlor) against the trust *unless* reasonable and prudent not to do so

☑ *Obtain insurance* on trust assets if and to the extent a reasonably prudent person with like responsibilities would do so

h. Liability in Event of Loss

(1) Modern Trend

Some cases (which appear to represent the modern trend) hold that the trustee is liable only for losses *caused* by the failure to earmark or segregate.

Do not confuse commingled investment devices with the commingling of trust and personal funds. The trustee does **not breach her fiduciary duty** if the trustee **commingles funds from multiple trusts to purchase a common investment**, provided units in and receipts from the common investment are allocated to each trust. On the other hand, if the trustee **commingles trust funds with her own** to purchase an investment, the trustee **is liable for any resulting profit or loss**.

i.   In General

The trustee normally has a duty to the beneficiary promptly and continuously to make the trust property productive. The trustee must use reasonable care and skill to provide a reasonable rate of income where there are beneficiaries entitled to income. Some courts have required this with respect to each and every asset of the trust estate, compelling the trustee to rid the estate of assets that are nonproductive or underproductive (in the absence of provision to the contrary). Today, recognizing the importance of impartiality and **portfolio** total return (including efforts to maintain purchasing power), the asset-by-asset view is generally (if not universally) superseded by a requirement that the trust estate **as a whole** produce a reasonable income yield.

(1) Duty with Respect to Land and Tangible Personal Properties

Where land and chattels are involved and are not being used by the life beneficiary personally, the trustee is under a duty to lease or otherwise manage or use the property so as to produce income, or to sell the property (unless the trust terms require its retention), all within a reasonable time and in a prudent manner.

(2) Cash

Money is to be made productive through investment, but the questions of whether to invest particular cash and the proper method to invest it depend on the remaining term of the trust and upon its cash needs. Even if under the circumstances there is no duty to invest the cash in other assets, there is a duty to maintain it in a safe place and to earn interest as reasonable; this ordinarily requires the trustee to keep trust funds in a reputable bank in an appropriate account in the name of the trust. [Rest. 3d § 76 cmt. d(1)] Thus, it would be a breach of trust to keep trust funds in an excessive amount or for an unreasonably long period in a non-interest bearing checking account.

STATUTORY LISTS	Trustee must act with prudence and impartially and invest in *eligible investments* specified on jurisdiction's statutory list.
TRADITIONAL "PRUDENT MAN" RULE	Trustee must exercise care, skill, and caution and invest as *"men of prudence"* would *in managing their own affairs*.
MODERN "PRUDENT INVESTOR" RULE	Trustee must exercise reasonable care, skill, and caution (*prudence*) and consider the purposes, terms, distribution requirements, and other circumstances of the trust when making investment decisions, which are evaluated in the context of the *entire trust portfolio* and as part of an *overall investment strategy*.

j. Standards Under Rules of Prudence

(1) Protection of Remainder Beneficiaries

Under these rules, the trustee must consider the interests of the remainder beneficiaries (preservation of corpus) as well as the interest of life beneficiaries (usually, but not always, income productivity). This duty properly includes some reasonable effort to protect capital (and also the income stream) against loss of purchasing power through inflation; the law was in some doubt and little developed in this matter under the "prudent man" rule, but the "prudent investor" rule explicitly requires this effort under ordinary circumstances.

(2) "Prudence" Determined as of Time of Investment

Whether an investment decision is "prudent" depends on the circumstances *at the time it was made*; foresight, not hindsight, is the test. [Rest. 2d § 227; Rest. 3d § 90] Factors to be considered include whatever is relevant—liquidity, risk of loss or volatility, role (and other assets) in the portfolio, tax implications, etc.

(3) Imprudent Investments May Not Be Retained

Upon the trust's creation, the trustee must review the original assets transferred to the trust (called *inception assets*) to see whether the type and range of assets comply with the applicable investment rule. If some do not, the trustee must make revisions in the portfolio as necessary. The trustee may not simply retain the inception assets. In addition to doing this initial review of the assets, the "prudent investor" rule requires the trustee to *continually review* the trust investment plan and holdings, and to make revisions as investments (or strategies) become imprudent or "unsuitable" to the trust's circumstances. The trustee ordinarily should not retain investments that would be improper to purchase for the particular trust or that have become unsuitable to its strategy, except as different considerations (*e.g.*, taxation of capital gains) might apply to purchase versus retention. Personal liability might result from improper retention of investments or for delaying action for an unreasonable time after the duty to adjust arose.

(4) Diversification

A cardinal principle of prudent investment is *diversification*. Even though an investment is otherwise proper, it may be, in context, an improper investment for the trustee to make because too large a portion of the trust assets are invested in it or because, by reason of that investment, an unreasonably large portion of the trust estate has become concentrated in a single investment or in a single industry or type of investment. This duty has not been clearly established at common law in all states, howeve*r; nor is there total agreement on the manner of its application, especially regarding what constitutes a justification for not diversifying. [See* **Americans for the Arts v. Ruth Lilly Charitable Remainder Annuity Trusts**, 855 N.E.2d 592 (Ind. 2006)—effect of "retention" language; **Wood v. U.S. Bank**, 828 N.E.2d 1072 (Ohio 2005)—"special circumstances" exception]

(a) Conduct, Not Performance, Is Crucial

These various principles, however, do not mean that the trustee is a guarantor against all losses; the test of prudence (and thus of liability) is one of trustee conduct and not of an investment's performance or a portfolio's performance. Thus, as long as investment decisions are proper, the trustee is not responsible for resulting losses. (Performance matters, however, in measuring damages when a breach of trust occurs.) And it is not (as some have suggested) a real obstacle to the use of modernized investment practices or portfolio concepts that a trustee *cannot offset* gains or profits obtained from some improper trust investments against losses from others, *i.e.,* that the trustee cannot view breaches of trust as a whole, reducing improper losses by improper gains. Again, that is a matter of measuring liability, not of determining the *existence* of a breach.

k. Specific Types of Trust Investments

No one form or type of permissible investment is suitable for every trust and investment strategy. The fact that a particular investment may be "proper" in one case does not mean that it would be so in another. The trustee must always use independent judgment under the circumstances.

SUMMARY OF TRUSTEE'S DUTIES			GILBERT
DUTIES	**DEFINITION**	**EXAMPLE OF BREACH**	**REMEDY**
TO ADMINISTER TRUST PERSONALLY ACCORDING TO TRUST TERMS AND LAW	Trustee must comply with trust terms and applicable law and *delegate only as a reasonably prudent person* would	Delegation of entire administration of trust	Trustee is liable for the amount of loss to trust
TO SECURE AND SAFEGUARD TRUST PROPERTY	Trustee must *take control* of property and *preserve* trust assets, collect claims	Imprudent failure to collect claims due, pay taxes, defend trust	Trustee is liable for losses resulting from breach; trustee may be sued to enjoin

	due, pay taxes, and defend trust from attack		improper or to compel proper conduct
TO SEGREGATE AND EARMARK PROPERTY	Trust assets must be identified ("earmarked") and kept separate from trustee's personal assets and assets of other trusts; *i.e., no commingling*	Placing personal and trust funds in same account	Trustee is liable for any resulting loss; lost or destroyed property is presumed to be trustee's, and increased value of commingled property presumptively belongs to trust
TO INVEST AND MAKE TRUST PROPERTY PRODUCTIVE	Trustee must use reasonable care to invest the property according to the *"prudent investor"* rule	Failure to diversify or review investments, improper retention of unproductive investments	Trustee is liable for losses resulting from breach, plus interest, or (by the modern view) for any profit that would have accrued to the trust if properly invested
LOYALTY	Trustee may not represent both personal and fiduciary interests; *e.g., no self-dealing*	Buying assets from or selling assets to trust, borrowing from or lending to trust	Beneficiary may affirm the transaction or set it aside, recovering damages to trust or profits of trustee
TO ACCOUNT	Trustee must keep and render *accurate accounts* of her administration of the trust	Failure to account periodically (if required) to beneficiary or to court	Beneficiary may sue trustee to compel her to account for properties, receipts, and expenditures, and prove proper administration

D. Trustee's Liabilities and Beneficiaries' Remedies

1. Standing to Enforce Trust

If a trustee has breached a fiduciary duty, only the *beneficiaries* (or a successor trustee, co-trustee, or guardian or other person acting on the beneficiary's behalf) can complain; outsiders have no standing to enforce the trust and cannot hold the trustee liable for duties that do not run to them. Even the settlor can complain only if he is also a beneficiary [Rest. 2d § 200], although this rule may be changing (usually by statute) especially in the case of charitable trusts.

2. Beneficiaries' Remedies

a. Equitable Relief

(1) Suit to Enjoin or Compel

The beneficiaries may institute suits to enjoin or instruct the trustee, or to compel proper performance of particular duties.

(2) Suit to Remove

In appropriate circumstances (*e.g.,* serious or repeated breach), the beneficiaries may obtain a court order removing a trustee or one or more of several co-trustees, or may deny or reduce compensation for the period involved.

(3) Constructive Trust

Where a trustee has misappropriated trust assets or used trust funds to acquire other property, the beneficiaries can enforce a constructive trust (tracing the property and requiring it or its proceeds and the profits from the property to be used exclusively for the trust and its beneficiaries) or enforce an equitable lien on the property to secure a claim for damages.

b. Damages

Where the beneficiaries seek damages, the following principles usually apply. [*See* Rest. 2d §§ 205–211]

(1) In General

The trustee is personally liable to the trust estate or to the beneficiaries directly, depending upon the circumstances, for any loss or depreciation in value of the trust estate and loss of income resulting from his breach of trust, plus interest. A growing number of modern decisions have recognized "losses" in the trustee's failure, as a result of making improper investments (*e.g.,* by not diversifying or by excessive conservatism including favoring the income beneficiary by investing excessively in bonds), to achieve the gains proper investments should have produced. This recovery for "lost profits" is expressed as restoring the trust estate to what it would have been "if properly administered." [Rest. 3d: Prudent Investor Rule § 211(2)]

(2) Failure to Make Property Productive

A trustee has a duty to make the trust property reasonably "productive." This term is usually used to refer to productivity of a reasonable amount of income (*i.e.,* "yield"), but the duty in its broader, but less frequently used, sense includes total return (often just "return"), *i.e.,* income plus other return, mainly in the form of appreciation in the market value of principal. A trustee who fails to make funds productive is liable to the adversely affected income beneficiaries and to the trust (or its remainder beneficiaries).

(3) Improper Investment

A trustee who does undertake to keep the property productive is nevertheless personally liable to the beneficiaries for losses resulting from any investment that is determined to be improper or imprudent under the principles stated above.

(a) Note

Competent beneficiaries who knowingly consent to a particular investment may be *estopped* to hold a trustee liable for their portions of any resulting losses.

(4) Losses to Principal

Where improper investment or improper conduct has led to a diminution in the value of the trust principal, the trustee is liable (along with other possible liabilities) to make up that loss.

Example: A $10,000 investment of trust funds in X Co. stock is found to have been imprudent. It is now worth only $2,000; the trustee is liable (traditionally) for the $8,000. But what if the trustee has made other improper investments that have increased in value (*e.g.,* the same trustee imprudently invested $10,000 in Y Co. stock, which is now worth $15,000)?

(a) General Rule—Gain from Improper Investment *Cannot* Offset Loss

It is a primary principle of trustee liability that, where there are two distinct breaches of trust, the trustee cannot offset the profits from one against the losses on the other. [Rest. 2d § 213] The policy of the rule is to avoid temptation to recoup losses (or to gamble the gains) from an earlier breach by undertaking another.

(b) Exception—Same Breach of Trust

If, however, the gains and losses are attributable to the same breach of trust, absent aggravated circumstances, a court will allow the balancing of losses against gains from that transaction.

(c) Single Breach vs. Distinct Breaches

It is often very difficult to determine whether a particular situation involves more than a single breach of trust; courts generally phrase the question in terms of ascertaining whether the breaches are "severable," or whether they are "substantially separate and independent." Factors to be considered in ascertaining the severability of breaches include: whether the same or different portions of the trust res are involved whether the breaches arise out of the same or different transactions, or out of the same or different investment policy decisions; the length of time between the transactions; and the like. Usually, two separate "imprudent" or otherwise improper investments are to be dealt with independently and without offset: The trustee is generally held liable for the loss on the investment that turned out badly, while the beneficiaries are allowed to retain the gain on the one that turned out well. But if the trustee made a single improper investment, part of which could be sold at a profit while the other had to be sold at a loss, his liability is the net loss after deducting the gain. But when are a series or set of investments all part of one investment action? [Rest. 2d § 213 cmt. e; Rest. 3d: Prudent Investor Rule § 213 cmt. f]

3. Trustee's Improper Transfer of Trust Property to Third Parties

a. General Rule

When a trustee improperly transfers trust property to a third party, the third party's liability depends on whether the jurisdiction follows the UTC or not.

(1) UTC: Acting in Good Faith

Under UTC § 1010, a person who deals with a trustee in good faith will not be liable for the trustee's breach. Courts in other jurisdictions presume that a third party. receiving the property was on real or constructive notice that the property transferred was trust property, and so that person must disgorge the property, usually under the doctrine of a constructive trust unless she can rebut the presumption. If the person receiving the property was a good faith purchaser for value, the person need not return the property. But the trustee may be required to compensate the trust for the property out of the trustee's own funds.

b. Consequences

If the trustee improperly transfers property to a party who is on actual or constructive notice, and that property appreciates in value, the third party is liable for the appreciation as well, since the appreciation would otherwise have accrued in the trust. [*In re* **Estate of Rothko**, 43 N.Y.2d 305, (1972).]

(1) Profits

A trustee is liable for any profit made by him personally through his breach of trust. The purpose of this rule is to remove any personal incentive a trustee might have to commit a breach of trust even at an "opportune" time.

Example: The trustee improperly borrows $10,000 from the trust and invests it; his successful investments go up in value to $100,000. The entire profit of $90,000 belongs to the trust.

(a) Identifiable Profits

A trustee is liable for identifiable profits that would have been made by the trust estate but for the breach.

Example: A particular security that the trustee was directed to retain in the trust estate was improperly sold but at its full value, and the proceeds were placed in a bank account. Subsequently, the stock, which had been sold for $20,000, has now increased in value to $50,000. The trustee is liable for this $30,000 in lost appreciation that should have accrued to the trust estate, in these facts, even under the traditional rule on damages.

(2) Interest and Earnings

The trustee is also chargeable with income lost (net of income received) as a result of the violation of fiduciary duty. Thus, he is, under appropriate circumstances, chargeable with interest at prevailing market or statutory rates on the sums owing to the beneficiaries or the trust estate from the time of the breach. [Rest. 2d § 207]

BENEFICIARIES' EQUITABLE REMEDIES FOR TRUSTEE'S BREACH OF TRUST	**GILBERT**
RESTITUTION (DAMAGES)	• *Loss or depreciation* in value of trust estate due to breach • *Interest* on sums owed from time of breach • *Profits* made by trustee personally due to breach
OTHER EQUITABLE RELIEF	• *Injunction*—trustee may be enjoined from committing a breach or compelled to perform his duties • *Removal*—trustee may be removed from office for committing a breach • *Constructive trust*—property misappropriated by trustee may be traced and applied exclusively for the trust and its beneficiaries

c. Relief from Liability

(1) Effect of "Exculpatory Clause"

The trust instrument may contain a provision to the effect that "the trustee shall not be liable for errors of judgment or carelessness, nor for any breach of trust." Such exculpatory clauses are generally given effect by the courts within reasonable limits.

(a) Limited by Public Policy

The clause is not valid or effective insofar as it attempts to relieve liability for bad faith, intentional breach of trust, or gross negligence. Such a provision would be contrary to public policy.

EXAM TIP **GILBERT**

If you encounter a clause in a trust instrument purporting to relieve the trustee from liability for breach of trust, remember that such exculpatory clauses are *strictly construed* but are *enforceable* to the extent *no bad faith, intentional breach, or recklessness* is involved.

---

(2) Consent of Beneficiaries

Under appropriate circumstances, *all* of the beneficiaries may modify a trust, at least as long as the modification does not undermine a material purpose of the settlor. Such unanimous action can constitute an *amendment of the trust* making thus authorizing the trustee's otherwise impermissible act. The unanimous action serves to prevent all beneficiaries from surcharging the trustee, giving the trustee complete immunity from liability for that particular act.

(a) Consent of Some Beneficiaries

Absent unanimous consent, the proper consent of some of the beneficiaries serves to estop those who consented but will not impair the rights of other beneficiaries to sue the trustee.

(b) "Consent"

Here, again, it is important to emphasize the full range of duties the trustee has to the beneficiaries. As a result of those duties, courts are cautious in finding effective "consent" and require full disclosure by the trustee and a properly informed action by a beneficiary who understands the applicable rights and alternatives. In addition, some affirmative approval or act of encouragement, inducement, or participation by the beneficiary may be required; mere silence is usually not enough.

(3) Other Instances of Relief from Liability

(a) Laches and Statutes of Limitation

A statute of limitations or by laches on the part of the beneficiaries may protect the trustee from suit. Because beneficiaries often do not learn of a wrong for some time, the statutory time period generally does not begin to run during the existence of the relationship *unless and until* the beneficiary is of age and knows or reasonably should know of the facts constituting the breach of duty.

(b) Effect of Trustee's Insolvency

In general, a trustee's liability may be discharged in bankruptcy, but not with respect to losses caused by fraud, embezzlement, or other intentional misappropriation.

E. Trustee's Liability to Third Parties

1. Contract Liability

Under traditional principles, a trustee (as principal), rather than the trust estate, was *personally liable* to all parties with whom the trustee contracted in the course of the trust administration, unless he specifically limits his personal liability by the terms of the contract

a. Statutes

Today, legislation in most states explicitly eliminates the personal liability of the trustee as "principal." Where the common law has been modified by statute, only the trust estate—*i.e.,* the trustee in his fiduciary capacity—is liable on contracts properly executed by the trustee if his status as trustee was known to the other party.

b. Trustee's Right of Indemnification

The trustee's right of "indemnification" under the traditional view for a proper and prudent contract in the course of administration means that the trustee can either satisfy his personal liability directly from the trust estate ("exoneration") or pay the creditor from his own funds and then obtain "reimbursement" from the trust estate.

(1) Includes Cost of Defense

The trustee's right of indemnification from trust assets includes all costs reasonably incurred in defending suits against him by third parties, *unless* the suit arises out of a breach of duty or from some fault of the trustee. (Note that a trustee usually may not charge the estate for attorneys' fees in an unsuccessful attempt to defend a surcharge action brought by a beneficiary.)

(2) Creditor's Rights

If the trustee is insolvent, it has been held that the trustee's right of indemnification can be reached (via creditor's bill in equity or its current counterpart) by the creditors to whom he is liable in the course of administration. The right of the creditor is derivative and thus subject to all defenses the trust or beneficiaries would have had (*e.g.,* breach of trust) in a suit directly by the trustee. To the extent the creditors had a *direct* action against the trust estate (*see* above), however, their rights are not derivative and thus probably are not subject to offset for beneficiaries' claims against the trustee.

2. Tort Liability

a. Trustee's Right of Indemnification

A trustee cannot indemnify himself from the trust estate for tort liability where the trustee was *personally at fault* (either for intentional or negligent torts). If not personally at fault, however, indemnity is allowed.

(1) Where Proper

Exoneration is allowed a trustee who is not personally at fault for: (i) torts committed by agents *selected and supervised with reasonable care* to undertake duties that can *properly be delegated*; (ii) torts based on *absolute liability*; and (iii) torts committed by the trustee as a normal incident to the kind of activity in which the trustee is *properly* engaged (*e.g.,* a trustee running a newspaper has been held not liable for inadvertent libel).

(2) Where Not Proper

Indemnification is not proper where the loss resulted from the trustee's breach of duty, in which case the fact that some third party actually caused the harm or damage is immaterial.

e.g. **Example:** The trustee, operating an apartment building in trust, fails to obtain liability insurance under circumstances that constitute a breach of duty. A visitor to the building falls under circumstances rendering the trustee personally liable for a janitor's negligence. The trustee is not entitled to indemnification because the loss should have been covered by liability insurance, for the lack of which the trustee is personally and ultimately liable.

	IS TRUSTEE PERSONALLY LIABLE TO THIRD PARTY?	MAY TRUSTEE SEEK INDEMNIFICATION FROM TRUST?
CONTRACT LIABILITY	*Traditional view:* Yes, **unless** the contract specifically provides otherwise *Modern view:* No, only the **trust estate** (*i.e.,* the trustee in his fiduciary capacity) is liable, absent personal fault of the trustee	Yes, if the contract was **within the trustee's powers** and he acted with reasonable **prudence**
TORT LIABILITY	Traditional view: Yes, including for torts committed by agents Modern view: No, unless the trustee was personally at fault or liable under respondeat superior	No, if the loss resulted from the trustee's **breach of duty** (*e.g.,* failure to insure) or the trustee was **personally at fault**

F. Duties and Liabilities of Beneficiaries

1. Beneficiaries' Duties Generally

a. No Affirmative Duties

Unless a beneficiary is also a trustee or has an obligation imposed by provision of the trust (in which she has expressly or impliedly accepted her interest), the beneficiary owes no affirmative fiduciary or other duties to the co-beneficiaries or to the trust estate.

b. Duty Regarding Breach of Trust

A beneficiary does, however, owe a duty (as do third parties) to other beneficiaries not to participate in a breach of trust by the trustee and a duty not to profit by the trustee's breach. [Rest. 2d § 256]

(1) Mere Consent Not "Participation"

The mere consent of a beneficiary to a trustee's breach of trust (*e.g.,* consenting to a proposed investment that proves to be improper) does not constitute a participation in that breach; however, there may be a fine line between mere consent and participation. A beneficiary who **induces** a breach of trust has been a participant in it.

(2) Liability of Beneficiary

An innocent beneficiary who profits from a breach of trust (but did not participate in it) is liable only to the extent of the improper benefit—*i.e.*, the "unjust enrichment." (A beneficiary *who participates* in a breach is liable not only to the extent of the improper benefit but also for the damage to the trust estate or other beneficiaries.)

(3) Beneficiary's Change of Position

The liability of an innocent beneficiary who profits from a breach of trust (even from a good faith mistake by the trustee) is based on the theory of unjust enrichment. If, however, the beneficiary has changed her position in reasonable reliance upon (for example) an overpayment or other improper distribution by the trustee, this is generally held to preclude recovery by the trustee or other beneficiaries (who may nevertheless surcharge the trustee).

c. No Duty to Indemnify Trustee

A beneficiary has no duty to indemnify a trustee for liabilities incurred in the course of administration, even under circumstances in which the trustee is properly entitled to indemnification from the trust estate. Of course, if a beneficiary has contracted to do so, she may be liable to the trustee; it also appears that such an obligation of indemnification may arise with respect to the beneficiary-settlor of a trust created for business purposes.

2. Remedies Against Beneficiary

Where a beneficiary has participated in or benefited from a breach of trust, the beneficiary may be held personally liable (as may the trustee) to the extent of the liabilities described above.

a. Beneficiary's Share Impounded

Whether the beneficiary's liability is purely as beneficiary or in her role as trustee as well as beneficiary, her beneficial interest is subject to a lien or charge to insure payment of that obligation. Benefits accruing to such a beneficiary are suspended and impounded until the trust estate has been restored or resulting obligations to other beneficiaries have been paid.

(1) Rationale

This impounding is an application of the general equitable principle that one entitled to participate in a fund cannot receive its benefits without first discharging any obligations to the fund.

EXAM TIP **GILBERT**

Although a beneficiary generally does not owe any fiduciary duties to the trust or other beneficiaries, she does owe a duty *not to participate in a breach of trust*. If you encounter a fact pattern in which a beneficiary has participated in a breach of trust (*e.g.*, by inducing the trustee to make an improper investment), she is *personally liable* for any loss incurred by the other beneficiaries as a result of the breach, and her *beneficial interest is subject to a lien or charge* for the amount of the loss incurred by the other beneficiaries. But remember, mere *consent* does not constitute participation.

G. Liabilities of Third Parties

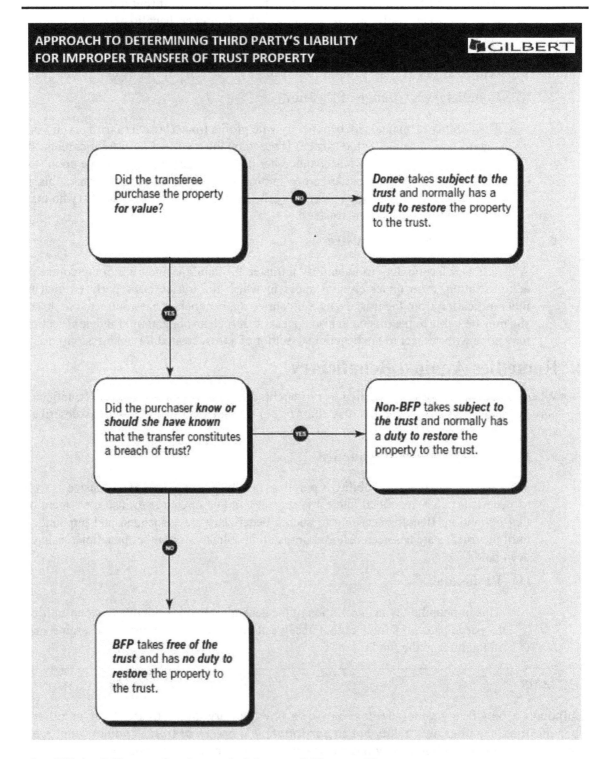

APPROACH TO DETERMINING THIRD PARTY'S LIABILITY FOR IMPROPER TRANSFER OF TRUST PROPERTY

GILBERT

Did the transferee purchase the property *for value*?

NO → *Donee* takes *subject to the trust* and normally has a *duty to restore* the property to the trust.

YES ↓

Did the purchaser *know or should she have known* that the transfer constitutes a breach of trust?

YES → *Non-BFP* takes *subject to the trust* and normally has a *duty to restore* the property to the trust.

NO ↓

BFP takes *free of the trust* and has *no duty to restore* the property to the trust.

1. Third Party's Acquisition of Trust Property

Of course, where a trustee improperly transfers trust property, a bona fide purchaser for value takes good title and has no liability to the trust estate or its beneficiaries (except, of course, for contractual or other obligations incurred in consideration of the transfer). The present discussion is concerned with the situation in which the transfer constitutes, for one reason or another, a **breach of trust** on the part of the trustee.

a. Donee

In such a case, if the transferee is a **donee** (even in good faith and without notice), the donee may be required to restore the property to the trust.

b. Bona Fide Purchaser

If, however, the transferee is a BFP, the transferee takes good title to the property free of the beneficial interests and has **no duty** to restore the property to the trust estate or other liability to the beneficiaries. "A bona fide purchaser takes free of latent equities," and in this situation the bona fide purchaser doctrine has generally been applied even where the trust property transferred was itself an equitable interest held by the trustee as a part of the trust res.

c. Purchaser Not Bona Fide

If the transferee is a purchaser but is not "bona fide," the transferee (like the donee) takes **subject to** the beneficial interests and has a duty to restore the property to the trust estate.

(1) "Non-BFP"

Clearly a purchaser who knows that the trustee is committing a breach of trust is not a bona fide purchaser. However, the mere fact that the transferee knows of the trust (*i.e.,* that the property is trust property) is not sufficient to deny the purchaser BFP status unless he knows or should know that the trustee's transfer is in breach of trust.

(a) Knows or Should Know

The transferee is not a BFP not only if he actually knows of the breach of trust but also if, under the circumstances, he **should know** of the breach or if, by reason of statute or otherwise, he is deemed to know (*e.g.,* by having a duty to inquire and thereby being charged with such knowledge as a reasonable inquiry would have produced). The laws of the several states differ with respect to the circumstances under which a party is under a duty of inquiry into the terms of the trust and into the circumstances surrounding the transaction when he knows or should know that he is dealing with a trustee.

2. Tort Liability

a. General Rule

Over half the states recognize a tort for third party liability for participating in breaches of fiduciary duty (TPLFD).

b. Elements

This tort requires the following elements:

(a) a breach of the fiduciary duty;

(b) the third party must have knowledge of that breach;

(c) the third party must have assisted in the breach; and

(d) the person to whom the fiduciary duty is owed—who will be referred to as the beneficiary—must have suffered damage as a result of the breach

Exam Tip: Consider how delegations may relate to this tort. For example, an accountant knowingly helps conceal a trustee's misappropriation of trust funds may satisfy these elements.

Chapter Seven

Accounting for Income and Principal

CONTENTS	PAGE
Key Exam Issues	150
A. Introduction	150
B. Specific Rules of Trust Principal-Income Accounting	153

Note to students: The material in this chapter is beyond the purview of most Trusts and Estates courses. This material is intended to serve as additional reference material for those who need or want it. What you need to know for the basic Trusts and Estates course is included under Trustee Duties, the Duty of Impartiality, in Chapter 4. Issues of income and principal will usually arise in that context, when a trust has one or more income beneficiaries and one or more remainder beneficiaries.

Key Exam Issues

In the event that your exam raises any question involving principal-income accounting issues, the first thing you should do is analyze the (expressed or implied) *trust terms* as the trust terms prevail over the general statutory rules or common law principles. Next consider those general statutory rules and common law principles. Be alert to possible applications of the trustee's duty of *impartiality* in balancing the almost inherently competing interests of income and remainder beneficiaries.

Particular problem areas to watch for include:

(i)   The handling of income from *transition periods* (*i.e.,* income during estate administration or income of periods within which the testator or life beneficiary died) in terms of both what the trust is entitled to receive and how those receipts are allocated between income and principal;

(ii) *Extraordinary stock dividends or splits*; and

(iii) *Underproductive or overproductive* (*i.e.,* wasting) *property* problems.

Also watch for distinctions between ordinary expenses and extraordinary or capital expenditures, and for the possibilities of apportionment or depreciation/amortization treatment of the latter.

A. Introduction

1. General Nature of the Principal-Income Problem

a. Successive Interests

In the typical trust situation, interests are generally divided between one or more *income beneficiaries* (usually for life or sometimes for other periods) and one or more *remainder beneficiaries*, whose eventual rights are in trust principal. In most trusts, the economic rights of these two types of beneficiaries will conflict.

(1) Classification of Funds

The resolution of conflicting claims among beneficiaries often turns on the classification of funds in the hands of the trustee either as *"income"* (the net income usually being payable currently to the life beneficiary) or as *"principal"* (generally to be retained in the trust estate for "future interest" holders). Accordingly, it is essential to classify receipts and disbursements so that they may be credited or charged to (or apportioned between) income and principal accounts.

b. Discretionary Benefits

The importance of accounting issues and rules is affected by the nature of the successive rights of the various beneficiaries, depending on whether trust accounting "income" may determine the rights of one or more of the beneficiaries.

(1) Discretionary Power over Distributions

The seriousness of the problem is lessened but not eliminated where, as is often the case, a life income beneficiary may receive principal in the discretion of the trustee (who holds a "power of invasion"); the maximum rights of the beneficiary are *not confined* to "income," but the *minimum* rights are set by the "income" account. The problem, however, is not present in a trust that is (or for so long as it is) *wholly discretionary*, with or without a standard (other than the trustee's fiduciary obligations) to guide the trustee's exercise of discretion over distributions (*e.g.,* a trust "to pay L such amounts of income or principal or both as necessary for L's support"), provided the discretionary benefit is limited to "income."

(2) Annuity or Unitrust Interests

Nor does the distinction between income and principal matter for *strict* (*i.e.,* without an "income" ceiling or floor) annuity trust interests (a specified, even indexed, *dollar* amount to be paid periodically) or unitrust interests (paying a specified *percentage* of principal, usually valued annually).

2. Sources and Priority of Accounting Rules

a. Trust Terms

Like most questions of trust administration, unless there is a controlling public policy restricting the settlor's freedom of disposition, the terms of the trust govern trust principal-income accounting questions whenever the matter is covered expressly or by an intention that can be found by construction of the trust provisions (*i.e.,* implied).

b. Legally Implied Rules

(1) State Law

If a particular accounting issue is not covered by the terms of the trust, the issue will be resolved in accordance with the applicable state law, usually by the terms of the state's "principal and income" statute—which all states, at long last, have in one form or another. Many still have a version of the Revised Uniform Principal and Income Act ("1962 Act"), and a rapidly growing number have adopted a revised Uniform Principal and Income Act ("1997 Act"). Gaps in statutes may be filled (perhaps under statutory mandate) by common law principles or resort to "generally accepted accounting principles."

(2) Accounting Rules

The specific rules of trust accounting often differ from general accounting principles because trust law is influenced by special factors. (Individuals will accounting expertise may be, for example, surprised at the trust law's strange lack of respect for normal financial concepts of "net" income.) In trust law, there is a tendency for some types of issues to favor income beneficiaries (reflecting the settlor's probable intent because income beneficiaries typically have the closest relationship to the settlor); there will be a tendency in other situations to avoid a forced income distribution of properties or funds likely to be important to maintaining a properly functioning trust estate.

e.g. **Examples:** Examples of an *income bias* include apportionment of certain routine expenses between income and principal and a lesser inclination (than in other accounting fields) to charge depreciation against income. An example of the less frequently occurring *principal bias* is the usual retention of stock dividends entirely as principal without acknowledging underlying differences in the practices of various corporations.

c. Trustee Discretion

By the terms of a trust, the trustee may be given private "rulemaking" authority in principal-income matters. What the settlor intended is a matter of interpretation of the trust provision. (A settlor, of course, should attempt to be clear about the scope and nature of the discretion.) The power may be interpreted: (i) to allow the trustee to *override* other trust provisions or legally implied rules *if in the trustee's judgment it appears appropriate* to do so (*e.g.,* in the trustee's judgment the provisions or rules appear unfair or unduly harsh as applied to the particular trust and situation, especially in light of the trustee's chosen investment program); or (ii) to be used *only* where the instrument or the law *does not provide clearly or at all* for a particular matter.

(1) Broad Construction of Trustee's Authority

Many courts have construed the trustee's authority broadly under such powers. Even on this issue, courts not only differ, but a given court may waver from time to time given a particularly compelling set of facts. Sometimes, courts may differ based on nuanced distinctions.

(2) Note

Within the scope of the discretionary power, the trustee's decision is usually controlling as long as the decision is made reasonably and in good faith.

d. Trustee Duties

In general, as in other aspects of trust administration, the law is designed and the trustee's accounting judgments are expected to reflect an overall fiduciary duty of fairness and impartiality to all beneficiaries, while at the same time respecting expressed or implied purposes, preferences, and intentions of a particular settlor.

(1) Adjustment Power

The trustee's duty to make trust property reasonably productive of income while observing the duty of impartiality may inhibit the trustee's efforts to invest optimally on a total return basis. Thus, the 1997 Act (prompted by the modern "prudent investor" rule) allows a trustee to "compensate" a beneficiary whose interest suffers (usually the income beneficiary) when the trustee undertakes an investment program that has a greater total-return expectation (emphasizing, *e.g.,* stocks heavily over bonds), intended for the long-term benefit of all, but that does not fulfill the usual dictates of the duty of impartiality. To satisfy those requirements, the trustee may exercise an "adjustment power." [1997 Act § 104] Increasingly, statutes are adding a "unitrust" option as a proxy for the income right if the trustee so elects. [*Compare* Rest. 3d § 79 cmt. i—use of common law power/duty of "equitable adjustment"]

If you encounter an exam question that involves principal-income accounting issues, remember that the first thing you should do is analyze the **expressed and implied terms of the trust**, which prevail over the general statutory rules or common law principles. Next you should determine whether there is a **statute** that governs the particular issues. Keep in mind that a court may broadly construe a trustee's **discretionary power** over accounting matters. Finally, remember that, if a trustee determines that by following the trust terms or statutory rules the trustee is unable to comply with the trustee's duty to administer the trust **impartially**, the trustee may **make adjustments** between principal and income to the extent necessary.

B. Specific Rules of Trust Principal-Income Accounting

1. Allocation Rules Are Default Rules

Where the trust instrument is silent and the trustee is not expressly given accounting discretion, the rules for allocating benefits and burdens between income beneficiaries and remainder beneficiaries are as follows.

2. Allocation of Benefits (Essentially Receipts)

Trust "income" is payable to the income beneficiary while trust "capital" belongs to the remainder beneficiaries (and is invested for any future income beneficiaries). Trust "income" includes all *ordinary receipts* from use or investment of the trust property; in this category fall rents, dividends, interest, etc. *Extraordinary receipts* are generally trust "capital" (unless they are in some manner to be apportioned); this includes proceeds from the sale or exchange of assets, settlement of most claims for injury to trust property, etc.

a. When Right to Income Commences

The income beneficiary is entitled to the net income from the *date of creation* of an *inter vivos trust*, or from the *date of death* in the case of a *testamentary trust* (even though there is an intervening period of administration of the settlor's estate). [Rest. 2d § 234]

b. Earnings of Testamentary Trusts During Estate Administration

Earnings on the trust corpus during administration of the decedent's estate are generally allocable to the income account from the testator-settlor's date of death (even though not payable, of course, until the trustee receives distribution of the trust funds).

(1) Distinguish—Nontrust Gifts

If *no trust* is involved, the amount of payment and date from which it is computed would depend on whether the gift was a general or specific one. The usual rule is that the legatee of a *specific* bequest (*e.g.*, "*my* 1,000 shares of ABC Inc. ") is entitled to actual earnings on the funds or property bequeathed from the date of death, whereas the legatee of a *general* (dollar amount, or "pecuniary") bequest (*e.g.*, $10,000) is entitled only to the statutory rate of interest (not necessarily the actual earnings) on the funds involved *commencing* one year after the date of death. (*See* Wills Summary.)

(2) Rule Where Trust Involved

In trust accounting the general rule is that the income beneficiary is entitled to **all earnings** on the trust estate **from the date of death**. What these "earnings" are, however, may follow the wills rule recited above, or—perhaps more often—any interest payable to the trust may commence at the date of the testator's death.

Example: If Testator devises Greenacre to Trustee in trust, income to Beneficiary, Beneficiary is entitled to Greenacre's actual net earnings from the time of Testator's death. This is the standard result, with or without the statute.

(3) Residuary Trust—Earnings of Other Estate Properties

Note that there is a conflict of authorities where there are earnings during probate that are derived from assets that do **not** ultimately become **part of the trust estate**.

Example: Testator creates a trust of the residue of her estate, and various assets are sold and used during probate to pay off pecuniary bequests, taxes, administration expenses, and claims against the estate. The income from such assets clearly becomes part of the trust estate (it falls into the residue). Should the trustee regard such receipts as trust income or as capital (and hence added to the corpus)?

(a) Majority View—Income

The majority view is that such receipts are **income**. This is the so-called Massachusetts Rule and is adopted in section 5 of the 1962 Act and continued in the 1997 Act.

(b) Minority View—Principal

There is some authority that limits the income beneficiary to income attributable to the assets that come into the trust. Under this view, the earnings from any other source (*i.e.,* the earnings here in question) are entirely allocable to the trust corpus.

(c) Minority View—Apportionment

Still other cases apportion the earnings between the income and principal accounts based on a formula like that applied to apportion receipts from the sale of unproductive property. Although often said to be a sound answer, this rule is less popular than the other rules because of its supposed complexity.

TYPE OF GIFT IN TRUST	EXAMPLE	WHO IS ENTITLED TO INCOME EARNED DURING ADMINISTRATION?
SPECIFIC	T bequeaths "Blueacre in trust for L for life, remainder to R"	L is entitled to net earnings on Blueacre (*e.g.*, rents) from date of T's death
GENERAL (PECUNIARY)	T bequeaths "$50,000 in trust for L for life, remainder to R"	L is entitled to net earnings (minus net income of specific devises and bequests) ***on a portion of T's estate equal to $50,000*** from date of T's death
RESIDUARY	T bequeaths "all the rest, residue, and remainder of my estate in trust for L for life, remainder to R"	*Majority view:* L is entitled to all earnings (that fall into residue), ***even on assets that do not eventually become part of residue***, from date of T's death
		Minority view: L is entitled **only** to earnings from date of T's death on ***assets that come into the trust***; earnings from date of T's death on ***assets that were sold to pay*** debts, expenses, and pecuniary bequests are principal
		Minority view: Earnings from date of T's death are ***apportioned*** between income and principal

c. Timing of Receipts—Apportionment of Income as Between Successive Beneficiaries

A frequent issue between successive beneficiaries is whether income received after the death of the testator or a life beneficiary should be allocated on the basis of when it was *received* or on the basis of when it *accrued*.

e.g. **Example:** On the death of life beneficiary B, income becomes payable to another income beneficiary, C. Do income items *received* by the trust *after* B's death, but *accrued during* her lifetime, belong to B's estate or to C?

d. Special Rules Governing Dividends

Difficult problems arise in connection with the dividends received by a trust from corporate stock—*i.e.*, determining whether a particular corporate distribution is "trust income" or "trust principal."

(1) Ordinary Cash Dividends

Ordinary cash dividends are easy; they are *income*.

(2) Extraordinary Dividends (Cash or Stock)

Extraordinary dividends raise several important classification issues. A *cash dividend* is "extraordinary" either because of its size or circumstances. *All stock dividends* are "extraordinary."

(3) Other Corporate Distributions

The same statutory rules and common law principles allocate corporate distributions of *stock rights* and *options* (and proceeds of their sale) to *principal*.

---

e. Allocation of Proceeds from Sale of Trust Assets

(1) Sales in General

All proceeds from the sale of most trust assets are *principal—i.e.,* become part of the trust *capital* account.

(a) Effect

Under ordinary circumstances, only the principal account is credited with profits and charged with losses realized on the sale.

(b) "Income Elements"

Gains on the sale of investments and other capital assets go to trust corpus even when they represent increases in value that eventually would have been realized and distributed to the income beneficiary (as rents, royalties, dividends, etc.) had the trustee retained the investment.

(2) Un(der)productive Property—Allocation of Proceeds of Delayed Sale

Except for a special provision on marital deduction trusts [*see* I.R.C. § 2056], the rule on unproductive or underproductive property (below) is expressly abandoned in the 1997 Act, as being inappropriate when income productivity is based on the trust portfolio as a whole and in light of the trustee's adjustment power under section 104 of the Act; over time, judicial decisions and amendments to other statutes can be expected to follow.

f. Treatment of "Wasting Assets"

A wasting asset is any property that is *depletable or perishable through use—e.g.,* timber, minerals, patents, annuities, copyrights, etc.

(1) Bequest or Devise of Properties Generally

Where a "wasting asset" becomes part of the trust estate under general terms in the settlor's will (*e.g.,* "all my estate" or "the residue of my estate"), it has typically been presumed that the settlor intended both the income beneficiary and remainder beneficiary to enjoy the benefit of the property. Hence, the trustee must *either* provide for *amortization* (deduct from income and set up a reserve) or *sell* the property and invest in "permanent" securities. [Rest. 2d § 239]

(2) Specific Testamentary or Inter Vivos Gifts

On the other hand, where the settlor makes a *specific gift*, during life or by will, of a "wasting asset" to the trust (*e.g.,* "my oil well to T in trust for B for life, remainder to C"), the income beneficiary has typically been allowed to receive all receipts, on the rationale that this is what the settlor must have intended in making a gift of the "income" from an asset that is depletable.

---

g.   Bond Premium and Discount

Bonds often sell at a premium or discount as a means of adjusting the bond's contractual rate of interest to the market rate at the time of sale. If the bond's rate is higher than the market rate, the bond will be sold at a premium; if it is lower than the market rate, the bond will be sold at a discount. Some bonds bear no interest but in lieu thereof sell only at a larger discount, reflecting the full amount of "interest" to be earned upon redemption.

(1)   Noninterest-Bearing Bonds

In the case of noninterest-bearing bonds, the increment on sale or redemption traditionally has belonged to *income*; that same result may be achieved by anticipating the eventual profit on redemption (or sale) and by making appropriate periodic payments from cash flowing into the principal account. [1962 Act § 7(a); *and see* Rest. 2d § 233 cmt. d; *but see* 1997 Act § 412(b)—payment received on zero-coupon bonds and the like is generally principal (relying on the adjustment power, to cope with any resulting overall unfairness to the income beneficiary)]

(2)   Other Cases—Interest-Bearing Bonds

(a)   Premium

The Restatement rule has *allowed* but has not required amortization of premium (by retention of excess interest in the principal account to repay that account for the "loss" on redemption) unless not to amortize will be unfair in light of the trust investments as a whole. [Rest. 2d § 239 cmt. f]

(b)   Discount

That rule provides that discount *cannot* be amortized (to increase the income payments out of anticipated profit to principal on redemption) prior to the sale or redemption of the bond, but then the proceeds may or may not be apportioned as fairness dictates. [Rest. 2d § 239 cmt. b]

(c) Uniform Act

Legislation in some other states precludes amortization of either premium or discount on bonds *except* on noninterest-bearing bonds. [1962 Act § 7(a)] Note that this rule effectively casts the responsibility for impartiality upon the trustee's "balanced" investment decisions, which is easier said than done.

3. Allocation of Burdens (Essentially Expenditures)

The general rule is that the trustee should pay the *ordinary*, *current expenses* of trust administration out of trust income, whereas expenses that are *"extraordinary"* or *solely beneficial to the remainder beneficiaries* should be paid from the capital account. Generally, the cost of keeping the trust property productive and secure is borne by the income account. Likewise, the income account is chargeable with all expenses of trust operation that go to the production or collection of income, while the principal account is chargeable with expenses that go to the improvement or preservation of the trust corpus.

a. Losses from Operation of Business

Any loss sustained in the operation of a business owned by the trust has been held to fall on *principal*; *i.e.,* such losses are not carried forward into any other year in determining profits or income.

b. Taxes, Assessments

Ordinary property taxes are charged to the *income* account.

(1) Assessments for Permanent Improvements

In contrast, assessments for "capital" or "permanent" improvements are generally handled as follows: Usually the entire assessment is charged to the *principal* account; under appropriate circumstances the income account thereafter may be charged with depreciation or amortization of the amount involved. The 1997 Act allocates expenditures related to *environmental* problems to *principal*. [1997 Act § 502(a)(7)]

(2) "Permanent"

Of course, the big problem lies in determining when a relatively *long-term* improvement is a "permanent" improvement. It has often been treated essentially as a question of fact or judgment, but generally if the benefit is one that is "likely to last" until the remainder beneficiaries come into possession, it is considered "permanent." With amortization, the handling need not be so arbitrary.

c. Upkeep

Current repairs, maintenance expenses, and assessments for temporary improvements are chargeable entirely to the *income* account. [Rest. 2d § 233 cmt. e; 1962 Act § 13a; 1997 Act § 501(3), (4)]

(1) Insurance

In many states, premiums for insuring trust property are also chargeable to *income*. Other states call for *apportionment* because principal is protected as well as income—probably reflecting "income bias."

(2) Initial Costs

When a trust is initially established, the cost of *putting trust property into rentable or income-producing condition* is chargeable against *principal*, even though the expenditure is of a type that would subsequently be a "repair and maintenance" item chargeable against income. [Rest. 2d § 233 cmt. i]

(3) Distinguish—Capital Involvements

Long-term, substantial improvements are treated and even defined differently in different states. Some *apportion* between income and principal (based on the life beneficiary's life expectancy or other supposedly appropriate basis); others charge these expenditures initially to the *principal* account and then *depreciate*; and others simply charge to *principal*.

d. Mortgage Payments

Interest on a mortgage debt secured by trust property is charged against *income*, whereas the *principal* element of each mortgage payment is charged to *principal*.

e. Trustee's and Attorneys' Fees and Other Administrative Expenses

(1) Income Charged by Some

Some of the earlier cases charged the trustee's compensation and related administration expenses entirely to the *income* account, at least in the absence of special justification for contrary treatment. Premiums on a trustee's bond are still generally held chargeable entirely to the *income* account.

(2) Generally Today—Apportionment

Such administrative expenses, however, including the fees that are payable to the trustee and to attorneys for their services (and usually also costs of accountings and judicial proceedings), are now generally *apportioned equitably* between the income beneficiary and remainder beneficiary. [Rest. 2d § 233 cmt. h]

(a) Discretionary Apportionment

In many jurisdictions, the amount that each interest must bear is within the reasonable *discretion of the trustee* (subject to review by the court) and varies with the circumstances of each case (*e.g.,* nature of services rendered, whether services benefited one interest rather than others, values of respective interests, etc.).

(b) Presumptively Equal Apportionment

In many states, however (often by statute), such expenses are *split equally* between the income and capital accounts in the absence of a showing of special circumstances.

f. Reserves for Depreciation

Considerable litigation has centered on whether the trustee may pay the income beneficiary the earnings from depreciable income-producing property (*e.g.,* commercial real estate) without setting up reserves for depreciation to protect the interests of remainder beneficiaries. Any explicit instructions by the settlor will be given effect. Where the trust instrument is silent, there is a split of case authority and considerable diversity among statutes.

	INCOME	PRINCIPAL
RECEIPTS	• *Ordinary cash dividends*	• *Stock dividends and splits*
	• *Ordinary receipts* from use or investment of trust assets (*e.g.,* rents, interest)	• *Extraordinary receipts* (*e.g.,* proceeds from sale of trust assets)
	• *Rental payments* (perhaps reduced by depreciation); *portion of production payments* from *wasting assets* (perhaps subject to depletion)	• *Portion of production payments* from *wasting assets*
	• *Increment (profit)* on sale or redemption of *noninterest-bearing bonds*	• Remaining proceeds from sale or redemption of *noninterest-bearing bonds*
EXPENDITURES AND LOSSES	• *Ordinary property taxes* and *depreciation or amortization* for *long-term improvements*	• *Assessments* for *long-term improvements*
	• *Current repairs, maintenance expenses, and assessments* for *short-term improvements*; *insurance premiums*	• *Initial cost* of making trust property *rentable or income-producing*; *long-term improvements* (perhaps with depreciation charged to income)
	• *Interest* on *mortgage debt*	• *Principal payments* on *mortgage debt*
	• *Portion of trustee's and attorneys' fees* and *administrative expenses*	• *Portion of trustee's and attorneys' fees* and *administrative expenses*

Chapter Eight
Modification and Termination of Trusts

CONTENTS	PAGE
Key Exam Issues	162
A. Revocable Trusts	162
B. Irrevocable Trusts	164

Key Exam Issues

Remember that the terms of the trust will tell you what procedures are available within the terms of the trust for modification and even termination. Exam questions concerning the modification and termination of a trust involve the possibility of termination of the trust before the trust would conclude according to the trust terms. The most critical exam material covered in this chapter has to do with the ability of courts and beneficiaries to modify or terminate trusts after the settlor has died.

1. When determining whether the beneficiaries may modify or terminate an irrevocable trust, consider the following factors:

    a. Whether the consent of *all possible beneficiaries*, present and future (including contingent beneficiaries), has been or can be obtained (being mindful of issues related to legal competency or obstacles presented by potential unborn beneficiaries); and

    b. Whether modification or termination will defeat a *"material purpose"* of the trust. If so, there can be no modification or termination unless, in the case of a living settlor, the settlor herself waives the material purpose. Keep in mind that if the settlor is living, the settlor could waive the material purpose.

2. A petitioner may ask the court to authorize equitable deviation without the need for the beneficiaries to consent. The petitioner, who is often the trustee, must establish the following:

    a. The existence of *changed circumstances* that were not anticipated by the settlor; *and*

    b. These changed circumstances *threaten the accomplishment of a trust purpose,* which requires more than merely convincing a court that the contemplated modification would improve the administration of the trust or would be in the best interests of the beneficiaries.

A. Revocable Trusts

1. The majority view today presumes that a trust is revocable unless it states otherwise, and can be modified or terminated according to its terms. [UTC § 602; Rest. § 63(3)] This is true for Totten Trusts as well.

2. Despite the general rule that a will cannot change the disposition of a nonprobate instrument, some jurisdictions allow a provision in a will to do so if the will specifically refers to the trust or devises property to the trust. Be aware, however, that some jurisdictions that have adopted the UTC have not adopted this particular provision.

3. The standard method of revocation of a revocable trust, unless the trust instrument specifies otherwise, is written notice delivered by the settlor to the trustee, who are often the same person.

    a. Note that the failure to comply with the manner prescribed in the trust instrument is not necessarily fatal to an attempted revocation, but in that case, there must be clear and convincing evidence of the settlor's intent to revoke.

    b. If the trust instrument does not prescribe a method for revocation, or does not provide that the method set out in the trust is exclusive, a provision in a will, or any other method showing the settlor's clear and convincing intent to revoke is allowed.

c.   If a Settlor loses capacity, a conservator or guardian may revoke the trust with the approval of the court supervising the conservatorship or guardianship.

4.   Rescission and Reformation

This requires proof of some recognized ground for relief—such as fraud, abuse of confidential relationship, undue influence, or mistake. [Rest. 2d § 333] The UTC provides more flexibility of judicial power to reform for mistake. [UTC § 415—requiring clear and convincing evidence; *and see* Rest. 3d § 62; *but see* **Flannery v. McNamara**, 738 N.E.2d 739 (Mass. 2000)—rejecting the counterpart Rest. 3d of Property § 12.1 with respect to *testamentary* trusts and reviving the traditional distinction between wills and inter vivos trusts]

EXAM TIP   **GILBERT**

If you encounter an exam question that asks whether the settlor can modify (which might be phrased as "amend") or revoke a trust, look at the terms of the trust. The settlor *cannot* modify or revoke an *"irrevocable"* trust. However, if the settlor has reserved a *power to revoke* (*i.e.,* the trust is "revocable"), the settlor can *revoke or modify* the trust. If the settlor has reserved an *unrestricted power to modify*, the settlor can generally *also revoke* the trust.

---

a.   Exception—Totten Trusts

Similarly, Totten trusts *can* be revoked by the settlor's will *if* the intention is manifested expressly or by clear implication.

(1)   Conservator

These powers can be exercised by a conservator (guardian, custodian, or whatever term is locally applied) if the settlor becomes incompetent, to the extent necessary for support, if other funds are sufficient, and most likely, absent contrary provision and with court approval, for the purposes of amending the settlor's estate plan. [*See* Rest. 3d § 11(5) and cmt. f—also agent so authorized under a durable power of attorney; UTC § 602(f)].

(2)   Trustee, Beneficiary, or Third Party

In creating (or, unless restricted, in amending) a trust, the settlor can grant to others, including a trustee or beneficiary: the power to modify the trust, the power to terminate it (and thereby, if a beneficiary, receive part of the trust estate), or the power to appoint interests under the trust.

5.   What Does the Settlor's Power or Revocation Mean for the Settlor's Creditors?

a.   Creditors of a settlor *can* reach the trust property if the trust is revocable. [Rest. 3d § 25(2) cmt. e; UTC § 505(a)(1)]

b.   **Bankruptcy**

If the settlor declares or is forced into bankruptcy, the trustee in bankruptcy obtains and can exercise the settlor's powers: thus, the creditors can reach assets held in a revocable trust.

B. Irrevocable Trusts

1. Modification with Settlor's Consent

If all beneficiaries agree, they may modify or terminate an irrevocable trust at any time *with the settlor's consent*

a. All Possible Beneficiaries

"Consent of all beneficiaries" means not only all existing but also *all potential* beneficiaries—born or unborn, ascertained or unascertained—*of all interests*, present or future, and no matter how uncertain or contingent.

(1) "Children"

A deceased settlor's children (as, *e.g.*, a class or remainder beneficiaries) are all ascertainable because the settlor cannot have any more children after death. But if the settlor is still alive (as in an inter vivos trust) or if the "children" are those of another who is still living, this class of beneficiaries cannot (at least under the common law's conclusive presumption of lifelong fertility) be ascertained or complete because of the possibility of additional members.

(2) "Issue" or "Descendants"

A remainder to a class designated as the issue (or its equivalent) of a person, whether living or deceased (unless leaving *no* issue), creates an indefinite class of *potential* beneficiaries. Accordingly, in such a case it is *not possible to obtain the consent of all* beneficiaries—*e.g.*, some may be minors, and necessarily some may not yet be born.

(a) Note

The above represents the traditional view and literal meaning of the generally stated rule and the holding of a modest number of reported cases. The modern view is to recognize the possibility of vicarious consent.

(3) "Heirs"

Under the term's usual meaning, the "heirs" of a *deceased person* are all ascertainable and are (or were at the time of ascertainment) alive. But this rule is not absolute.

(a) Deferred Class of Heirs

If the trust expressly or impliedly refers to a *deferred*, "artificial" class of heirs, even of a person who is already dead, such a class of remainder beneficiaries may not be ascertained or confined to living persons.

> **e.g.** **Example:** Testator devised "to Trustee in trust for Son for life, remainder to go to those who would then be my heirs as ascertained at Son's death."

(b) Heirs of a Living Person

The class membership is also unascertainable and open to afterborn persons if the "heirs" are those of a *living person*.

b. All Beneficiaries Existing and Competent

The requirement that all beneficiaries must be legally competent (sui juris) and give otherwise valid consent has been held to mean what it says. Under this meaning, it would not be possible to obtain consent from all beneficiaries when any possible beneficiary (i) *may be afterborn*, or (ii) *is a minor*.

(1) Possibility of Vicarious Consent

The consent by a minor's guardian is probably sufficient, and consent by a guardian ad litem for unborn or unascertained persons in such situations is beginning to receive some recognition, as has the doctrine of virtual representation. [*See also* Rest. 3d § 65 cmt. b; UTC §§ 302–305.]

EXAM TIP

If your exam asks whether the beneficiaries can compel modification or termination of a trust, the first thing you must do (under all views) is determine who are **all the possible beneficiaries** (whether born, unborn, ascertained, or unascertainable) **of all the interests** (present, future, vested, or contingent). Second, you must decide whether it is possible to obtain consent from all such beneficiaries. Keep in mind that **unborn or unascertainable** beneficiaries (*e.g.,* a living person's "heirs") and **minor** beneficiaries **cannot consent**, but also note the possibility of vicarious consent.

---

2. Termination Without Settlor's Consent (Usually After Settlor's Death)

a. Note

Termination without the settlor's consent is more difficult because of the deference of courts for the settlor's intent.

b. Material Purpose Doctrine/Claflin Doctrine

This rule states that without the settlor's consent, the beneficiaries may not modify a trust in any way that interferes with its "material purpose," that is, with any aspect of the trust that the settlor considered important and part of the reason for the trust's existence. [**Claflin v. Claflin,**149 Mass. 19, 20 N.E. 454 (1889)]

c. "Intent" Differentiated from "Material Purpose"

Obviously, by its very nature, a proposed modification or premature termination of the trust involves a departure from a "specific intention" of the settlor as manifested in the terms of the trust. Thus, the *Claflin* doctrine does not seek to protect every intention or desire of the settlor. The doctrine is concerned with the trust's *purpose* or purposes, and even then, only those that are *"material."*

d. Inferring Purposes

Trust instruments rarely include specifications of the settlor's purpose but, in most cases, only contain the terms that implement *some* unstated purpose or purposes. Thus, it is generally necessary to speculate about or to attempt to infer the purpose(s) and whether any such purpose is *material*. In determining whether termination or modification would defeat a "material purpose" of the settlor, courts consider the *wording of the trust instrument* and the *circumstances of its execution*. Parol evidence of various kinds is also admissible—including the *settlor's statements* both before and after the creation of the trust, as long as they are indicative of the *original* purpose and state of mind. Most frequently, however, the material purpose that proves to be the obstacle to modification or termination is found in the *nature of the trust* or in the types of provisions it contains.

Example: In a trust "for Child for life, remainder to Grandchild," is the settlor's goal to provide for successive enjoyment by Child and Grandchild, or is it to protect Child from what the settlor believes to be Child's bad judgment (although, traditionally at least, Child must be *legally* competent or the question would not arise)?

(1) Judicial Interpretations of "Material Purpose"

(a) Delayed Interests

Claflin itself involved a trust that provided for termination and distribution to the beneficiary when he turned 30. The beneficiary petitioned the court for early termination when he was 27. The court refused, holding the settlor had set up the trust precisely to delay distribution until the beneficiary was 30. Courts will generally determine that delayed interests such as the one in *Claflin* constitute a material purpose of a trust.

(b) Successive Interests

The key question is whether these are part of the material purpose of the trust or not. There is conflicting law on this question: courts have differed. In one case, a trust provided for a lifetime interest for parents with the children as remainder beneficiaries. The parents asked the court to terminate the trust and distribute the assets to them. The court refused, holding that having the assets professionally managed during their lifetimes was a material purpose of the trust. On the other hand, another court found that a lifetime beneficiary who transferred her interest to the remainder beneficiaries during her lifetime did not violate a material provision of a trust because the settlor's only material purpose was to preserve the assets for the remainder beneficiaries. Although the authorities are divided and often unclear on the point, the usual view seems to be that courts will generally require some evidence (language, circumstances, etc.) from which to infer a material purpose, or else they will infer only a general purpose of providing for successive enjoyment by the beneficiaries (so that all beneficiaries together are free to modify the trust or to terminate it and divide the assets as they wish).

(c) Spendthrift Clauses

The traditional presumption was that spendthrift clauses represented a material purpose of the trust. This likely meant that any trust with a spendthrift clause could not be terminated early because that would allow a beneficiary's creditors to reach her assets. Today, because these clauses are boilerplate in most trusts, the UTC and the Restatement reverse that presumption and state the mere existence of such a clause does not necessarily mean, without more, that it was material purpose of the trust, UTC 411(e), Rest (Third) 65 cmt. 3 (2003). Nevertheless, this is still not the majority view.

(2) Discretionary Terms

Traditionally, granting the trustee discretion in making distributions constituted a material purpose of the trust, but today the UTC and some jurisdictions have changed this position and require more than the mere existence of discretionary terms to show a material purpose.

(3) Removal of Trustee

The removal or replacement of a trustee can frustrate the material purpose of the trust, of evidence shows that the settlor chose the particular trustee because for particular personal characteristics or qualifications.

EXAM TIP   ▮GILBERT

If the question involves a petition to modify a trust with a spendthrift provision, remember that such a clause may or may not count as a material purpose of the trust. In jurisdictions that have adopted UTC § 411(c), a court would require further evidence. beyond the mere existence of the spendthrift clause, to show that the clause constituted a material purpose of the trust.

---

e. Termination or Modification with Consent of the Beneficiaries and No Frustration of Material Purpose

If the termination or modification would not frustrate a material purpose of the trust, and all the beneficiaries agree, a court will authorize termination or modification of a trust. [UTC § 411(b)]

(1) Even if not all the beneficiaries consent, a court may modify or terminate a trust if 1) the trust could have been modified or terminated if all the beneficiaries had consented, and 2) the interests of the non-consenting beneficiaries are adequately protected. [UTC § 41(e)]

(a) Beneficiaries who are under a legal disability, such as minors or the unborn require representation to adequately protect their interests in a modification proceeding.

DETERMINING MATERIAL PURPOSE THROUGH NATURE OF TRUST		▮GILBERT
TYPE OF TRUST	**EXAMPLE**	**MATERIAL PURPOSE**
SUPPORT TRUST	S "to T in trust, to pay or apply such amounts of income or principal or both **to or for the support of** X for life, remainder to Y"	Perhaps, but not necessarily, to protect X from want and her own imprudence
TRUST UNTIL STATED AGE	S "to T in trust, to pay the income to X **until she reaches age 30**, then to distribute the principal to X"	To keep the property out of X's control until the stated age

SPENDTHRIFT TRUST	S "to T in trust, to pay the income to X for life, remainder to Y; the interests of X and Y **cannot be transferred or reached by their creditors**"	To protect X and Y from their own imprudence *Note:* Spendthrift provision alone does **not** constitute material purpose under Third Restatement and UTC (but this is controversial and many UTC states have declined to adopt this view)

f. Purpose Frustrated or Impermissible

(1) Spendthrift Protection Not Needed

Where the beneficiary whose interest the spendthrift provision was to protect has died or no longer holds his interest, the trust may be terminated (unless to do so would violate another material purpose).

(2) Perpetuities Period Expired—Trust No Longer Indestructible

By operation of law, the restraint upon the freedom of the beneficiaries ends, as does the law's deference to the settlor's purpose, once the applicable perpetuities period has expired—"lives in being plus 21 years" under the common law Rule Against Perpetuities. Although (as long as all interests are vested) a trust may **endure** beyond the period of the Rule, the trust can no longer be "indestructible."

3. Modification for Special Circumstances—Equitable Deviation

Judicial Power to Allow a Trustee to Deviate from or Modify Trust Terms to Effectuate the Settlor's Purpose under Changed or Unanticipated Circumstances

a. Administrative Versus Dispositive Terms

Under the traditional view, a court of equity could authorize or direct the trustee to deviate from, or even modify, only the **administrative** terms of a trust (and thus to perform acts otherwise forbidden) in order to carry out the settlor's material purpose under changed or unanticipated circumstances. The more recent view, expressed in UTC § 412(a) and Restatement (Third) § 66, however, allows for modification of both administrative and dispositive terms (that is, terms involving distributions to beneficiaries).

b. What Changed or Unanticipated Conditions Justify "Equitable Deviation"?

Equitable deviation is justified whenever, due to *changed circumstances unforeseen by the settlor*, compliance with the original terms of the trust would *defeat* or *substantially impair* one or more of the trust purposes. [Rest. 2d § 167]

(1) Unforeseen Circumstances Required

The rule is intended to protect—not to disregard—the actual or probable intentions of the settlor. Therefore, circumstances must have changed since the trust was established such that deviation is necessary to carry out the trust's purpose. Under the traditional view, these circumstances had to be ones not contemplated by the settlor, but under the UTC and Third Restatement view (*supra*), it is sufficient that the circumstances involved were not anticipated by the settlor.

c. Effect of Express Trust Provision

The mere fact that the settlor has, in the trust instrument, directed or forbidden the trustee to perform the particular act which the trustee now seeks to perform (or a beneficiary now seeks to have the trustee directed or authorized to do) does *not* preclude deviation. The question is whether the settlor *would have so intended had she known* of the circumstances.

(1) Explicit Prohibition or Direction

(a) Sale Forbidden

Even under the stricter traditional view, if the settlor forbade the trustee to sell or encumber trust property, the trustee may be authorized by the court to do so if the circumstances have changed (in a way not foreseen by the settlor) and the sale or encumbrance is now necessary to preserve the trust estate or to provide for the beneficiaries.

e.g. **Example:** Even though the trust terms direct the trustee to retain the shares the settlor owned in his longtime employer, the court may allow (or require) the trustee to sell those shares if necessary to prevent such a serious loss of trust income or value that a trust purpose would be threatened.

(b) Termination of Trust Activity

Even a termination of the trust's *principal activity* may be authorized if the court finds that continuance of the activity would jeopardize the settlor's original purpose. [Rest. 2d § 336]

e.g. **Example:** Where a trust was created with the direction "to retain and carry on my farm," the farm operation may be terminated and the property sold if it appears that, due to unforeseen changes affecting the farm, continued operation would inevitably result in loss of the farm.

(2) Provision Forbidding Any Modification

If the settlor expressly provided against *any* modification of the trust, courts might be particularly reluctant to authorize deviation from the original terms. Nevertheless, if a court were convinced that the settlor had not considered the particular unforeseen circumstances that have occurred, deviation would probably be ordered. [*In re Estate of Pulitzer*, 139 Misc. 575 (1931), *aff'd*, 237 A.D. 808 (1932)]

e.g. **Example:** Joseph Pulitzer instructed his trustee to continue to publish the *New York World* newspaper and prohibited sale of the stock of the publishing company. Losses incurred in publishing the *World* jeopardized not only the profits but also the other assets of the trust. The court directed the trustee to sell the publishing company stock. [*In re Estate of Pulitzer, supra*]

d. Liability of Trustee

Where the trustee knows or should know of circumstances justifying a deviation from the original terms of the trust, he may be *liable* if he carries out those original terms. A trustee's fiduciary duties include a duty to apply to an appropriate court for instructions under such conditions, with liability for a loss if he fails to do so. [Rest. 3d § 66(2)]

(1) Exception—Emergency

A trustee may be exempt from liability if he deviates from the original trust terms without first obtaining court permission if an emergency exists requiring immediate action (and perhaps even if he reasonably believes such an emergency exists). [Rest. 3d § 66 cmt. e]

e. Distinguish—Cy Pres Doctrine and Charities

The judicial power to modify not only applies to the administrative provisions by equitable deviation, but also the *purposes* of *charitable trusts* under the cy pres power in appropriate circumstances. (*See* Chapter 5 of this Summary.)

EXAM TIP   **GILBERT**

Recall that the cy pres doctrine allows a court to deviate from the trust's original purpose and modify it to fit current circumstances. To invoke cy pres, the court must find (i) that the designated purpose has been *fulfilled* or has become *illegal, impossible, or impracticable* to carry out, and (ii) under the traditional view, that the settlor had a *general charitable intent*

WHO CAN MODIFY OR TERMINATE TRUST   **GILBERT**

SETTLOR	If the trust is revocable
TRUSTEE	If power to modify or terminate is *expressly conferred or implied*; or changed circumstances require e equitable deviation
BENEFICIARIES	If *all potential beneficiaries* (present and future) *consent* and *no material purpose* of settlor will be *defeated*
COURT	Under traditional view, if there are *unforeseen changed circumstances* that *threaten the accomplishment of a trust purpose* and proposed change does not involve taking from one beneficiary and giving to another

4. Decanting Statutes—Definition

"Decanting" allows a trustee to distribute trust assets to new trust which might have different terms. The trustee can do this either under the auspices of Decanting Statutes, available today in many states, or under trust provisions that allow for decanting.

a. Permissibility

(1) Permissible Under Trust Terms

If the trust itself gives the trustee authority to decant, it will specify the circumstances and procedures under which it can be done

(2) Permissible Under State Law

If the state has a decanting statute, it can provide the trustee with the authority necessary to decant the trust assets.

b. Fiduciary Obligations

Decanting must be done in compliance with the trustee's fiduciary duty.

c. Decanting Statutes

(1) Power to Invade Principal

Almost of the statutes allow the trustee to decant if the trustee has power to invade the principal, even if the trust terms do not specifically authorize decanting.

(2) Changing Beneficiaries

The statutes generally allow the trustee to remove beneficiaries but not to add new beneficiaries.

(3) Change of Interests

The statutes do not typically allow for the acceleration of interests. Likewise, the statutes do not typically allow for the reduction of a beneficiary's fixed income interest.

d. Reasons to Decant

(1) Tax Purposes

To achieve beneficial tax treatment, the trustee may decant to permit moving trust assets to another state where there is no income tax.

(2) Administrative Purposes

Decanting can be used to expand or reduce the trustee's authority to engage in transactions not authorized by the original trust terms.

(3) Changing Beneficiaries or Their Interests

Decanting allows for some changes to the beneficiaries or their interests. This includes limiting distributions to a beneficiary with substance abuse problems, or to increase distributions to a beneficiary whose needs turn out to be greater than the settlor anticipated, perhaps though illness or disability.

Chapter Nine
Trusts Arising by Operation of Law

CONTENTS	PAGE
Key Exam Issues	174
A. Introduction	174
B. Resulting Trusts	176
C. Constructive Trusts	179

Key Exam Issues

In writing an answer to an exam question involving trusts arising by operation of law, keep in mind the distinctions between resulting trusts and constructive trusts:

(i) A *resulting trust* involves a *reversionary interest* when the equitable interest in the property is not completely or effectively disposed of. The revision is based on the *presumed intent* of the settlor.

(ii) A *constructive trust* is not a trust at all but a *remedial device* based on principles of equity, usually imposed to *cure wrongdoing or prevent unjust enrichment*.

1. Watch for the following fact scenarios that may involve a *resulting trust*:

   a. The trust makes an *incomplete disposition* of trust assets.

   b. An express trust is *unenforceable* (*e.g.*, the beneficiary is not properly designated).

   c. An otherwise valid express trust *fails* for illegality, impossibility, or impracticability.

2. Watch for the following fact situations that may implicate a *constructive trust*:

   a. The facts involve an *unenforceable oral trust*.

   b. There has been a *breach of fiduciary duty*.

   c. Title was acquired by some *wrongful conduct* (*e.g.*, fraud, mistake, or conversion, etc.).

A. Introduction

1. General Nature

Constructive trusts and resulting trusts may arise out of situations in which an actual intention to create a trust intention is present but the trust fails. Thus, these trusts are inferred *by law* or *imposed by courts*, rather than being the product of a settlor's intentional act.

a. Resulting Trusts

Resulting trusts arise from *reversionary interests* that can come about in situations involving trusts, but they may arise in situations that involve other areas of the law as well.

b. Constructive Trusts

Constructive trusts are remedial devices. They are *imposed* by courts in the exercise of their equitable powers *to remedy wrongs or to avoid unjust enrichment*. They arise out of diverse situations and in virtually all areas of the law; they may and often do arise in the context of trust law.

2. Failed Trust or Trust Provision

Trust Assets with Nowhere to GoFor present purposes, the most significant resulting trusts are those that are recognized by law on the basis of the legally *inferred* intent of the transferor to re-acquire equitable interests where the legal title has been transferred, accompanied by an expressed intention to create a trust, but where the transferor has failed, in whole or in part, to make a complete or effective disposition of all equitable (or beneficial) interests in the property. This incomplete disposition may result simply from the transferor's failure to create interests covering all possible rights and situations (*i.e.,* provision is omitted or the provisions are incomplete), or it may arise because an actually expressed provision cannot be complied with (*e.g.,* proof is barred by the Statute of Frauds or Statute of Wills) and therefore fails. Alternatively, it may arise because an otherwise properly created interest fails (*e.g.,* the trust purpose is illegal or the beneficiary dies before date of transfer with no alternate beneficiary provided for in the trust instrument) or is rejected (*e.g.,* the intended beneficiary disclaims with no alternate beneficiary provided for in the trust instrument).

3. Statute of Frauds Not Applicable

Recall that the Statute of Frauds does not apply to trusts arising by operation of law. As a matter of fact, both as originally formulated in 1676 and as enacted in most jurisdictions to date, there is a specific exception in the statute for trusts of real property "created by operation of law."

a. Constructive Trusts

A constructive trust, even involving real property, may be founded entirely on oral evidence, provided the pleadings have alleged a cause of action and circumstances (*e.g.,* unjust enrichment) under which such a remedy is appropriate.

b. Resulting Trusts

Although a resulting trust is usually established without the use of parol evidence, it may be established with the aid of such evidence as necessary.

4. Retroactivity, Tracing, and Accounting

A decree establishing a constructive trust or resulting trust is normally retroactive to the date of the transferee's acquisition of title. The "trustee" is thus required to account for and pay over to the beneficiary or beneficiaries all profits realized from the property or its proceeds, and if the "trustee" has personally used or occupied the property, then for the fair value of such use or occupancy.

5. Duty to Convey Title

In most instances, a resulting trust or constructive trust is basically a "dry" or "passive" trust, in which the "trustee's" *sole duty* is to convey the property.

a. Constructive Trusts

A court decree establishing a constructive trust simply directs the trustee/title holder to make the appropriate transfer or empowers the "beneficiary" to demand the transfer. Where the constructive trust is to implement an intended express trust that requires more than placing title in an appropriate transferee (*e.g.,* to carry out the purposes of a "secret trust" that involved an intended but unenforceable *express* trust for X for life, remainder to X's issue), it is likely that the directed conveyance will be to another as trustee to carry out the terms of the intended trust.

b. Resulting Trusts

When a resulting trust is recognized and other provisions of an incomplete express trust have been fully implemented, the trustee's only remaining duties are passive, involving a conveyance to the settlor or other reversionary successor in interest. Where terms of an expressed trust remain to be implemented, the trustee may continue to have active duties to other beneficiaries plus resulting trust obligations (including active duties) to distribute excess earnings (and sometimes even unneeded portions of corpus) or to preserve, manage, and hold trust property for future distribution to the settlor or the settlor's successors.

B. Resulting Trusts

1. General Nature of Resulting Trust

The best way to understand the general nature of a resulting trust, or of a resulting trust interest, is to consider it equity's way of recognizing an equitable *reversionary interest*—*i.e.*, an interest remaining in a prior owner who, in making a transfer, made what turned out to be an incomplete disposition of the "beneficial" (*i.e.*, equitable) ownership. Thus, a resulting trust arises where the transferor, in conveying the property, did not intend for the person receiving legal title to have the beneficial interests—or at least the transferor is legally presumed not to have so intended—but failed to make a *complete or effective* disposition of the beneficial interests in the trust property. [Rest. 3d §§ 7, 8] There are three general types of situations that give rise to resulting trusts (*see* below).

---

a. Failure to Express Intent as to Some or All Beneficial Interests

In some resulting trust situations, the transferor did not express (presumably by oversight) an intention with respect to some or all of the beneficial interests in the property; *i.e.*, the transferor *did not make a complete disposition of the equitable interests*.

(1) Excessive Trust Res

Where the *amount* of property transferred to the trust proves, whether temporarily or permanently, excessive for the purposes of the trust, and no disposition of the surplus is indicated, courts may infer that the settlor did not intend to make a disposition of the surplus or to allow the trustee to retain it, but rather intended to retain it herself by way of "resulting trust" for her benefit or that of her successors in interest.

Example: Transferor conveys Blackacre "to Transferee in trust to pay such amounts of income as are necessary for the support of Beneficiary, and on Beneficiary's death to convey Blackacre to Charity." The income from Blackacre significantly exceeds the amount reasonably appropriate for Beneficiary's support. If the court infers that Beneficiary is not to receive *all* income and that the surplus is not to be accumulated for future needs or for future distribution to Charity, then the right to the excess income has not been disposed of (which may be considered to have been overlooked) and is payable to Transferor or Transferor's successors by resulting trust.

(2) Unanticipated Circumstances for Which No Interest Expressed

Where expressed interests are provided covering some but not all *circumstances* (other circumstances that may be considered to have been overlooked), the unused interests are held upon resulting trust for the transferor or the transferor's successors.

Example: Transferor bequeaths "to Transferee in trust to pay the income to Beneficiary for life, and on Beneficiary's death to transfer the principal to Beneficiary's then living issue." Beneficiary dies without having had issue. Because no provision has been made and no interest has been created for the circumstances that have materialized, the property reverts; *i.e.,* Transferee holds upon resulting trust for Transferor, Transferor's residuary beneficiaries, or, if none (or if the trust was itself a residuary trust), Transferor's heirs at law.

b. Expressed Trust Unenforceable

Where the transferor *has* sought to dispose of the equitable interests by express trust, but that trust is not expressed in a *form* that permits it to be enforced (*i.e.,* the transfer is not effective), a resulting trust may arise.

(1) Effect Where No Appropriate Remedy

If, under the circumstances, a constructive trust is not appropriate and the terms of the transfer are such that the transferee is clearly not allowed to retain the property (hence no need for a restitution remedy), then the beneficial interest has not been effectively disposed of but remains as a reversion in the transferor (or her successors) by way of resulting trust.

Example: Consider the following two examples. Transferor creates a will that gives the residuary estate "to Transferee, as trustee" but specifies no beneficiaries or other trust terms in the will. Alternatively, Transferor creates a will that gives the residuary estate "to Transferee in trust upon such terms as I have or may communicate to Transferee during my lifetime" and no other trust terms are included in the will. Assuming no special circumstances exist (such as actual fraud) requiring a constructive trust for Transferor's estate or others, it is clear on the face of the instruments that Transferee takes in trust but (under the general rule today) the terms of the trust cannot be proved and cannot be carried out. In each example, Transferee holds on resulting trust for Transferor's estate for the benefit of Transferor's residuary beneficiaries or, if none, Transferor's heirs at law (*i.e.,* an equitable reversion remained in Transferor's estate).

c. Expressed Trust Fails for Other Reasons

Where the intended expressed trust fails, in whole or in part, for other reasons, the interests that fail (assuming the gaps are not to be filled by construction, allowing the transferee or other beneficiaries to take by implication or acceleration) remain in the transferor so that the property is held upon resulting trust for the transferor or her successors.

(1) Failure of Interest for Illegality, Impossibility, or Impracticability

Such a situation may arise because the failure is immediately or subsequently discovered that some (or all) of the beneficial interests cannot be carried out because such carrying out would be illegal, impossible, or impracticable to do.

Example: Transferor, a chef, bequeaths her residuary estate "to Transferee in trust to provide scholarship funds for the benefit of the outstanding students of my alma mater, the National Culinary Institute for Excellence." Ten years later when Transferor's dies and the will is admitted to probate, the National Culinary Institute of Excellence is closed. Transferor had never updated or altered her will. The court in a proper proceeding holds that the cy pres doctrine is inapplicable, and the charitable trust fails. In that instance, Transferee now holds the residuary estate upon a resulting trust for Transferor or, in this case, Transferor's successors in interest, who would be Transferor's heirs at law.

e.g. **Example:** Transferor bequeaths "to Transferee in trust for the benefit of Beneficiary until Beneficiary reaches age 25, the principal and any unexpended income then to be paid over to Beneficiary." Beneficiary, however, predeceases Transferor and all of Beneficiary's interests lapse and others are not substituted by antilapse statute (*see* Wills Summary). Had Beneficiary survived Transferor there would have been a complete disposition (because, by normal rules of construction, Beneficiary's future right to the property is indefeasibly vested so that even her death before attaining age 25 would not cause her interest to fail, rendering the disposition incomplete). Because here Beneficiary predeceased Transferor, the intended interest fails and the equitable rights in the property are not effectively disposed of. Transferee holds upon resulting trust for Transferor's estate (*i.e.,* for Transferor's residuary beneficiaries or heirs at law).

(2) Failure of Interest Due to Disclaimer

Sometimes a transfer is altogether complete on its face, but one or more of the beneficiaries renounces his equitable interests. Often the gaps in these situations are filled by statute, by construction, or by acceleration of a remainder interest (*e.g.,* S devises to L for life, remainder to R; on disclaimer by L the remainder to R will accelerate, as if L had died). But if no gap filling provision applies, the void created by the disclaimer leaves a part of the equitable interests in the property undisposed of, *i.e.,* there is a reversionary interest, and the trustee holds (in part at least) upon a resulting trust for the transferor or the transferor's successors in interest.

2. Consequences of Such Cases

In all of these cases, a resulting trust arises by operation of law with respect to all or some equitable interests in the property (either some quantity or portion or some present or future interest) because the deed or will failed to make **complete, effective disposition** of the property. In other words, some interests remain in the grantor (or the grantor's estate) after the court has considered the various possibilities for filling in the gaps or deficiencies by construction of the instrument and has also considered any alleged grounds for remedial action in the form of a constructive trust either in favor of the intended beneficiaries or to effect restitution to the transferor or her successors in interest. The recognition and enforcement of resulting trust interests also assumes that the failure to make effective disposition was not the result of any illegality of a type that leaves the transferor with "unclean hands" such that a court of equity will refuse to intervene.

COMMON TYPES OF RESULTING TRUSTS	GILBERT
A RESULTING TRUST MAY ARISE BY OPERATION OF LAW WHEN:	
☑ The transferor has *failed* (in whole or in part) *to make a complete or effective disposition of all equitable* (or beneficial) *interests* in the property	
☑ An otherwise properly created interest *fails due to illegality, impossibility, or impracticability*	
☑ An otherwise properly created interest is *rejected* (*e.g.,* disclaimed or renounced)	

C. Constructive Trusts

1. Remedial Device—Not Really a Trust

A constructive trust is not really a "trust" at all. [Rest. 3d § 1] Like a resulting trust, a constructive trust arises by operation of law. But, quite differently from the resulting trust, a constructive trust serves as an *equitable remedy* to redress wrongful conduct or prevent unjust enrichment. A constructive trust is imposed whenever a court of equity is convinced that the person who acquired title to the property is under an equitable *duty to convey it to another* because the property acquisition was by fraud, duress, mistake, etc., or because (in certain appropriate circumstances) the holder of title would be unjustly enriched if the holder were permitted to retain the property. In essence, a constructive trust is not designed to effectuate an expressed trust intention but rather is to serve as *a remedial device to prevent injustice*.

EXAM TIP

Keep in mind that despite the term constructive "trust," a constructive trust is not really a trust at all. A constructive trust is an *equitable remedy* imposed to *redress wrongful conduct* or *prevent unjust enrichment*. Usually, the constructive trustee's *only* duty is to convey the property to the person who would have owned it *but for* the wrongful conduct.

---

2. When Oral Trust Unenforceable

Courts often apply the constructive trust remedy when property was transferred by one person to another on an intended trust but the trust is unenforceable. Usually, in such cases the express trust fails because of lack of formalities (*e.g.,* oral promise to hold in trust made with respect to land or assets passing by will). Then, if the trustee refuses to carry out the unenforceable oral trust agreement, courts of equity will, *in appropriate circumstances*, impose a constructive trust. The rationale is that failing to do so would encourage and reward wrongdoing or constitute unjust enrichment to permit the trustee to retain the property outright.

3. As Remedy for Breach of Fiduciary Duty

A constructive trust may also be imposed when property is obtained by one person through breach of a fiduciary duty owed to another.

Example: A trustee absconds with trust funds and uses the money to buy a house for himself; a constructive trust may be imposed on the house in favor of the beneficiaries whose funds were taken.

a. Other Situations

A constructive trust is by no means limited to the wrongdoing of trustees. Constructive trusts may be imposed whenever fiduciary duties are owed by one person to another, *e.g.,* an attorney to a client, a guardian to a ward, an executor or administrator to the beneficiaries of a decedent's estate, the director of a corporation to the corporation or its shareholders. (*See* Corporations Summary for discussion of duty of a director not to appropriate for himself a "corporate opportunity" and other such breaches.)

4. As Remedy in Nontrust Situations

The constructive trust remedy is also available as a remedy to prevent unjust enrichment and to rectify wrongs in nontrust situations. The following are the most common applications.

a. Fraud

Suppose the transferee defrauds the transferor into transferring title and possession of Greenacre to the transferee by falsely promising to make valuable improvements on the property, which will benefit other property owned by the transferor. In transferring the property to the transferee, the transferor in no way intended to retain any interest, and the transferee certainly did not intend to assume any fiduciary duties; neither intended to create a trust. Nevertheless, upon discovery of the fraud, the transferor can sue to impose a constructive trust upon the wrongfully obtained profits and property (or its proceeds if the property has been sold); *i.e.,* the law will impose a fiduciary status with an obligation to reconvey title (or proceeds) and profits, even though this was not the actual intention of the parties.

(1) Actual Fraud

In such situations, the constructive trust remedy is generally appropriate only where the transferee is guilty of actual fraud. One who makes a promise *never intending to perform* is guilty of fraud, and if this can be shown, a constructive trust would be proper. A mere broken promise is normally not enough; however, other remedies may be available even where a constructive trust is not.

(2) Abuse of Fiduciary or Confidential Relationship

If the promisor (transferee) stands in a fiduciary or confidential relationship to the party from whom the promisor acquired the property, most courts will then impose a constructive trust for breach of promise *without* actual fraud, the breach being a violation of the transferee's fiduciary duty (and hence, as some courts would put it, a "constructive" fraud).

b. Mistake

Likewise, a transferee who obtains property from another by *mistake* (innocent or otherwise) holds on constructive trust for the transferor.

Example: Grantor conveys two tracts of land to Grantee, while intending to convey only one. Grantee holds the second tract on constructive trust for Grantor, whether Grantee knew of the mistake or not. (*See* Remedies Summary.)

c. Other Situations

Imposition of a constructive trust is often appropriate where a transferee obtained title to property by conversion, theft, or duress, or where a transferee acquired title as beneficiary under the will of a decedent whom the transferee murdered, or as surviving joint tenant where the surviving joint tenant murdered the other joint tenant(s). A constructive trust may even be imposed on an inheritance where an heir (or even another person) wrongfully prevented the decedent from making a will.

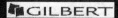
A CONSTRUCTIVE TRUST MAY ARISE BY OPERATION OF LAW WHEN:

☑ When a *fiduciary breaches a fiduciary duty*

☑ When the transferee obtains title to the property by *fraud, mistake, conversion, theft, duress, or homicide*

☑ Sometimes, when an express trust fails due to *lack of formalities* (*e.g.,* oral trust)

5. Effect of Transfer to a Third Person

If the wrongdoer sells the wrongfully obtained property to an innocent purchaser who purchases in good faith and for value, the wronged party's right to have a constructive trust imposed with respect to that particular property will be cut off. This is because, under the general rule, a transfer of legal title to a *bona fide purchaser* cuts off all hidden "equities."

a. May Reach Proceeds

Aa constructive trust, however, may be imposed upon the proceeds of the sale (and profits) in the hands of the wrongdoer under the "tracing" doctrine.

e.g. **Example:** Trustee misappropriated trust funds and used the misappropriated trust funds to purchase a television and stereo for Trustee's personal use. Later, Trustee sells the television and stereo to BFP, a good faith purchaser for value, and deposits the sale proceeds in a bank account. The trust beneficiaries (or a successor trustee) can have a constructive trust imposed on the sale proceeds (and interest thereon) in the bank account.

b. Not a Bona Fide Purchaser

If, however, the transferee did not give value (*i.e.,* was a donee), or if at the time of purchase, the transferee knew (or should have known) of the source of the funds used by the wrongdoer to acquire the items in question, or in some other way was on *notice* concerning the goods, In that instance, the transferee is not a bona fide purchaser and is not entitled to retain the goods. The transferee does not cut off the equities of the beneficiaries. In this case, a constructive trust can be imposed upon the items in the transferee's hands. The beneficiary then will have a choice of either of two possible constructive trust remedies to pursue: against Trustee for the proceeds or against BFP with respect to the television and stereo.

COMPARISON OF TRUSTS ARISING BY OPERATION OF LAW

	RESULTING TRUST	CONSTRUCTIVE TRUST
DEFINITION	Reversionary interest recognized where transferor *fails to make a complete or effective disposition of beneficial interests* in property	Remedial device imposed to *cure wrongdoing or prevent unjust enrichment*
IMPLIED OR IMPOSED IN FAVOR OF	Settlor or his successors in interest	Intended beneficiary or settlor

Review Questions
and Answers

Review Questions

1. Evaluate the following statements to classify each of the statements as true, false, or dependent upon additional information (and if so, what information).

    a. The main characteristic of an "active" trust is that the trustee must exercise discretion.

    b. Both a trust and a bailment can apply to any type of property, but legal title passes only under a trust.

    c. A trustee generally has more limited powers than an agent.

    d. If someone transfers money to someone else, the test for whether the transfer created a trust is whether the transferor intended to create a trust relationship with respect to the specific property transferred.

    e. The sole distinction between a private trust and a charitable trust is what purposes are permissible.

    f. A trustee would breach the trustee's fiduciary obligations if the trustee were to deviate from standard accounting principles for the allocation of expenses between income and principal.

    g. A constructive trust is not a fiduciary relationship with respect to property.

2. A would like to ensure that B is taken care of. To do that, A decides to convey certain property in trust to T, to be used for the benefit of B. The prepared written instrument does not use the word "trust."

    a. Does the absence of the use of the word "trust" prevent creation of the trust?

    b. Would the result be different if A expressed A's intentions in writing to create a trust but failed to communicate these intentions to B?

c. Assume that the written instrument uses the following language:

"To T with the hope and expectation that T will use the funds to provide support for B as T determines in T's absolute discretion." The quoted language is sufficient to manifest an intent to create a trust. _____

3. O obtains an option to purchase Greenacre. O writes to L, "I hereby convey Greenacre to you in trust for the benefit of my two children M and P." Assume that O exercises the option and takes title to Greenacre 10 days after writing to L.

   a. Is a valid trust created when O writes the letter? _____

   b. Is a valid trust created when O takes title? _____

   c. Assume that O receives the deed 30 days after exercising the option. At that time O sends the deed to L with a note paperclipped to the deed that reads as follows: "This is what you need to effectuate the trust I previously wrote to you about." Is a valid trust created now? _____

4. C owns various commercial real estate properties in Metroville. C conveys one commercial property to J "for life, remainder to Y in trust for H." J is uninterested in managing the property. J continues to ensure that property taxes are paid, but J does not rent the property and does not undertake any maintenance of the property. Y is concerned that the property is not being properly managed. Does Y have any cause of action against J? _____

5. D owns Blackacre. S properly obtains a lien on Blackacre. S writes a letter to T that reads as follows: "I convey all interest that I have in Blackacre to you in trust for B." Do T and B each have interests in Blackacre? _____

6. G borrows $5,000 from C and immediately deposits the sum in G's general checking account in G's sole name. G later becomes insolvent. C seeks to establish priority as a creditor by showing that G held the $5,000 in trust for C after the loan became due.

   a. Assume C has a signed letter from G to this effect. Is C likely to prevail? _____

   b. Would the result be different if the bank, rather than G, became insolvent? _____

   c. Would it make any difference if C had given G the $5,000 to hold in trust for B, and C now seeks priority over other creditors of the insolvent G? _____

7. S creates a trust for the benefit of B with T as trustee. S expressly reserves certain rights with respect to investments that may be made with trust property. May S properly transfer such reserved rights to another individual named Q? _____

8. K conveys certain property to M and L to be held in trust for Y.

a. Assume that M is a minor at the time the trust is created. Does this affect creation of the trust? _____

b. Would the result be different if neither M nor L qualify as trustees? _____

9. T owns an extensive collection of paintings. T validly creates a will that devises "my entire collection of paintings to A in trust for my child B for life, then to State Art Museum."

   a. If A becomes insolvent, do A's creditors have any recourse against A's interest in the paintings? _____

   b. If B becomes insolvent, do B's creditors have any recourse against B's interest in the paintings? _____

   c. Assume that A accepts the trusteeship. Five years later, A dies. A is survived by B. Upon A's death, does title to the paintings then pass to the State Art Museum? _____

   d. Assume now that A and C were co-trustees of the trust. A dies. B and C survive A. Would the result be different from any of the responses above? _____

10. A owns a thriving local restaurant. A conveys to E with a legal instrument reading as follows: "I hereby appoint you to hold and manage the restaurant in trust for J."

    a. May E refuse to serve as trustee because E does not want to manage the restaurant? _____

    b. If E accepted the trusteeship, may E resign even though the instrument does not designate a successor trustee? _____

    c. Assume that E accepts the trusteeship and commences operation of the restaurant. At the same time, E opens a bar next door to the restaurant and uses the same name as the restaurant for the name of the bar. The bar becomes popular with declining sales occurring at the restaurant. If J wishes to remove E as trustee, will J likely prevail? _____

11. F devises a farm that has been in F's family for over 50 years "in trust" to F's two sole surviving family members named G and E. At the time of F's death, G is insolvent. G's creditor C argues that C is entitled to satisfy C's claim from G's share of the estate. Will C prevail? _____

12. R has a beloved pet dog named Fido. R decides to create a valid will that reads "my residuary estate to T in trust to care for Fido." R dies with R's will properly admitted to probate. Has a valid trust been created? _____

13. W conveys W's securities holdings to V "in trust for my son Q, all holdings to be paid to Q when he reaches age 21." A further provision of the trust requires V to employ the services of I, an investment analyst, in managing the portfolio. If V decides to handle the investments, may I sue to enforce the trust provisions? _____

14. F conveys a parcel of real property "to X in trust for H for life, then in trust for those designated as beneficiaries in my last will and testament." Has a valid trust been created? _____

15. U devises U's stamp collection to W "in trust for the family of my late sister O, to be allocated as W so chooses."

    a.   Is this a valid trust? _____

    b.   Would the result be different if the devise were to W "in trust for yourself or for the family of my late sister O"? _____

16. T creates a valid will that gives $100,000 to E "in trust for all of my good friends from my fraternity days." Is this a valid trust? _____

17. P conveys Blueacre "to Y in trust for my cousin C"

    a.   Does C have any interest in Blueacre? _____

    b.   Would C's interest, if any, change if the conveyance were "to Y, to sell for the best available price and to hold the sale proceeds in trust for C"? _____

18. V conveys an office building to F "in trust for my grandchildren, provided no distribution of income is made until they reach majority."

    a.   Has V created a valid trust? _____

    b.   Would the result be different if the conveyance were "to F in trust for my cousin L for life, remainder to my grandchildren"? _____

19. D wrote an email to D's niece Q that states as follows: "In consideration for your assistance in editing my latest book, I promise to hold one-fifth of the royalties therefrom in trust for your children, G and H." Does this result in creation of a trust? _____

20. W declares in writing to L, "I hereby appoint myself trustee of my City apartment building for L." W properly executes and records a deed that provides W is the grantor and W as trustee is listed as the grantee. Is this sufficient to create an enforceable trust? _____

21. C bequeaths C's fracking company, C's collection of vintage automobiles, and C's first-edition book collection in trust for the benefit of C's sole grandchild E. E has actively campaigned against fracking and refuses to own an automobile. E does, however, love books and want the first-edition book collection. May E renounce an interest in the fracking company and the automobiles while accepting the interest in the book collection? _____

22. S orally agrees to hold the recently acquired proceeds from the sale of S's single-family house in trust for J. S then uses the proceeds to buy a condominium. Can J enforce the trust as to the condominium? _____

23. Z deeds Z's bed-and-breakfast inn to K, upon an oral trust for O. With K's knowledge and consent, O finances an expensive marketing campaign to increase business at the bed-and-breakfast.

    a. If K denies any trust agreement, may O enforce O's rights as beneficiary? _____

    b. Suppose that K and O operate the bed-and-breakfast inn for several months, whereupon K files for personal bankruptcy and K's creditors seek to have the motel declared a part of K's estate. Will the creditors be successful? _____

24. M conveys all of M's real property to T, upon T's oral representation that T will hold the property in trust for M's spouse U and will properly manage the property after M's death. After the conveyance, T refuses to perform as trustee and asserts title to the property outright. Can U enforce the trust? _____

25. H asks H's friend I if I will manage H's property as trustee for H's spouse L, should H die before L. I agrees, whereupon H executes a will leaving all of H's property to I. After H's death, the will is admitted to probate. I and L survive H. I asserts full title to the property.

    a. Can H's spouse L enforce any rights to the property? _____

    b. Would the result be different if H's will had devised the property to I "pursuant to the trust previously agreed to by us"? _____

26. F conveys certain property to R "in trust for my child A, this trust to be irrevocable by me." Later F executes a will devising the bulk of F's estate "to R upon the existing trust for A."

    a. Will this devise be upheld? _____

    b. Would the result be different if F had retained the power to modify the trust? _____

    c. Would the result above be affected if the jurisdiction in question had adopted the Uniform Testamentary Additions to Trusts Act? _____

27. D insures D's life for $100,000, naming K as the beneficiary under the life insurance policy. In a typewritten memorandum, K agrees to hold the proceeds in trust for Z's family and acknowledges D's power to revoke the trust or change the beneficiary at any time. Is this a valid inter vivos trust? _____

28. Y opens a savings account in Y's own name "as trustee for my cousin, P." Subsequently, Y executes a will leaving "all my personal property, including savings and bank deposits" to W. Is P the beneficiary of an inter vivos trust at this point? _____

29. L conveys L's farm "to Q in trust for O and P." O then orally agrees to transfer O's interest in the ranch to R, who notifies Q of the transfer. Some time later, O prepares a written deed of gift transferring the farm to E, who fails to notify Q of the conveyance.

    a. May Q properly pay income from the farm to R?   _____

    b. Would the result be different if the trust property consisted of L's municipal bonds?   _____

    c. Suppose that prior to either attempted conveyance, O files a petition in bankruptcy. Can O's creditors attach O's interest in the farm?   _____

30. S conveys $100,000 "to A in trust for B, with corpus and income to be paid to B and no other." Shortly thereafter, B becomes insolvent.

    a. Are B's creditors entitled to attach B's interest in the trust?   _____

    b. Would the result be different if A had paid $5,000 in income to B under the terms of the trust?   _____

31. K purchases Purpleacre from N, but has title conveyed to I "in trust, with income to K for life and the remainder to the heirs of K." K is paid income by I until K's death. May K's creditors attach Purpleacre to satisfy their claims against K?   _____

32. O devises O's personal property "to D as trustee, to pay to my nephews and nieces in such proportion as D shall deem proper." Shortly after O's death, one of O's nieces named G attempts to assign G's interest in the trust to R.

    a. Is the assignment valid?   _____

    b. Suppose D indicates D's intention to pay a specified portion of the property to G, whereupon G makes the assignment to R. D has notice of the assignment, but conveys the property to G. Can R proceed against D?   _____

33. W deposits $30,000 in U's name "in trust for the education of my child Z, and for that purpose only." U calculates that Z's educational expenses will be less than $30,000. May U properly pay the excess amount to Z for Z's general use?   _____

34. T bequeaths the bulk of T's estate in trust to Private College, "to be used to defray the educational expenses of needy students of Private College from Ruralville, Montaska."

    a. Is this a proper charitable trust?   _____

    b. Would the result be different if, in addition to the above provision, T's trust also provides that a portion of the trust property be devoted to the care and feeding of T's pet parrot Petunia?   _____

35. L conveys property to F in trust "for use in spreading the conservative philosophy of government to the general public." Is this a charitable trust? _____

36. H bequeaths certain property in trust to an order of Franciscan monks "for the purpose of daily masses for my soul and for the perpetual care of my grave site." Has J created a charitable trust? _____

37. E discovers that E has an incurable illness and is told that E has no more than six months to live. Two weeks before his E's death, E conveys all of E's property in trust for the advancement of the Next Life Church, in order to enhance E's chances for reincarnation. Is this a proper charitable trust? _____

38. I bequeaths $5 million in trust to found a private school, with P (a private individual) as trustee, that will be "exclusively for Caucasian females." Is this a valid charitable trust? _____

39. W devises $250,000 in trust to provide shelter for the homeless in Metro City, which has a population over 10 million "but if such purpose fails, then to the heirs of my grandchildren." W dies survived by two children. Several months after W's death, Metro City commences its own plan to provide public housing for the homeless, a plan which had been in progress for several years. Will the trust fail? _____

40. O conveys certain property to X and Y in trust for Q. Shortly thereafter, Y's personal creditors attempt to attach the trust property to satisfy claims against Y. X seeks a temporary restraining order against this action, but Y refuses to join in the application. May Y's creditors have the application denied on this ground? _____

41. E is appointed trustee of an investment portfolio, to be managed for the future educational expenses of the settlor's children.

    a. If E administers the trust as would a reasonable person, has E fulfilled E's duty of care as trustee? _____

    b. If E is an investment analyst by profession, will E be held to a higher standard of care than the ordinary trustee? _____

42. O conveys a large apartment complex to D, a businessman, in trust for J. D hires C as a live-in manager at the complex. Several months later, D discovers that C has embezzled $2,000 in rental income.

    a. Is D liable to J for this loss? _____

    b. Would the result be different if D and C were appointed as co-trustees, with C in charge of day-to-day operations? _____

43. S conveys certain property to W in trust for R. Thereafter, W (knowing R is in the market for a house) wishes to sell W's house to R.

    a. If the house is totally unrelated to the trust property, does W owe any special duty to R regarding such a sale? _____

b. Would the result be different if the trust property consisted of real estate holdings and W proposed to have the trust purchase W's house? _____

c. Would the result be different if W negotiates the sale of certain trust holdings to Z and receives a bonus from Z for the sale? _____

44. C, who owned a car dealership, is appointed trustee of certain property. May C properly compensate himself for arranging the purchase of a car for the beneficiary out of trust funds? _____

45. State Bank is a corporate entity with fiduciary powers. State Bank has been properly serving as trustee for five separate and unrelated trusts. State Bank learns of a large real estate development that it considers a good investment.

a. May the bank properly pool assets from the five trusts to meet the minimum capital contribution required for the development? _____

b. Prior to making the investment in question, the bank obtains insurance against its own liability to the trusts as a result of the investment. Is this proper? _____

c. Assume that State Bank consults its general counsel to determine whether such investment may be appropriate. General counsel replies as follows: "Regardless of the prudence of a particular investment, it must be of a *type* approved by statute before the trustee can commit trust funds to it." Is this statement correct? _____

46. V is named trustee of property for the benefit of A. Thereafter, V purchases a bar in her V's name, using both trust funds and V's personal assets. The bar fails to open for business due to zoning changes that V should not have anticipated. Is V liable to the trust for the funds invested? _____

47. G is appointed trustee of L's bank accounts "to pay a yearly income of $10,000 to N for life, then to P." G continues to maintain the checking accounts in proper form and to make the specified disbursements. Has G thereby fulfilled G's duties as trustee? _____

48. J is trustee of certain property for the benefit of D. W, a highly successful entrepreneur, tells J that if the trust lends W a substantial part of the corpus, W will pay the highest possible interest rate and will see that the trust has first opportunity to invest in W's next venture.

a. If W is clearly solvent, may J make the loan? _____

b. Suppose J obtains D's consent to the loan. Several months later, W loses W's entire operation (along with the loaned funds). Is J personally liable to D for the loss? _____

c. Suppose instead that J makes the loan without D's consent. W is able to repay only 50% of the principal. J makes a similar loan to F, who repays the entire loan plus interest and a "bonus" to the trust. D then sues J for the loss on W's loan. Can J offset the gains on F's loan against the losses on W's? _____

49. T is trustee for certain property under a trust instrument with a provision exculpating the trustee from liability for errors of judgment, carelessness, or negligence in administering the trust. T invests substantial time in a risky venture to which T has committed trust funds. Despite T's best efforts, the trust assets invested are lost. The investment was improper but not grossly negligent. Is T entitled to compensation for T's services on the venture? _____

50. L is trustee of a trust holding various parcels of real property. L contracts with M, an electrician, to make certain repairs on trust property. The written agreement for the repairs is signed by L "as trustee."

a. Can M sue L personally for monies owed to M under the agreement? _____

b. Can M proceed against the trust estate if the contract was imprudent or in excess of L's trust powers? _____

c. Could M proceed against the trust estate if the contract was proper *and* if there was an *effective* disclaimer against personal liability? _____

51. H is trustee of a trust that owns a flower shop. On a delivery run on Valentine's Day, one of the shop's employees negligently injured a pedestrian. Can the pedestrian hold H personally liable for the tortious conduct? _____

52. T is trustee of property for A, B, and C as co-beneficiaries. C makes an improper investment that impacts the trust property and results in a loss to the trust.

a. Do A and B have any recourse against C? _____

b. Would the result be different if, before A and B discover the breach of trust, C assigned C's beneficial interest to P, a bona fide purchaser without knowledge of the impropriety? _____

53. S devises S's apartment building "to U in trust to pay income to P for life, remainder to Q." S dies on March 1, and a final decree of distribution for his estate is entered on October 18.

a. Is P entitled to income from the apartment from March 1? _____

b. Would the result be different if the trust property devised by S was $250,000 and not the apartment building? _____

c. Suppose that P dies two years after S. Two days after P's death, U receives rental income on the apartment house for the previous month. Should this income go to P's estate? _____

54. S conveys property to D in trust for K and P, reserving the power to revoke the trust.

    a.   Does S have the power to modify the trust? _____

    b.   Could S exercise the power to revoke the trust in S's will? _____

    c.   If K and P agree, may they modify or even terminate the trust? _____

55. A devises A's house to C "in trust for B, provided, however, that the house not be sold prior to B's death." After A's death, the neighborhood is rezoned for industrial use as a stockyard. The house can no longer be used a residence.

    a.   May the court permit C to sell the house? _____

    b.   Could C be personally liable to B if C adheres to A's instructions and fails to seek court instructions respecting the sale of the house? _____

56. J purchases Q's farm for $50,000 but directs that title to the farm be transferred to L. J and L are not related. Some time thereafter, L attempts to sell the farm to W and retain the proceeds. J moves to enjoin L, on the ground that L holds the farm for J on a resulting trust. L seeks to introduce evidence of an oral agreement with J, whereby J had advanced the $50,000 purchase price as a loan to L (which L would repay out of the sale proceeds from W). J moves to exclude such evidence because of the Statute of Frauds. Should J prevail? _____

57. A executes a deed conveying A's mountain cabin to Y, upon Y's representation that Y will improve the property and convey it to A's adult grandchild, H, in one year. After the year has passed, Y asserts full title and refuses to convey the property to H. Will a constructive trust be imposed in favor of A? _____

58. M validly created a trust for the benefit of M's two children named D and K. T was properly appointed as trustee. The terms of the trust provide as follows: "T is permitted to distribute as much income and principle to and among the beneficiaries as T determines appropriate in T's absolute discretion."

    a.   Assume that D is 15 years older than K. K has requested that T pay for all of K's tuition and fees at Private College because T had previously paid for all of D's tuition and fees at Public University. T declines to pay for K's expenses. K files a petition in court to compel a distribution. Will K prevail? _____

    b.   Assume that M transferred 1,000 shares of Big Tech stock to T. T, knowing that M had a long employment at Big Tech, decides not to sell any of the shares. Is such decision appropriate? _____

    c.   Assume the terms of the trust are silent as to trustee compensation. T decides that T is devoting significant amount of time to the trust management. T decides to pay T $75,000 for "services rendered." Is such payment permissible? _____

Answers to Review Questions

1.a. **TRUE** — A trust is active if the trustee has *any* power or duty thereunder that involves the exercise of discretion.

b. **FALSE** — It is true that title passes only under a trust. However, a trust can apply to any type of property; a bailment can exist only as to *chattels*.

c. **FALSE** — The agent's authority is limited to what power is expressly *granted* by the principal, whereas a trustee is held to have all powers appropriate to a trustee's duties *unless* limited by the settlor in the terms of the trust instrument or by law.

d. **TRUE** — If the transfer is made without an intention that *those particular* funds be held or returned, only a debt is created.

e. **FALSE** — A key distinction between a private trust and a charitable trust is permissible trust purpose, but that is not the sole distinction. A distinction also exists with the beneficiaries.

f. **FALSE** — A settlor may in the terms of the trust instrument alter allocation of expenses. In addition, the statutory rules and common law principles related to allocation of expenses is not necessarily consistent with standard accounting principles.

g. **TRUE** — A constructive trust is an implied (aka remedial) trust. Although the word trust is used, a constructive trust is not best described as a fiduciary relationship with respect to property.

2.a. **NO** — Although use of the word "trust" may be helpful to establish intent, no magic words are needed to create a trust. The intent must be to create a relationship that the law would deem a trust that is essential.

b. **NO** — As long as there is an external expression of A's intent, communication to the beneficiary B is not required to create the trust. Notice that *neither* the beneficiary nor the trustee need be notified of the trust, as long as an effective transfer is made; nor need the trustee expressly accept the appointment (such acceptance being presumed in the absence of evidence to the contrary) for the trust to be created. As a practical matter, of course, the trustee will almost always be made aware of the trust when the trustee takes delivery of the property.

c. **DEPENDS** — Mere use of precatory words ("hope") will not create a trust under modern law. Use of the word "expectation" does create some complication as "expectation" is not one of typical precatory words, such as hope, wish, or desire. Added to that is the additional language of "to provide support" and "T's absolute discretion." An argument can be made that A intended to create a trust.

3.a. **NO**   O must ***own*** the trust property to create a valid trust. An option is not a sufficient property interest to create a trust.

b. **YES**   O must <u>***own***</u> the trust property to create a valid trust. While no trust is created when O writes the letter, when O takes title, a trust is created.

c. **YES**   Courts will generally hold a trust intent expressed prior to acquisition of the property to be sufficient if there is a manifestation of intent ***after*** acquisition that is consistent with the earlier expression.

4. **YES**   A trust of a future interest (here, a remainder) can be created immediately. Y as the remainderperson may exercise Y's right to prevent waste, etc.

5. **YES**   S has no legal title to Blackacre, but S ***can*** convey S's ***equitable interest*** (a lien) in trust. The trustee has the paramount equitable interest, while the beneficiary B has the subordinate interest.

6.a. **NO**   G and D cannot create a "trust" from a mere debt owed by one to the other. Instead, C has a general claim against D (absent some other type of security) and thus would have no priority over the other general creditors.

b. **NO**   In this case, the "trust" fails not only because it represents a general debt but also because there was no segregation of the monies deposited by D. G simply deposited the $5,000 into G's general checking account. Even if C had given G the $5,000 ***specifically*** to hold in trust, it is unlikely that C could establish any priority.

c. **PROBABLY YES**   Here, there is no underlying general debt; and the only possible question would be segregation of the monies held in G's checking account in G's sole name. However, if there were sufficient evidence of separation—*i.e.*, a "special deposit" of the $5,000 by G—then the trust would probably be upheld.

7. **YES**   Any rights that a settlor has may be transferred by the settlor to another.

8.a. **NO**   M's minority ***may*** affect M's capacity to administer the trust, and hence may mean that M fails to qualify as trustee. In that event, M's co-trustee, L, acquires the title to the property as trustee.

b. **DEPENDS**   The absence of a trustee in an inter vivos trust may cause the trust to fail because there can be no effective transfer of the trust res. However, there is no delivery requirement for ***testamentary*** trusts, and so the court could simply ***appoint*** a trustee—and this might also be done for an inter vivos trust if the trustees' failure to qualify is due to incapacity (minority, etc.). In the few cases where the settlor *explicitly* requires a particular trustee, *no* court appointment can be made and the trust will fail.

9.a. NO Whether A has full title or merely a life estate, it is a *"bare" legal title* without any beneficial interest. Hence, A's personal creditors cannot satisfy their claims against the trust property. Notice that the question specifically states that the creditors are A's personal creditors and do not thus have a claim on the trust property.

b. DEPENDS Additional information about the trust, specifically whether a spendthrift provision is included, and additional information about the creditors, such as whether the creditors are B's minor children, are needed to answer whether the creditors of the beneficiary may access the trust property.

c. NO In most states, A's "bare" legal title would pass to A's heirs (but without any beneficial interest in the paintings) *subject to the trust*. (In some states, title would vest in the court until a new trustee was appointed.) However, title would *not* pass to the State Art Museum until B's death (absent some other provision in the trust).

d. YES Absent contrary circumstances, co-trustees are deemed to hold title as *joint tenants*. Hence, upon A's death, the legal title would not pass to A's heirs but would vest solely in the surviving co-trustee C.

10.a. YES E is not required to accept the trusteeship and may refuse to accept the trustee for any reason whatever.

b. YES Now E has accepted the trusteeship. E may not simply stop serving as trustee. E must (1) follow the terms of the trust for resigning or (2) obtain a court *order* relieving E of E's appointment. E remains personally liable for E's trust duties until the proper resignation procedures are followed. As a result, E must continue to manage the trust property until the resignation is effective.

c. PROBABLY YES The standard to remove a trustee is high. E's action may involve a breach of trust responsibilities *and* possible conflict of interest, J would probably obtain a court order removing E as trustee.

11. PROBABLY NOT Here, G and E are both trustees and beneficiaries, which raise the issue of merger. Most courts, however, would hold that *no merger* has occurred (*i.e.,* that G and E each hold as trustee for the benefit of both). Thus, G's creditor C could *not* reach the estate. A few courts would hold that a merger *did* occur (in which case C could reach G's beneficial interest in the farm).

12. **DEPENDS**   R has attempted to create a trust for the benefit of a personal pet, who is not an ascertainable beneficiary. Thus, under traditional trust rules, R has not created a private trust (because no beneficiaries capable of enforcing the trust) and has not created a charitable trust (because the trust is limited to R's personal pet and lacks a charitable purpose). Courts may recognize this relationship as an *honorary trust*—if T is *willing* to apply the property for Fido's care, T will be allowed to do so. The vast majority of states today specifically authorize creation of so-called pet trusts, which a special purpose trusts that do not met the requirements of a private trust. If R lives in such a jurisdiction, a valid trust will have been created.

13. **NO**   I would be regarded as merely an *incidental* beneficiary, without rights to enforce the trust. Only the beneficiary Q (or if Q is a minor, Q's guardian) could commence such a suit.

14. **YES**   A valid trust has been created. Should H predecease F, X would hold a *resulting trust* for the benefit of F until the beneficiaries of F's will could be ascertained. Of course, the will must comply with the requisite *formalities* under the Statute of Wills.

15.a. **YES**   "Family" is a sufficient class description, and because W's power of selection among the class members is *mandatory*, W's discretion as to manner of allocation does not affect the validity of U's gift.

   b. **YES**   Now W has the power to include W. For that reason, no trust has been created. U has instead made a *gift* to W, subject to a general power of appointment.

16. **PROBABLY NOT**   A question arises about whether the beneficiaries are ascertainable. Although somewhat more limited than "all my friends" with the modifier "good" and the caveat "from my fraternity days," T's class of beneficiaries is still probably *too indefinite*. Accordingly, E would hold the property for T's successors in interest. Notice that E does not simply inherit the property.

17.a. **YES**   Under modern law, C as the beneficiary is regarded as having *equitable* ownership of the estate, while Y, as trustee, holds legal title thereto as trustee.

   b. **YES**   Here, C has an equitable interest in the trust property, which is equitably converted from one in land to one in the sale proceeds. Hence, it is an interest in *personalty* rather than real property.

18.a. **NO**   The conveyance violates the Rule Against Perpetuities, the rule against suspension of power of alienation, *and* the rule against accumulations; *i.e.,* in each case, it is beyond the period of lives in being plus 21 years.

b. **YES**	The gift to V's grandchildren would still fail (as violating the Rule Against Perpetuities and the rule against suspension of power of alienation), but the gift to L does *not* violate the rules and is therefore enforceable.
19. **PROBABLY NOT**	To create a trust, there must be an effective *present* transfer of the trust property to the trustee (who would likely be D); a mere promise is not sufficient. However, because there was *consideration* for the promise, it can be enforced against D even if no trust arises until royalties accrue.
20. **NO**	Even where the settlor is also the trustee, the settlor must demonstrate "delivery" of the trust res by *segregating* it from settlor's other property. Here there has been the execution and recording of a deed in the building to W as trustee for L. But such actions are probably not sufficient.
21. **PROBABLY**	It is doubtful that a beneficiary's acceptance must be of the whole of the property rights under the trust.
22. **YES**	The Statute of Frauds applies only to *real property*, and property is characterized by its *original status*. Here, the trust res was originally personal property (money), and its subsequent conversion into real property does not affect enforceability of the oral trust.
23.a. **POSSIBLY**	Even though it is unclear whether there was any transfer of possession, O's efforts to increase business by financing an expensive marketing campaign may constitute sufficient *part performance* to create an enforceable trust.
b. **NO**	As long as the trustee K performs under the oral agreement (and/or the trust is otherwise enforceable, as by part performance), *no one else* can challenge the trust under the Statute of Frauds. The statute merely bars enforcement against the *trustee*.
24. **NO**	U cannot enforce the trust directly because the Statute of Frauds renders it unenforceable. If, however, T *never* intended to perform, T is guilty of fraud and a *constructive trust* will be imposed in favor of U. Moreover, parol evidence to show the agreement and the fraud can be introduced. If T intended to perform at the time of conveyance, but *later* changed T's mind, there is a split of authority—although the modern view would still impose a constructive trust to prevent unjust enrichment. Many courts would impose the constructive trust in favor of the *settlor* M, rather than U.
25.a. **SPLIT OF AUTHORITY**	The oral trust agreement cannot be enforced directly, but most courts would allow H's spouse I to enforce the agreement as a *constructive trust*. Other courts would impose a constructive trust, but only in favor of H's *estate* (so that H's heirs, including

H's spouse, would take the property). In *either* case, I will not be allowed to keep the property for herself.

b. **SPLIT OF AUTHORITY**	Here, most courts would find that I holds upon a *resulting* trust for H's heirs (*i.e.,* that the provision is simply a defective testamentary trust). Other courts (and the preferred view) would find a *constructive* trust in favor of I's spouse the intended beneficiary.
26.a. **YES**	F has created a pour over will. The "pour-over" provision is effective because it was executed after the trust was in existence and the trust itself is nonmodifiable.
b. **DEPENDS**	If F did not actually modify the trust, the "pour-over" is clearly valid. If the trust *was modified*, the trend is to hold that the "pour-over" is valid and applicable to the trust as amended. Some courts would hold the "pour-over" invalid altogether or would uphold it only on the trust terms at the time the will was executed. Note that if the will was *republished* after the amendment, the "pour-over" is effective on the amended terms in all jurisdictions.
c. **YES**	The Uniform Act requires only that the trust be *sufficiently described* in F's will. It can be any preexisting trust.
27. **YES**	Life insurance trusts are considered nontestamentary, and retention of powers by the settlor-insured will not affect this result (unless *complete* powers are retained).
28. **DEPENDS**	The primary factor is Y's *intent*. If there is clear evidence that Y intended a trust after the will (*e.g.,* deposit book given to P), there is an inter vivos trust (a Totten trust). Absent such evidence, there is a split of authority. Some courts *reject* the attempted trust as an ineffective testamentary transfer; while the majority would uphold the trust even in the face of Y's will, unless there is evidence that Y intended *this* bank account to be included in the bequest (*i.e.,* had *revoked* the trust).
29.a. **NO**	Ordinarily, the first assignee *in point of time* (and in some states the first to *notify* the trustee) will prevail. Here, however, the conveyance to R was *oral* and is thus void under the Statute of Frauds.
b. **DEPENDS**	In most jurisdictions, an oral transfer of beneficial interest in *personal property* is effective, and R would prevail. Some courts, however, require *symbolic "delivery"* of the equitable interest in the form of a writing, and thus R would probably not be entitled to the income.
c. **YES**	O's creditors can reach O's interest in the farm (although they could not reach the farm itself because O is not the sole beneficiary).

30.a. **SPLIT OF AUTHORITY**   Nearly all courts would recognize the conveyance as a valid *spendthrift trust* and would thus bar B's creditors from reaching it. Few, if any, courts would either reject the trust as invalid or permit B's creditors to reach all or a portion of the *income* from the trust.

b. **NO**   While the creditors could reach the income actually paid, their rights to B's *interest* in the trust (to both income and corpus) would be the same as if no income had been paid.

31. **YES**   This is a self-settled trust. A spendthrift trust created by the settlor for *himself or herself* cannot be used to evade creditors; the creditors may attach the trust property even after the settlor's death.

32.a. **NO**   The beneficiary of a discretionary trust cannot assign any interest until the trustee has exercised the trustee's discretion.

b. **YES**   Once the trustee *exercises* that discretion by electing to pay some part of the trust to a beneficiary, the beneficial right vests and is assignable. Hence, D is personally liable to the assignee, R, for failing to convey the property to R.

33. **NO**   The critical language of the trust is "for that purpose only." A support trust is confined to the purpose of the trust, and *every* payment by the trustee must be applied towards that purpose.

34.a. **PROBABLY YES**   It is possible that the class of needy students from Ruralville, Montaska is so small that the requisite indefiniteness of beneficiaries would be lacking. However, the majority view would uphold the trust because the *group is indefinite* and the purpose (education) is ultimately *beneficial to the general public*.

b. **YES**   The trust must be *exclusively* for charitable purposes, and care of T's pet parrot does not meet the criteria for such a purpose (*e.g.,* sufficient public benefit).

35. **YES**   Dissemination of political views is considered an "educational" purpose, which is generally charitable *per se*.

36. **PROBABLY YES**   Most courts hold that masses for a deceased settlor are a sufficient religious purpose to make the trust charitable. Perpetual care of a grave is now generally held to be a charitable purpose; but even in those states that consider it a noncharitable purpose, a willing trustee likely may carry out the purpose as an *honorary trust*.

37. **PROBABLY YES**   Few, if any, states still restrict "last minute" gifts, and those that do apply such limitations only to *testamentary* trusts. Because E conveyed the property in an *inter vivos* trust, it would probably be upheld.

38. PROBABLY NOT — Even where a trust is *privately* administered, there may be sufficient *state involvement* to prevent racial discrimination under the Fourteenth Amendment.

39. DEPENDS — The gift over to W's grandchildren appears to violate the Rule Against Perpetuities; thus, it would fail. However, under the cy pres doctrine, the court might apply the trust res for other needs of the homeless (food, etc.) if this seems consistent with W's trust purpose. Otherwise, a *resulting trust* would be imposed for W's heirs (*e.g.,* the two children).

40. NO — While powers within the framework of the trust must be exercised *jointly* by co-trustees, there is no requirement that they act jointly in litigation. Hence, X's application cannot be dismissed because Y refuses to join in it.

41.a. NOT NECESSARILY — The standard of care and skill applied to trustees is that of the *reasonably prudent person* dealing with similar property for similar purposes (and, in some jurisdictions, of such a person handling her own property or the affairs of others). This may well *exceed* the "reasonable person" standard in many cases.

b. YES — A trustee is bound to use any special skills or abilities the trustee possesses—*i.e.,* to do the best possible job.

42.a. DEPENDS — Delegation by a trustee of day-to-day apartment operations is probably proper (*i.e.,* a *"ministerial"* function of the trust). Hence, D would be liable for C's embezzlement only if D had not exercised prudence in making the delegation (*e.g.,* C had a criminal record, etc.) or in general supervision of the accounts. Notice that the embezzlement was discovered within a matter of months, suggesting that D was regularly reviewing the accounts. If the embezzlement was not discovered for an extended period of time, it may be the case that D was not properly supervising the trust.

b. PROBABLY NOT — Each trustee owes the same duty of care in monitoring accounts to guard against mismanagement or malfeasance by a co-trustee (although D is *not an insurer* of C's honesty).

43.a. YES — W owes a duty of *utmost fairness* in *any* transaction with the beneficiary, R. This would probably include disclosure of all relevant facts regarding the value of the property, fairness of price, etc. Also, W would have the burden of proving that W had met this standard.

b. YES — The trustee *cannot* sell personal assets to the trust estate; such a sale is *voidable* by the beneficiary, R, *regardless* of W's good faith or "fairness" to the trust, because it constitutes prohibited self-dealing.

c. **NO**		Here again, this sale is *voidable* because W violates W's fiduciary duties by accepting compensation from a third person (Z) in connection with administration of the trust.
44. **DEPENDS**		If this was reasonably related to C's trust duties (*e.g.,* trust to "provide necessaries" to beneficiary), C might be entitled to some compensation. However, the purchase of a car through C's *own* dealership may be voidable, and any profit or commission received would be owed to the beneficiaries.
45.a. **YES**		It is not improper for a corporate entity to pool funds from several trusts for a common investment, as long as the trustee is acting in good faith in its capacity as trustee.
b. **YES**		As part of its general *duty to safeguard* the trust estate, the trustee is obliged to obtain insurance on the trust property—including insurance on its own liability (because this serves to protect the trust res as well as the trustee).
c. **NO**		The majority of states follow the Prudent Investor Rule that applies the usual standard of care, skill, and caution to the trustee's investment decisions. Some states still have "statutory lists" of approved types of investments. In those instances, the statement is accurate. However, the trust instrument itself can always approve an investment not on the list, and other statutory lists are *permissive* rather than mandatory.
46. **SPLIT OF AUTHORITY**		Some states hold the trustee *absolutely liable* for trust assets commingled with the trustee's own funds, and in such states V would be liable for the loss. In most states, however, V would be liable only where the commingling *caused* the loss—which is not the case in this situation.
47. **NO**		A trust estate consisting of *money* should at least be placed in an interest-earning account, where this will not interfere with the trust purpose. Disbursements to the beneficiary N are predictable enough for the trustee G to structure the accounts to earn interest and still pay the beneficiary N as required.
48.a. **PROBABLY NOT**		Despite W's solvency, the high interest rate, and the promise of future investments, this is still an *unsecured* loan, and such loans of substantial trust assets are generally improper.
b. **DEPENDS**		Ordinarily, the trustee would be liable to the beneficiary for the loss on this improper investment. Here, however, the beneficiary provided consent in advance of the investment. D is competent, D's affirmative consent to the loan may *estop* D from holding J liable.
c. **PROBABLY NOT**		The two loans appear to be separate "imprudent investments." Accordingly, such the gains from one *cannot* be offset against

the losses on the other by a trustee sued for breach of trust. The trustee J would thus be liable for the loss on W's loan.

49. **NO**

Although the exculpatory clause probably relieves the trustee of any liability for the improper investment, it ***does not authorize*** such investments so as to permit compensation for the trustee's time devoted thereto.

50.a. **NO**

The signature "as trustee" is probably a sufficient disclaimer by the trustee L of personal liability on the contract.

b. **PROBABLY NOT**

If the contract was ***improper***, no disclaimer would be given effect. Only if the trustee was ***insolvent*** would a possible suit for restitution against the trust be permitted.

c. **YES**

Most courts allow direct action against the trust estate under such circumstances.

51. **YES**

The trustee is personally liable for torts by agents as well as torts by the trustee. T would, however, be entitled to ***indemnification*** from the trust for any such liability, ***and*** the pedestrian can reach the trust estate in equity if the trustee is insolvent.

52.a. **YES**

As innocent beneficiaries, A and B each have a direct ***lien*** on C's beneficial interest for the amount of the loss. If C's interest is not sufficient to cover the loss, each has a personal claim against C for the deficiency.

b. **NO**

A BFP in this situation takes ***subject to*** the lien of A and B because an ***equitable*** (rather than legal) title is involved. And, presumably, A and B would still have their personal claims against C for any deficiency.

53.a. **YES**

The right to income from a ***testamentary*** trust commences from the ***date of the settlor's death***, even if there is an intervening period prior to distribution.

b. **DEPENDS**

Under the general rule, the result is the same whether the bequest is general ("pecuniary") or specific. Under the statutory rule, however, P would be entitled to the ***net earnings on a portion of the estate equal to the pecuniary amount*** from the date of S's death.

c. **SPLIT OF AUTHORITY**

Under most statutes, the income would be ***apportionable***—so that P's estate would receive the portion of income that accrued before P's death, and Q would receive the income that accrued after P's death. A minority of states would pay the ***entire*** amount as income to Q. The same result would obtain under common law rules.

54.a. **YES**

If the power to revoke is ***unrestricted***, a power to modify the trust is also generally implied.

b. **DEPENDS**   If the trust property is a savings account (*Totten trust*), revocation by will is allowed. Also, such revocation is allowed if the trust instrument ***expressly authorizes*** it. Otherwise, the revocation must be made inter vivos.

c. **PROBABLY NOT**   ***All*** beneficiaries must consent to the modification or termination; all must be legally competent (or in some states represented by a guardian); and the action cannot defeat a "material purpose" of the settlor in creating the trust. Here, insufficient facts are provided to evaluate whether the modification or termination would defeat a material purpose.

55a. **YES**   Here, an ***unforeseen change of circumstances*** has created a need to sell. The settlor's instructions to the contrary are not conclusive where (as here) a sale is required to preserve the trust estate and provide for the beneficiary.

b. **YES**   The circumstances justifying a deviation from the settlor's instructions are clear, and the trustee would be in breach of the trustee's fiduciary duties if he failed to apply for appropriate court instructions.

56. **NO**   Evidence tending to rebut a trust arising by operation of law (*e.g.,* a resulting trust) is ***not*** governed by the Statute of Frauds and can be entirely oral.

57. **DEPENDS**   If Y made the promise to reconvey, never intending to perform, Y is guilty of ***fraud*** and a constructive trust could be declared. If, however, Y made the promise intending to perform but later changed her mind, no constructive trust could be declared and A would be limited to contractual relief.

58.a. **PROBABLY NOT**   The trust is discretionary. Unless the beneficiary can establish that the trustee's decision is capricious or malicious, the beneficiary will have difficulty compelling a distribution. Here, the trustee has previously paid for one of the beneficiary's educational expenses and is now declining to pay for another beneficiary's educational experiences. Additional facts would need to be known as to whether this decision is problematic. The trustee, for example, may have made significant distributions for K's benefit. The amount of requested funds may be dramatically different. The trust property may have declined in value. Although the trustee has a duty of impartiality, that does not mean that the beneficiaries will receive an equal amount of funds from the trust.

b. **NO**   The duty of prudence requires the trustee to invest with regard to diversification. Although the trustee may be correct that the stock has sentimental value to the settlor, the trustee must act in the best interests of the beneficiary. An undiversified portfolio creates problems. Note that the trust terms do not specifically state that the trustee retain the original assets or invest without regard to diversification.

c. **PROBABLY NOT**   When the trust terms are silent, the trustee is entitled to reasonable compensation for services rendered and reimbursement of reasonable expenses. What is unknown here is how the $75,000 is being calculated. This may be calculation based upon the number of hours devoted to trust management or a percentage of the trust corpus. A flat rate, however, is likely to be problematic because no method of calculation is presented. Such flat rate may not be considered reasonable.

Exam Questions
and Answers

QUESTION 1

Mary is survived by her two children named John and Martie. Mary is also survived by her father-in-law Ed. Mary had expended modest but increasing sums for the support and care of her father-in-law, supplementing Ed's own pension funds, which (due to inflation) had become increasingly inadequate to maintain his admittedly comfortable lifestyle.

Mary's valid will is admitted to probate. Mary's probate estate is substantial. Mary's will nominated her son, John, as executor. Mary directed that one-half of her estate go to her daughter, Martie, and one-half of her estate go to John, "with the request that he provide any financial needs that his grandfather, Ed, may have during his remaining years."

John has come to you for advice. Specifically, John would like to know whether (as a note from Ed's lawyer has suggested) John "holds the one-half share of the estate in trust as necessary for his grandfather's benefit." For present purposes, do not concern yourself with the precise terms of the trust, if one exists, but merely address the question of whether a trust exists. Discuss the reasons for your answer, the arguments for and against the trust result, and any additional facts you need to ascertain.

QUESTION 2

Tyrone's valid will is admitted to probate. Tyrone's will includes the following three provisions.

Tyrone bequeathed 100 shares of Tyrone Enterprises stock to each of four named employees, provided each survived Tyrone and was employed at Tyrone Enterprises full-time by the company at the time of Tyrone's death.

Tyrone's will also provides: "I leave my art collection to my trusted friend, Ani, to distribute such of the paintings and sculptures to such of my relatives and friends as Ani deems appropriate."

Tyrone's will then provides: "I leave the residue of my estate, including property not effectively disposed of under other provisions of my will, to Ani, as trustee, to buy, sell, invest, and administer the trust assets and to pay the net income in equal shares to my sister and brother or to the survivor of them, and then to distribute the remainder thereafter in equal shares to my then living nieces and nephews."

Ani hires your law firm for advice. Ani asks you what Ani's legal rights and duties are with respect to Tyrone's art collection. How do you respond?

QUESTION 3

Bryan deeded Greenacre to his sister Sybil. Bryan died a year later. Bryan is survived by Sybil and four adult children. Caleb, one of the four children, has special needs. A conservator was duly appointed to handle Caleb's property.

Although the deed made no reference to a trust, the conservator for Caleb consults you, alleging that the transfer was made pursuant to Sybil's oral promise to hold and manage the land for the benefit of Caleb. According to the conservator, Sybil had suggested this idea to Bryan because Sybil had greater skills in land management than did the conservator, who does not dispute this statement.

What obstacles do you expect to encounter in attempting to enforce Caleb's alleged rights under the law of a typical American jurisdiction? What added information do you need? In particular, explain the theories you might pursue, including the results you might expect from each, the allegations you would need to make in your pleadings, and the crucial facts that might aid or undermine your case.

QUESTION 4

Sam and Glynne were lawfully married in the jurisdiction of New Calisota. New Calisota has adopted an intestate statute that provides a surviving spouse is entitled to one-half of the probate estate. New Calisota is a separate property jurisdiction and provides that a surviving spouse is entitled to claim an elective share in the amount of one-third of the augmented estate, which includes probate property and non-probate property.

Sam received a terminal diagnosis three years ago. At that time, Sam established a revocable trust and transferred almost all of the assets titled in Sam's name into the trust. The trust terms provide for the net income to be paid to Sam annually and provide that on Sam's death the principal is to be distributed to State University for scholarships for academically gifted students. Sam and County Bank & Trust Co. serve as co-trustees.

Glynne only learned of the trust recently, and Glynne is very upset. In addition, Glynne learned that Sam's debts greatly exceed the value of his nontrust assets, and Sam's creditors are becoming quite restless.

(1)   Can the creditors reach any of the trust funds to satisfy their claims, now or after Sam's death?

(2)   Will Glynne be able to assert a right to any of the trust assets after Sam's death?

QUESTION 5

When Lara's daughter Jess turned ten years old, Lara decided to do some planning. Lara deposited $30,000 of her own funds in a savings account at S&L Savings in the name of "Lara, as Trustee for Jess." A few months later and each year thereafter, Lara's father-in-law Otto deposited $3,000 in this same account on Jess' birthday. These deposits (the $30,000 by Lara and a total of $30,000 by Otto) are the only deposits that have been made to this account.

Ten years after the creation of the trust, Lara died. The savings account now shows a balance of $64,000, including accumulated interest. The account records show that only two withdrawals have been made over the entire period of the account, and both occurred within the last year. The first withdrawal was in the amount of $10,000. Lara's financial records showed this money was placed in her personal checking account and spent for her own living expenses. The other was a withdrawal of $15,000, which was given to Lara's favorite nephew as a wedding present.

Lara's will bequeathed her personal belongings to her spouse and then left "the rest, residue and remainder" of her estate "including all funds on deposit in my account with S&L Savings" in trust for her spouse for life and then for Jess for life, with the principal thereafter to be distributed to Jess' then living issue. In a jurisdiction that recognizes the doctrine of Totten trusts, is Jess entitled to the $64,000? Can Jess make a claim for any of the $25,000 withdrawn from the account?

QUESTION 6

Shortly before his death 15 months ago, Ben transferred his 500 shares in Wind Energy, Inc. to Metroville Bank in trust, to pay the income to the Metroville School District "for the sole and exclusive purpose of providing a free lunch program on school days for all students in grades one through six." The stock, originally thought to be worth $800,000, has suddenly skyrocketed in value due to a technological breakthrough by the company and is now worth nearly $4 million. Despite the company's increasingly conservative dividend policy and its growth orientation, the trust's income will apparently now jump from $20,000 to at least $40,000 per year.

By serving moderately nice lunches to all students at Metroville Grade School last year, the income was sufficient to cover the cost of a comprehensive free lunch program. The school principal, the Parent Teacher Association (PTA), the District School Board, and the trustee bank all agree that it would not be desirable to expend more than $25,000 for the lunch program and that much better use could be made of the money (such as by providing books, other meals, afterschool care, or the like for the children of Metroville's few needy families). The school board and bank consult you and would like to know:

(1)   Can the trust purposes be broadened, and are there any serious risks in attempting to do so?

(2) Is it likely, as is now being contended by Ben's disgruntled heirs, that this trust is invalid because its purpose is not truly charitable?

QUESTION 7

Thirty years ago, Elycee devised what had long been the family farm "to my daughter, Diane, as trustee, it being my desire that she retain the farm with full power to lease, manage, and otherwise deal with it and in all respects to administer the trust in her sound discretion, for so long as my son, Ward [who then was and still is considered to be mentally incompetent], shall live, with remainder on his death to Diane if then living, or otherwise to her issue who are then living. For the duration of the trust the net income shall be paid or applied annually, one-half to or for the benefit of Ward and one-half to or for the benefit of Diane or her issue." By reason of inflation and other factors since Elycee's death, the cost of living has greatly increased and the value of the farm has increased as well, but the net income produced by the farm has actually declined.

Ward is now 50 years of age and in reasonably good physical health, and his conservator would like the farm to be sold. The conservator is also considering a surcharge action against Diane for not having sold it earlier: the conservator points out that the normal rate of return on trust investments in the community has been higher than the rate of return of the functioning farm for the last 20 years and particularly for the last 10. The conservator can prove that Ward (as partial income beneficiary with no interest in principal) would have been better off financially now and almost certainly will be in the future had a sale occurred at any time, say, 15, 10, or even five years ago, with the funds then being reinvested in a diversified portfolio of securities.

Ward's conservator would like your opinion with respect to the theories upon which he might now seek to urge or compel sale and to surcharge Diane. He would also like a brief assessment of his chances of success. (Incidentally, it is possible that Diane would be willing to sell the farm now if it appeared appropriate, but it is clear that several of her adult children would be adamantly opposed.)

QUESTION 8

A few years before his death, Seth deeded Sheepacre and Cowacre to Farmers' Bank in trust "to pay the income to my wife, Wendy, for life, and also to pay her such amounts of principal as the trustee deems appropriate for her comfort and welfare, with the remainder upon her death to be distributed to such of my children as survive her." Seth passed away a few years ago. Wendy is now age 70, and Seth's only two children, Abe and Bea, are ages 46 and 42. The three of them have agreed to ask the bank to terminate the trust and to deed Sheepacre to Abe and Cowacre to Bea, the children having agreed to provide Wendy with any support she might need in the unlikely event that her rather substantial independent resources prove to be inadequate. The bank has refused to terminate the trust because that would be contrary to the terms of the trust. Wendy, Abe, and Bea have petitioned the court for an order directing termination of the trust based on their consent.

Assuming Seth is now dead (and that he died intestate), what result should the court reach? Explain. Would the analysis change if Seth were still alive? Would it matter whether Seth supported or opposed the petition for termination? Would it matter if the trust contained a spendthrift clause, restraining alienation of Wendy's income interest?

QUESTION 9

Dominique was a collector of collections. Over the course of several years, Dominique had assembled quite a collection of expensive designer handbags from the capitals of fashion all over the world. Dominique's other collections included depictions of the Morton Salt Girl, coins of countries of the former Soviet bloc, Bundt cake pans, and many others.

The handbag collection was by far the most valuable of all of them. Individual bags ranged in value from one dollar to ten thousand dollars. At the time of her death, there were about 200 bags in the collection. The collection as a whole was worth over a hundred thousand dollars. She kept the bags stored in an otherwise empty cedar paneled guestroom closet in her house, each wrapped in protective cloth and packaged separately. She only used them on special occasions like the opera or weddings; she had a few more modest handbags for everyday use.

Dominique had two daughters, Gladys and Leila. Gladys was as much of a handbag afficionado as her mother and had her own collection of handbags. Leila, on the other hand, thought handbags were stupid. Several years before her death, when Gladys was visiting, Dominique told Gladys: "These are yours when I die. You know your sister doesn't care about them, and I want you to have them because I know you'll treasure them." She showed Gladys where she kept the collection, carefully unwrapping each one for both of them to admire.

When Dominique died, Leila had been living with her and taking care of her for about five years before her death. Over that time, Leila had sold one or two of the handbags to meet household expenses without mentioning it to Dominique. Dominique's will had a provision devising her various collections to Gladys and Leila, with instructions that they were to "take turns choosing among the collections, starting with Gladys, because she is older."

At this point, Leila had found out what the handbag collection was worth. Gladys took her turn and picked the Bundt pan collection. When Leila took her turn, she chose the handbag collection. Gladys protested, "You can't take those—Mom was keeping them for me! She wanted me to have them! She put them aside for me years ago!"

Gladys comes to you for advice. What do you tell her? What questions do you have?

QUESTION 10

Your client, Bob Figueroa, is an obstetrician. He is a very conscientious doctor and his patients love him, but he nonetheless worries about malpractice lawsuits. He knows that his field of medicine sees the most malpractice suits and the highest damage awards, and he wants to protect himself, although he has so far not had any problematic births in his practice. He wants advice from you about setting up a trust to preserve his assets for his family and protect them from possible future creditors. The state where you both live has not adopted any new trust forms in recent years. What advice can you give him about his options? For each option, explain their advantages and disadvantages.

ANSWER TO QUESTION 1

The question of whether a trust exists requires consideration of the language used by Mary in the terms of her will. While no "magic words" are required to be used, Mary does need to manifest sufficient intent to create a fiduciary relationship with respect to property. Consideration includes the language of the will "with the request that he [i.e., John] provide any financial needs that his grandfather, Ed, may have during his remaining years." In addition, Mary's lifetime support of Ed can be considered.

Arguments for a Trust Result: The language may be interpreted to manifest intent to create a trust. In general, *precatory language* is not sufficient to create a trust. Precatory words (such as "hope," "wish, and "desire") are just that—mere requests or suggestions, and not expressions of trust intent or of obligation. Mary's will uses slightly stronger words by stating "with the request." This language could be interpreted to be an expression of an intent to create a trust.

Facts and circumstances may also overcome the judicial reluctance to base a trust upon precatory language.

The other provisions in the will may suggest that a trust was intended. In other words, Mary has already identified John as a fiduciary by nominating John to be her executor. Some authorities have indicated that precatory language is more likely to be interpreted as an expression of trust intent if it is addressed to a transferee (in this case John) who stands in a *fiduciary capacity*.

Mary's lifetime support of Ed may suggest that a trust was intended so that Mary's lifetime pattern of supporting Ed would continue after her death. Courts are influenced by whether the trust will produce, under the circumstances, what appears to be a *natural or an unnatural result*; here, the fact that Mary had been providing for Ed during her lifetime may invite the inference that providing for him is important to Mary. In those circumstances, the alleged trust would be a natural arrangement for her to make, particularly if Ed would otherwise be left in need. Without more information, this latter point is difficult to assess and thus requires further investigation into matters such as whether Ed's situation would be a serious one without some such provision.

Arguments Against a Trust Result: The language used "with the request" is ambiguous and could be interpreted as precatory. While Mary does not use the conventionally recognized precatory language of "hope," "wish, or "desire," Mary does not use words like "require" or "direct." Given the ambiguity, the language should be interpreted to be precatory.

Determining that a trust was created would create internal inconsistencies in the dispositive plan. A trust result would be inconsistent with the normally inferred intention to treat children equally. If John is found to take his one-half share of the estate in trust, subject to significant obligations to his grandfather, Mary's provision for John would not be comparable to the provision for her daughter, Martie. Martie's gift has no such language. Just how disparate the treatment of her children would be if a trust were found would depend on the terms and meaning attached to that intention. Furthermore, this uncertainty itself reinforces John's argument against finding a trust. Although the question does not ask for a discussion of the precise terms of the trust, the very fact that the language in the will is vague is likely to detract from any allegation that there was an intent to impose binding duties in the form of a trust.

While Mary had provided some support of Ed during her lifetime, Mary's support was of limited value. Given that Mary had substantial assets and provided most support, even though increasing over time, may be used to support the argument that Mady did not have an intend to provide continuing support.

ANSWER TO QUESTION 2

This question essentially raises the problem of whether Tyrone's will provision with respect to his art collection creates a valid trust or a power of appointment, or whether the plan of disposition with respect to such properties fails entirely. It is rather clear from the outset that Ani is not to take the art collection outright; thus, Ani is not free to retain the properties as Ani's own or to distribute the property between and among friends and relatives, as Ani chooses. A number of other problems and possibilities must therefore be examined as you respond to Ani's question about Ani's legal rights and duties with respect to Tryone's art collection.

Basic trust doctrine requires that a private trust have **sufficiently definite beneficiaries** to permit the trust to be enforced, or else the intended trust must *fail*. If the intended trust cannot be enforced, traditional doctrine would preclude Ani from voluntarily carrying out the intended purpose, even if Ani were ready and willing to do so.

Under typical American doctrine, one must consider whether the beneficiaries are **reasonably definite**. Clearly "friends" is **not** a sufficiently definite class of beneficiaries, even where a trust provides for discretionary selection. In contrast, terms such as "relatives" or "kindred" may or may not be treated by a particular court as sufficiently definite. A probable majority view would treat such classes as sufficient to sustain a trust on the theory that, if the trustee does not perform, the court can implement the trust by making distribution to those relatives that would take by intestate succession. A minority would consider "relatives" too indefinite, and the trust would fail. Even under the majority view, however, a court might well take the view that the trust in the present problem fails because of the intermixing of relatives and friends, resulting in an overall category of beneficiaries too vague to permit enforcement or implementation should the intended trustee fail to act. Then, standard theory continues, if the court cannot **compel** the carrying out of the trust, it cannot **permit** it; this non sequitur is criticized by many commentators and rejected by a tiny minority of American courts. The mixture of "relatives" and "friends" actually presents a more challenging question. It is possible that courts would take the position that, if "relatives" alone could be handled by applying intestate principles and disregarding the more vague class of relatives among whom distribution would be allowed but not required, one could do the same thing despite the addition of "friends." Among that admittedly less defined class, the intestate statutes could be used to carry out the trust if necessary, but allow Ani to exercise her broader discretion.

There is still another possibility here. Standard doctrine would allow Ani to carry out Tyrone's wishes if Ani's authority had been intended to be **permissive** rather than mandatory—*i.e., if Ani was intended to have a "power"* rather than to take in trust. It is not necessarily clear from the instrument that Ani was to be required to dispose of the collection; nor is it clear that the testator's residuary clause did not contemplate that very possibility. The residuary reference to properties not effectively disposed of by other provisions could relate simply to the Tyrone Enterprises stock, the bequests of which were conditioned; but that language could also have referred to portions of the art collection not disposed of by Ani, thus indicating that the testator had not intended to require but only to **authorize** Ani to dispose of that property, and to add it to the residuary estate if and to the extent he saw fit not to distribute it. The language in the provision for the art collection is similarly susceptible of more than one reading.

In short, it is possible to construe the provision with respect to the art collection as a power rather than as a trust, and it is also possible (though not probable) that a court would hold the provision sufficiently definite to permit Ani to carry it out as a mandatory trust intention.

ANSWER TO QUESTION 3

This question raises the issue of a potential secret trust. Such arrangements pose several obstacles, but some paths for recovery may be available.

Possible Obstacles: One obstacle to be considered in any instrument of transfer (whether the subject matter is land or personalty) is the **parol evidence rule**. In most states (and according to the Restatement), parol evidence is admissible in a case like this as long as the deed does not explicitly state either that a trust is or is not intended. In such a case the evidence is deemed not to contradict the writing but to **supplement** or complete it. Thus, although some jurisdictions do take a contrary view, in most states this rule would pose no serious obstacle.

The principal obstacle in the present case, which involves land, is the ***Statute of Frauds***. The Statute of Frauds precludes an oral promise from being proven to establish an ***express*** trust. There are, however, several bases upon which a ***constructive*** trust can be imposed for Caleb's benefit.

Theories of Recovery: The surest bases for having the intended trust carried out by way of constructive trust are ***fraud*** or ***breach of confidential relationship***, but each of these requires factual showings that may be difficult.

Fraud: In addition to the making of the oral promise, a fraud case (as distinguished from a simple breach of contract case) requires a showing that, ***at the time of the promise***, Sybil had no intention of carrying out her agreement; a subsequent change of heart by one who initially intended to perform is not a fraud. Further factual investigation will be required, with the allegations and factual concerns guided by these legal requirements for fraud. In this case, there is at least some indication that it was Sybil who suggested the idea, and this sometimes helps as a starting point for a fraud case.

Breach of Confidential Relationship: As far as abuse of a confidential relationship is concerned, the mere fact that Sybil was Bryan's sibling would ***not be enough*** to establish a confidential relationship, but it would be of some help if other facts also existed upon which to base and support an allegation of such a relationship. The facts here invite inquiry into whether Bryan had come to rely on Sybil's special expertise in the past in his management and decision making with respect to his properties. An actual ***prior dependence*** upon Sybil could lead to a finding that a confidential relationship existed.

Conveyance in Contemplation of Death: The facts also invite a consideration of whether Bryan's conveyance might have been made in ***contemplation of death***, although again the facts are not particularly strong without further evidence. There is at least some authority that an oral promise inducing a conveyance in contemplation of death can be enforced by constructive trust.

Unjust Enrichment: Beyond this, there is always the possibility of seeking a constructive trust as a remedy for simple ***unjust enrichment***. Most authority is against this, but there is at least a growing number of decisions allowing restitution via constructive trust where the grantor conveys to the grantee upon oral trust for ***the grantor***. Even this authority, however, poses difficulties in the present case for two reasons: (i) it is less likely to be applicable even by analogy to the grantor's transfer to the grantee orally in trust for a ***third party***; and (ii) even if a remedy is granted, it is likely that the constructive trust will be for the purpose of making restitution to the grantor (and here to the grantor's estate) rather than by "going forward" with the intended trust for the benefit of the third party. Such a result would likely be much less helpful to Caleb (depending, *e.g.,* on the terms of Bryan's will, if any).

ANSWER TO QUESTION 4

This question raises the issue of the consequences of a revocable trust both during the settlor's lifetime and upon the settlor's death.

(1) **Creditors:** By acting promptly, the creditors could reach Sam's life interest in the trust ***income***, but under the present facts this interest will have limited value given Sam's medical diagnosis. The question becomes whether the creditors reach the ***principal*** as a result of Sam's retained powers of revocation. In the absence of a statute, most jurisdictions have held that the creditors cannot, although there is a growing minority view on this point (and the property would be reachable under the federal Bankruptcy Code).

(2) **Glynne:** Glynne can attempt to have the trust declared wholly illusory and defective (*i.e.,* have it treated as a mere agency or an invalid attempt to make a "testamentary" disposition). Assuming Sam had no will (none is mentioned in the question), this would allow Glynne to seek a one-half intestate interest in the property ostensibly held in the trust. As mentioned above in connection with the creditors' claims, this line of attack is not particularly promising in the absence of further facts

that would undermine the reliability and seriousness of Sam's apparent intention to establish a trust during his lifetime.

Does Glynne's one-third elective share of the augmented estate stand on a different footing? This prompt requires you to connect concepts about trusts to concepts related to estates. In the absence of a statute, such as the UPC's augmented estate statute, which would bring it into the estate for purposes of the elective share. courts have held that it does not. In those situations, courts hold that a revocable trust *can* be used to circumvent a surviving spouse's elective share. Note that increasing case law (and an increasing number of statutes) give special protection to the surviving spouse's elective share. Many of these cases require a finding that the trust was intended to "defraud" the spouse, but most courts have rejected this highly subjective approach. There is very little other authority (absent legislation) recognizing a special status for a spouse's elective share with respect to such trust properties. It is fair to say, however, that on the more general question (mentioned in the prior paragraph) of whether a trust is entirely "illusory" and thus invalid, some courts have—without openly saying so—appeared to be more receptive than usual to such a challenge when it is brought by a surviving spouse.

ANSWER TO QUESTION 5

Under a normal application of the Totten trust doctrine, Lara's original deposit in the savings account would *presumptively* give rise to that special form of revocable or tentative trust known as a "Totten trust."

Under such a trust, the depositor is free to treat the funds as the depositor's own funds and to withdraw (*i.e.*, revoke) them for any purpose whatever (including to make a gift to another), but at the depositor's death the amount remaining in the account belongs to the person indicated as beneficiary in the account name (here, Jess). On the other hand, the nature of the account and the rights in it are ultimately dependent on the depositor's *intention*. The above-described arrangement is simply what is normally presumed, subject to rebuttal by a showing of different intention—*i.e.*, it may be shown either that, in depositing her funds in the account, Lara intended an irrevocable trust gift or that she had no intention to create any form of trust whatever.

The presumption is quite different with respect to funds deposited by someone *other* than the person whose name appears as trustee on the account. Thus, the deposits of Otto's funds in Lara's name as trustee for Jess would normally result in an irrevocable trust for Jess.

The whole of these circumstances may reflect upon and invite inquiry into the actual intention of Lara at the time of her deposit. The findings could lead to the conclusion that in this situation Lara's intention all along was to make a gift to Jess by irrevocable trust, into which she anticipated that Otto could likewise make gift deposits. If this were so, Lara would not be free to change her mind later and, in effect, revise the character of the trust.

Courts have also tended to treat the depositor's *disclosure* to the "beneficiary" of the existence of the trust account as some (but not conclusive) evidence of the depositor's intention to make an irrevocable trust gift. Thus, finding out how and when Jess learned of the account's existence would be a potentially relevant inquiry.

All of these facts and circumstances go to the primary question of whether and to what extent the funds may have been held irrevocably in trust for Jess, rather than in classic Totten trust form. This has a bearing on her right to claim the $25,000 (plus interest) withdrawn from the account, as a possible misappropriation by Lara. It also relates to Jess' claim to the $64,000 now remaining in the account. Under normal Totten trust doctrine, unlike the inference with respect to other revocable trusts, the *depositor's will can revoke the trust* and dispose of the funds. This, however, could not be done if the trust were irrevocable—as it would appear to be with respect to Otto's contributions, and as it would be even with respect to Lara's contributions if the initial presumption of revocability were found to be rebutted under the facts and circumstances of this situation. (Incidentally, it probably makes no difference whether the particular withdrawal was to meet the needs of the depositor or was for some other purpose, such as to make a gift to another.)

ANSWER TO QUESTION 6

This question asks you to focus on the potential modification of a charitable trust.

(1) **Modification of Trust Purpose:** The grounds upon which the purposes of charitable trusts can be modified under the *cy pres doctrine* are generally quite strict.

First, it must be shown that the trust's present purpose has become *illegal* or that it has become *impossible* to achieve *or impracticable* to use the intended funds for the intended purpose. Whether it is "impracticable" to use all the anticipated income from the trust for the purpose in question cannot really be ascertained from the facts here. Further and more precise inquiry into the issue of impracticability of the trust purpose must be made; it is *not* sufficient to show merely that all interested parties agree that spending all the funds for the present purpose is "not desirable" or that "much better use" could be made of the funds. Note that the new ground of *wastefulness* is not likely to be establish here. The funds relative to the purpose as not so excessive to constitute wastefulness.

Second, if investigation reveals that the purpose is illegal, impossible, impracticable, or wasteful, the possibility of cy pres modification requires, under the traditional view, a further finding that the settlor had, in addition to the specific trust intention, a *general charitable intention*. Otherwise, the surplus funds would revert via *resulting trust* to the settlor's heirs. Ben's heirs apparently would be inclined to object to cy pres on this ground, and a court might be influenced in their favor by the fact that the trust has been in existence for such a short period of time (although few courts openly state that time is relevant). The fact that Ben's expressed purpose was declared to be a "sole and exclusive" purpose should not be decisive if adherence to that purpose has become "impracticable" for reasons not anticipated by him.

Finally, even if it is appropriate to go forward with cy pres, the court would have to authorize the application of the surplus funds to a purpose that *approximates* the *settlor's original purpose*. This involves some risk that the funds would be used not for a related purpose within the same school district but rather, *e.g.,* for a grade school lunch program in a neighboring community. Further inquiry into this question might produce many relevant factors to be considered; *e.g.,* the nature and extent of Ben's attachment specifically to Metroville, or his interest in the grade school as distinguished from the high school or junior high school, etc., would be relevant.

(2) **Charitable Purpose:** It is unlikely that a particular court would find Ben's purpose noncharitable, although some might have their doubts. It is not fatal to a charitable purpose that it benefits persons who are not needy, as long as the purpose is otherwise charitable. The purpose in this problem could be to offer relief from poverty to some members of the community. The purpose may be to support good health by providing meals. The purpose could be deemed to serve a governmental or educational purpose, or to be a purpose of general benefit to the community or public. Even though Ben's heirs may be disgruntled, they would be unlikely to prevail on an argument that the purpose is not charitable. A finding of any of the above purposes would sustain this trust as a charitable trust.

ANSWER TO QUESTION 7

Under normal doctrine, this would not be an appropriate case for modification of trust terms based on consent of all beneficiaries, particularly because some of the remainder beneficiaries are opposed. Thus, discussion here will focus upon: (i) the meaning of the instrument; and (ii) whether there exists a basis upon which a court would order or authorize sale of the farm.

Elycee's "desire" that the farm be retained sounds *precatory*, and Diane was given "discretion" with respect to administration (although in context this language may refer to *how* to administer and manage the farm rather than whether to retain the farm). If this language is construed simply to mean that retention of the farm is recommended but not required, then Diane could have (and as time went on probably should have) sold the farm as an **underproductive investment**, inasmuch as it was—although not a disaster—an investment that produced noticeably lower income return for Ward than would have been produced by ordinary investments. If this is so, a court might even **surcharge** Diane for not having sold the farm sooner, if it found its retention to be an **abuse of "sound discretion."** Note the possibility of conflicting interests because Ward is dependent on the trust's income flow while Diane and particularly her issue likely want growth in the value of the principal. On the other hand, Elycee's expressed "desire" for retention, even if not mandatory, could lead to an interpretation that would allow reasonable retention even under circumstances in which it would otherwise be inappropriate to hold the property. (Notice that the facts of the problem offer the opportunity to discuss both sides of this issue, with the outcome uncertain.)

If, as a matter of interpretation, it is found that Elycee intended to **require** retention of the farm (Diane's discretion relating purely to its management), then the situation is very different. A **direction** to retain **must** be followed by a trustee **unless**, by reason of circumstances **not anticipated by the settlor**, adherence to the terms of the trust would jeopardize a trust purpose. Even if a purpose to provide for Ward's "support" can be inferred, it is not apparent that the purpose is failing or threatened if all one can show is that he clearly "would have been better off" with a different investment program. Thus, a more focused inquiry into the present facts would be required to ascertain whether the purpose of the trust is actually in jeopardy. An occasional decision has adopted a more receptive rule toward **equitable deviation**, but under traditional doctrine it is arguable that the trust is fulfilling its overall purpose, which relates to the economic welfare of the family as a whole. If, however, the facts establish that a trust purpose is jeopardized, Diane would have a **duty** to apply to the court for authority to deviate from the trust terms and could not only be forced to change investments, but might even be surcharged for failing to take appropriate action at an earlier time.

ANSWER TO QUESTION 8

The rules applicable to termination of trusts based on consent of beneficiaries vary somewhat from state to state, although the **consent of all possible beneficiaries** is uniformly required in the absence of a statute. Some courts hold (following English doctrine) that this consent is all that is required. Most courts require more than this; according to the *Claflin* doctrine as applied in most of these states, it must also be shown that the termination or modification requested by the beneficiaries will **not defeat a "material purpose"** of the settlor. Thus, applying this latter doctrine as the general rule, there are two basic concerns: (1) whether consent has been obtained from all possible beneficiaries (while it has generally been required that all be sui juris and consent personally, the trend is to allow **virtual representation**); and (2) whether the proposed modification or termination would defeat a material purpose of the settlor.

(1) **Consent from All Possible Beneficiaries:** Assuming Seth is dead, Wendy and the two adult children are the sole beneficiaries of the trust. This is so even though the children are required to survive Wendy in order to take, despite the contingency under which, if none survive, the remainder would be left undisposed of. In the latter event, the bank would hold upon a **resulting trust** (*i.e.*, a reversionary interest) for Seth's successors in interest, who happen to be Wendy and the two children because he died intestate. (Properly analyzed, the resulting or reversionary interest was left in Seth at the time the trust was created and passed on his death to his heirs at that time; the successors are not determined at the later time when the reversion materializes into a possessory interest.)

Settlor Alive: If Seth were still alive, Seth would be beneficially interested in the trust as the reversion holder; but it would be impossible to obtain consent of all possible beneficiaries inasmuch as there is no assurance that all possible children are alive to join in the petition—unless the particular court were prepared to reject the normal common law conclusive presumption of lifelong fertility (*i.e.*, the "fertile octogenarian" doctrine).

(2) **Material Purpose of Settlor:** Next, whether termination will defeat a material purpose of the settlor must be analyzed. In the original statement of the facts, nothing indicates any purpose that would be undercut by the proposed premature termination. In the absence of some affirmative indication of a particular purpose, courts are not inclined to imply a purpose other than the obvious objective of successive enjoyment by the successive beneficiaries (which is not in and of itself ordinarily viewed as an obstacle to termination). Although a protective or assured *support* purpose is sometimes found in the facts and circumstances or even implied from the form of the trust (*e.g.,* a wholly discretionary trust), it is unlikely that the mere inclusion of a discretionary power to invade principal has this effect.

Spendthrift Clause: A spendthrift clause *does* constitute a barrier to termination by consent in *Claflin* jurisdictions, but such a clause alone does *not* constitute a material purpose under the Third Restatement or Uniform Trust Code.

Settlor Alive: If Seth were still alive, the situation would be somewhat changed. The joinder of the settlor in a petition to terminate serves to remove any objection based on interference with a material purpose of a settlor. In other words, if all possible beneficiaries join the petition, they do have a right to terminate or modify with the *joinder* of the settlor. On the other hand, if there is no "material purpose" obstacle to termination by all beneficiaries, the settlor's *opposition* is properly irrelevant.

ANSWER TO QUESTION 9

This question invites consideration of whether a trust has been created. Personal effects may constitute trust property. The focus will be whether Dominique, the potential settlor, manifested intent to create a trust. Dominque did care for the collection, and she used items in the collection. Whether she does so in a way that is inconsistent with her personal ownership would be an inquiry.

The prompt invites consideration of what questions the attorney would ask of Gladys to gather additional facts. Those questions would include what writing (other than the will) references the collection, what the insurance rider (if any) states about the collection, and who may be able to testify about Dominque's statements about the collection. Remember that intent is critical to the analysis.

ANSWER TO QUESTION 10

This question raises the possibility of creating a self-settled asset protection trust. The prompt asks you to provide advice to Bob. You should raise both the legal implications and the non-legal implications.

Legal Implications: The question states that the jurisdiction has not adopted any trust forms in recent years. Nevertheless, Bob may create a trust with a situs (i.e., legal location) that is in a jurisdiction that does recognize self-settled asset protection trusts. The requirements of that jurisdiction would need to be reviewed but will typically include a requirement that a trustee (or at least a co-trustee) be domiciled in that jurisdiction. That likely means that Bob would need to hire a professional trustee, which can increase the cost of maintaining the trust. In addition, some jurisdictions have exceptions to which creditors may access the trust property. Research as to the particular requirements and exceptions would need to be undertaken. There may also be conflicts of laws and possible bankruptcy issues arising in the future if a creditor did try to reach Bob's assets.

Non-Legal Implications: It will be legally possible to have Bob create a self-settled asset protection trust that will hold the bulk of his assets. Such a trust would, as Bob is asking, protect his assets for his family and prevent his creditors (or at least most creditors depending upon the applicable exceptions) from accessing the trust property. Critics would point out that self-settled spendthrift trusts allow settlors to have the benefits of wealth without the responsibility. The cost of Bob's malpractice (if he were to commit malpractice) would be born by the individuals harmed and potentially broader society. Bob may face an impact on his reputation if it were discovered that he had chosen to create a self-settled spendthrift trust rather than obtain adequate malpractice insurance. That loss of reputation may also affect the number of patients seeking his assistance and the number of employees who wish to work with him in his practice.

Table of Cases

Americans for the Arts v. Ruth Lilly Charitable
    Remainder Annuity Trusts, 136
Berthot, In re Estate of, 27
Brainard v. Commissioner of Internal Revenue, 18
Broadway National Bank v. Adams, 89
Chapman's Estate, In re, 98
Claflin v. Claflin, 165
Feinberg, In re Estate of, 42
Flannery v. McNamara, 163
Fletcher v. Fletcher, 126
Howard v. Howard, 124
Huber, In re, 23, 90
Marsman v. Nasca, 121
Moore v. Jones, 79
Olliffe v. Wells, 72
Palozie v. Palozie, 14
Pulitzer, In re Estate of, 169
Rothko, In re Estate of, 140
Sullivan v. Burkin, 79
Toni 1 Trust v. Wacker, 91
Totten, In re, 76
Trust under Will of Stuchell, In re, 121
Ventura County Department of Child Support Services
    v. Brown, 127
Wood v. U.S. Bank, 136

Index

ABANDONMENT OF PURPOSE, XXXV
See also Modification and Termination

ABUSE OF CONFIDENTIAL RELATIONSHIP, 65–66

ACCEPTANCE
by beneficiary,
 acceptance presumed, 5
 assignment of interest, 56
 disclaimer, 55
 not essential to trust, 55
 partial acceptance, 55
 relation back, 55
 retraction, 56
by trustee,
 acceptance presumed, XV
 disclaimer, 55
 relation back, 54
 retraction, 55
 trustee's obligations, 54
 unaware trustee, 54

ACCOUNT, DUTY TO, XXVI

ACCOUNTING FOR INCOME AND PRINCIPAL, 149
accounting rules, 151–52
 impartiality, 152
  adjustment power, 152
 legally implied rules, 151–52
 trust terms, 152
 trustee discretion, 152
benefits, 153–54
 allocation, general rule, 153–54
 bond premium and discount, 157–58
  interest-bearing, 157
  noninterest-bearing, 157
 commencement of right to income, 153
 dividends, 155–56
 essentially receipts, 153–54
  unproductive assets, 156
 successive beneficiaries, 155–56
 testamentary trusts during administration, 153–56
 wasting assets, 156–57
burdens, 158–59
 assessments, 158
 business losses, 158
 depreciation reserves, 159
 general rule, 158
 mortgage payments, 159
 taxes, 158
 trustee's and attorneys' fees, 159
 upkeep, 158
  capital improvements, 159
  initial costs, 159
  insurance, 158
default rule, 150–51
generally, 5
 discretionary benefits, 151
 successive interests, 150

ACTIVE TRUSTEE, 4

ACTIVE TRUSTS, 4

ADMINISTRATION OF TRUSTS
beneficiaries, 144
 breach of trust, 145
 no indemnification, 145
 remedies against, 145
  impoundment, 145
duties of trustee, 120–44. *See also* Care, Skill, and Caution, 126
 impartiality, 123–24
 loyalty, 121–23
 prudence, 135–36
general responsibilities and authority of trustee, 120–26. *See also* Duties of Trustee
 preservation of res, 135
 productivity, 138
 sources of power, 120
powers of trustee, 120. *See also* Trustee
 amend or terminate, 121
 co-trustees, 128–29
  deadlock, 129
  majority vote, 128
  sale or transfer, 129
  unanimity requirement, 128
 delegation to third persons, 129
 discretionary, 36, 126–27
  absolute discretion, 127
  distributions, 128
  limited judicial review, 127
 generally, 126
  implied powers, 126
  improper exercise, 129
  passive trust, 4
 imperative, 127
 implied as "necessary or appropriate," 118, 120
 sources of, 120
  beneficiaries' actions, 120
  court instructions, 120
  law, 120
  trust instrument, 120
 successor trustees, 129
third-party liability, 119
 acquisition of trust property, 146–47
  bona fide purchaser, 147
  donee, 147
  "non-BFP," 147
trustee's liability, 142–44
 to third parties, 142–44
  contract, 142–44
  tort, 143–44

AFTER-ACQUIRED PROPERTY, 15
See also Creation of Express Trusts

AGENCY, 7–8
control, 7
distinguished from trust, 7

liability, 8
liability for agent's acts. *See* Administration of Trusts; Duties
      of Trustee; Trustee
powers, 7
termination, 8
title, 7

ALIENATION
See Beneficiaries; Res

AMBIGUITIES, 69
See also Statute of Frauds

ANIMALS, 31, 105–06

ASSIGNMENTS
See Beneficiaries

ATHEISM, 105
See also Charitable Purposes

ATTORNEYS' FEES
apportioned between income and principal, 159
trustee employing self, XXVI

BAILMENTS, 6–8
defined, 6
distinguished from trust, 6
income, 7
nature of property, 6
remedies, 7
title, 7
transferees, 6–7

BANK AS TRUSTEE
commingled investment devices, XXVI
deposits in own bank, XXVI
higher standard of duty, XXV, 131
own shares as investments, XXVI

BANK DEPOSIT TRUSTS, 17
See Totten Trusts

BENEFICIARIES
acceptance presumed, 5
ascertained or ascertainable rule, 3
      facts of independent significance, 34
      Rule Against Perpetuities, 33
      status until ascertained, 33–34
      Statute of Wills compliance, 69–70
      unascertained at trust creation, 34
assignment of interest, 56
defined, 30–31
disclaimer, 55
duties, 144–46. *See also* Administration of Trusts
identification requirement, 30–31
      class gifts, 35–37
incidental benefits, XII
modification and termination by, 164–66. *See also*
      Modification and Termination
nature of beneficiaries' interests, 39
      co-tenancies, 39
      equitable owner, 84
necessity of, 30–31
      charitable trusts, 31
      effect of lack of beneficiary, 31
      honorary trusts, 31. *See also* Honorary Trusts
      presently identifiable, 30
      trustee's awareness of intended beneficiary, 31
      unborn beneficiaries, 31
notice and acceptance, 55. *See also* Acceptance
remedies against, 145

remedies against trustee, 138–39. *See also* Trustee
retraction, 54
      alienability, 19
      assignment, 56
            form and manner, 84
                  consideration, 84
                  delivery, 84
                  formalities, 84
                  notice, 84
            involuntary transfers, 86–87
                  creditors' remedies, 87–88
                        creditor's bill in equity, 143
         restraints on alienation, 85–87
            discretionary trusts, 85. *See also* Discretionary
                Trusts
            protective trusts, 90–91
             spendthrift trusts, 85–89
                 arguments for/against, 88–89
            support trusts, XX, 169
who may be a beneficiary, 32
      incompetents, 32
      minors, 32
      unincorporated associations, 32

BENEFIT TO COMMUNITY, 105
See Charitable Purposes

BONA FIDE PURCHASERS
bailments, 6
constructive trusts, 63
Statute of Frauds, 63

BONDING, 24–25

BONDS
      See also Accounting for Income and Principal
allocation of interest from, 160
as investment, 3
premium and discount allocation, 157–58

"BREAKING THROUGH," XIX
See also Spendthrift Trusts

CAPACITY, 21–24

CAPITAL IMPROVEMENTS, 158

CARE, SKILL, AND CAUTION, 126
See also Duties of Trustee

CHARITABLE PURPOSES, 99–104
      See also Charitable Trusts Animals, 105–06
benefit to community, 105
      general standard, 99–100
benevolent purposes, 99
certainty of purposes, 100–01
conditional gifts, 109
constitutional limitations, 111–12
      "charitable," 100
      motive vs. purpose, 99
      specific purposes, 102–06
education, 102
      law reform, 103–04
      nonindigents, 105
      political parties, 102–03
      political views, 102
      profit-making institutions, 103
governmental purposes, 105–06
      animals, 105–06
      political change, 106
graves, 106

health, 107
historical or artistic merit, 107
illegal, immoral, or irrational purpose, 100
incidental benefits, 108
private social clubs, XXII
profit-making purpose, 103
qualification as private trust, 107–08
relief of poverty, 102
    nonindigents benefit, 102
Rule Against Perpetuities exception, 110–11
senior citizens, 107
split-interest trusts, 108

CHARITABLE TRUSTS, 93–115
charitable purposes, 95. *See* Charitable Purposes Creation
    and Purpose, 95–96
cy pres, 112–15
    application of, 112–13
        expressed gift over, 113
        frustration, 114
        general purpose, 113
        nearest purpose, 114–15
        restricted purpose, 113
        Rule Against Perpetuities, 113
        trust would terminate, 113
    nature and requirements, 112–13
        fulfillment or frustration, 114
        general charitable intent, 113
    resulting trust if inapplicable, 113
enforcement, 97
favored by law, 95
limitations on, 109–12
    constitutional, 111–12
    Mortmain Acts, 109
    Rule Against Perpetuities, 44, 110–11
modification, 112–115
public benefit requirement, 94
    direct benefit, 94
    indefinite number of beneficiaries, 97
    limited number of beneficiaries, 98
    noncharitable co-beneficiaries, 98–99
        separate or successive shares, 99
similar purpose result, 113

***CLAFLIN* DOCTRINE,** 165

CLASS GIFTS
See Beneficiaries; Duration of Trusts

CLASSIFICATION OF TRUSTS
See Trusts

CONDITIONAL FEE, 9
distinguished from trust, effect of, 10

CONDITIONAL GIFTS, 109

CONFLICT OF INTEREST, 26–28
See also Duties of Trustee

CONSIDERATION, 51, 56–57

**CONSTITUTIONAL LIMITATIONS ON
    CHARITABLE PURPOSES,** 111–12

CONSTRUCTIVE TRUSTS, 5
See also Statute of Frauds
accounting and tracing, 175
against trustee, 63
arises by operation of law, 4–5
breach of fiduciary duty, 179
defined, 3, 170

duty to convey title, 175
equitable remedy, 179
    when imposed, 179–80
nontrust cases, 180–81
    fraud, 64
    mistake, 64
    wrongful prevention of will-making, 180
oral trust unenforceable, 64. *See also* Statute of Frauds
retroactivity, 175
semi-secret trusts, 50
Statute of Frauds inapplicable, 63
transfer to third person, 181
    "non-BFP," 181
    tracing proceeds, 181
    unjust enrichment, 66–67

CO-TRUSTEES
See Administration of Trusts; Duties of Trustee; Trustee

CREATION OF EXPRESS TRUSTS, 50
    See also Intent
inter vivos, 51
    consideration, 56–57
        after-acquired property, 57
        ineffective transfer, 57
        promise to create future trust, 18
    parol evidence rule, 50
        ambiguity, 69
            silence as to trust, 68
            trust clearly stated, 68
            trust specifically excluded, 68
    registration of trust, 56
    Statute of Frauds, 58–60. *See also* Statute of Frauds
        delivery to trustee, 52
            no trustee, 53
                 constructive trustee, 53
            personal property, 52
            real property, 52
            settlor as trustee, 53
        notice to and acceptance by beneficiary, 54
            acceptance presumed, 5
            assignment, 56
            disclaimer, 55
            evidentiary questions, 54
            not essential, 55
            partial acceptance, 55
            relation back, 55
            retraction, 56
        notice to and acceptance by trustee, 56
            acceptance presumed, XV
            disclaimer, 55
            relation back, 54
            retraction, 55
            trustee's duties, 54
            unaware trustee, 54
        present vs. future transactions, XIV
    Uniform Probate Code, 56
life insurance trusts, 74–75. *See also* Life Insurance Trusts
methods, 75
revocable inter vivos trusts, 73–75. *See also* Revocable Inter
    Vivos Trusts Testamentary Trusts, 69–75
    pour-overs, 50. *See also* Pour-Over Wills, secret trusts,
        70–71. *See also* Secret Trusts, semi-secret
        trusts, 72–73. *See also* Semi-Secret Trusts
will substitutes, 173. *See* Revocable Inter Vivos Trusts

CREDITORS
bank accounts, 77
creditor's bill in equity, 143

fraud on, 23
revocable inter vivos trusts, 79
rights against beneficiaries, 84–86
rights against settlor, 85
spendthrift trusts, 85–88
trustee's indemnification, 131

CY PRES, 112–15
See also Charitable Trusts

DEBTOR-CREDITOR RELATIONSHIP, 8–9
distinguished from trust, 8
insolvency, 9
losses, 9
profits, 9

DECANTING, 170–71

DECLARATION OF TRUST, 15–16

DELEGATION
See Duties of Trustee

DELIVERY
See Creation of Express Trusts

DISCLAIMER
by beneficiaries, 55
by trustee, 55

DISCRETIONARY FUNCTIONS, 36

DISCRETIONARY TRUSTS, 82–83
beneficiary's interest not reached by creditors, 85
trustee's decision to pay, 85
abuse of discretion, 128
attachment, 84
misdelivery, 85

DIVERSIFICATION, 119, 125

DIVIDENDS, 153, 155–56
See also Accounting for Income and Principal

DOCTRINE OF WORTHIER TITLE, XII

DRY TRUSTS, 4
See Passive Trusts

DURATION OF TRUSTS, 42–43
reasons for limitations, 43
rule against accumulations, XIV, 13
charitable trusts, 110–11
Rule Against Perpetuities, 42–46
charitable exception, 110
class gifts, 44
cy pres, 112–15
effect of remoteness, 46
honorary trusts, 107
perpetuities period, 42–43
gestation period, 45
"life in being," 45
trust may continue beyond perpetuities period, 46
vesting, 43–46
class gifts, 44
interests subject to Rule, 44

DURESS, 64–65, 68

DUTIES OF TRUSTEE, 120–26
See also Administration of Trusts
administer personally according to trust terms, 136

delegation, 129
co-trustees, 131–32
delegation, 131–32
duty to participate, 131
liability for breach, 132
liability for acts of agents, 130
nondelegable duty, XXIV
proper delegation, 131
independent contractors, 131
liability to third parties, 142–44
ministerial vs. discretionary functions, XXIV
advice of others, XXIV
other trustees, 131–32
supervision, 131
predecessor trustees, 132
care, skill, and caution, 126
compensation, 122–23
property of others standard, XXV
trustees with special skills, 131–32
bank or trust company, 132
collect and safeguard trust estate, 133
collect assets, 133
defend trust, 133
against settlor, 133
insure res, 133
preserve assets, 136
fiduciary standards, 120–26
care, skill, and caution, 126
impartiality, 152
loyalty, 121–23
obey trust terms, 121
prudence, 135–37
inform beneficiaries, 125–26
invest and make productive, 137. *See also* Investments
loyalty, 121–23
borrowing from trust estate, 126, 133
compensation from third person, XXV
conflict of interest, 27
corporate trustees, 132
commingled investments, 125
deposits in own bank, XXVI
trustee's own shares, XXVI
exceptions, 123
beneficiaries' consent, 122
court authority, 122
loans to trust estate, XXV
self-employment, compensation for, XXVI |
transactions with beneficiary, 122
presumption of unfairness, 122
transactions with trust estate, 122
beneficiaries' remedies, 138–39
trust terms, 122
prudence, 135–37
segregate and identify, 118
earmark, 118
exceptions, 123

EARMARKING, 118
See also Duties of Trustee

EDUCATION, 102
See also Charitable Purposes

ELECTIVE SHARE, 78–79

EQUITABLE CHARGE, 9
distinguished from trust, 9

EQUITABLE CONVERSION DOCTRINE, XV

EQUITABLE INTEREST, 2

EXCULPATORY CLAUSE, 141–42
See also Trustee

EXECUTORS, 10

EXPENSES, TRUSTEE, XXV

EXPRESS TRUSTS, 5
See also Creation of Express Trusts
defined, 5
intent, 5
    charitable, 113. *See also* Charitable Trusts
    form of expression, 14
    immediate effect, 15–16
        postponing designation of essential elements,
           16
        savings bank trusts, 17 *See also* Totten Trusts
        testamentary trusts, 17
        Totten trusts, 17
        trust of a future interest, 16–17
        Trust of a promise, 17
    precatory expressions, 14–15
        construction, 14
        time and place, 15–16
    testamentary, 17. *See also* Testamentary Trusts
    time of expression, 18
        after-acquired property, 18
        gifts, 18
    words or conduct, 18

FACTS OF INDEPENDENT SIGNIFICANCE, 30, 34
See Pour-Over Wills

FIDUCIARY STANDARDS
See also Duties of Trustee

FORCED SHARE, 78–79

FRAUD
See also Statute of Frauds
constructive trusts, 64
on creditors, unenforceable oral trusts, 63–64

FUTURE INTERESTS, 16–17

GOVERNMENTAL PURPOSES, 105–06
See also Charitable Purposes

GRAVES, 31, 106

GUARDIANSHIPS, 14, 162

HEALTH, 107
See also Charitable Purposes

HONORARY TRUSTS, 31–32
graves, 106–07
interests created, 32
masses, 104
not a true trust, 31
pets, 31–32
resulting trust remedy, 107

IDENTIFICATION, 12
See Beneficiaries; Res

ILLEGAL PURPOSE, 42

ILLUSORY TRUST, 78–79

IMMORAL PURPOSE, 100

IMPARTIALITY, 123–24

IMPOUNDMENT, 145

INCOME AND PRINCIPAL, 149
See Accounting for Income and Principal

INCORPORATION BY REFERENCE, 34
See Pour-Over Wills

INDEMNIFICATION, 142–44

INDEPENDENT CONTRACTORS, 131

INSURANCE
duty to insure, 133
principal and income, 158
res, 133
trusts, 74–75. *See also* Life Insurance Trusts

INTENT
See also Express trusts

INTER VIVOS TRUSTS
See Creation of Express Trusts; Revocable Inter Vivos Trusts

INVASION OF PRINCIPAL, 151

INVESTMENTS
common trust funds, 134
generally, 134
    cash, 134
    land and chattels, 134
    prudent investor rule, 135
        diversification, 136
        imprudent investments, 138
           conduct, not performance, crucial, 136
        time of investment determinative, 135
    "prudent man" rule, 135
    statutory lists, 135

IRRATIONAL PURPOSE, 100

LAW REFORM, 103–04
See also Charitable Purposes

LEASE BY TRUSTEE, 134

LEGAL INTEREST, 2–3

LIENS
See Equitable charge

LIFE INSURANCE TRUSTS
creation, 74
irrevocable, 74
res, 74
revocable, 74–75

LOYALTY, 121–23
See also Duties of Trustee

MARRIAGE, RESTRAINTS ON, 40–41

MASSES, 104
See also Honorary Trusts

METHODS OF TRUST CREATION
See Creation of Express Trusts

MISTAKE, 64

MIXED TRUSTS, 40

MODIFICATION AND TERMINATION, 164–66
    See also Charitable Trusts; Cy Pres
by beneficiaries, 164–65
    Claflin doctrine, 164–65

consent of all, 164–65
    all competent, 165
        vicarious consent, 165
    all possible, 164
        children, 164
        heirs, 164
        issue or descendants, 164
    settlor's purpose not defeated, 170
        frustration, 167
        Rule Against Perpetuities, 168
        settlor's consent, 164
        spendthrift trust, 85–89
        support trust, 167
by courts, 168
    administrative provisions modified, 168
        acceleration of indefeasibly vested rights, 177
        cy pres compared, 170. *See also* Charitable
            Trusts
        equitable deviation rule, 168–70
            unforeseen circumstances, 168
        express trust provision, 169
            no modification provision, 169
            sale forbidden, 169
            termination of activity, 169
        trustee liability, 169
            emergency exception, 170
by operation of law, 168
    creditors' rights where power of revocation, 163
        bankruptcy of settlor, 163
        rescission and reformation compared, 163
        settlor as sole beneficiary, 85
        Totten trust exception, 163
by trustee, 162
    decanting, 170–71
    judicial, 168
    trust terms, 169
charitable trusts, 170. *See also* Charitable Trusts

MORTGAGE PAYMENTS, 159

MORTMAIN ACTS, 109
See also Charitable trusts

**NOTICE TO AND ACCEPTANCE BY TRUSTEE AND
    BENEFICIARY,** 56
See also Acceptance; Creation of Express Trusts

ORAL TRUSTS
constructive trusts, 63–64. *See also* Constructive Trusts
secret trusts, 70–71. *See also* Secret Trusts
Statute of Frauds, 58. *See also* Statute of Frauds

PAROL EVIDENCE RULE, 69
See also Statute of Frauds

PARTIES TO TRUST
See Beneficiaries; Settlor; Trustee

PASSIVE TRUSTEE, 4
duty to hold and convey, 4

PASSIVE TRUSTS, 4
See also Statute of Uses Defined
modern law, 4
passive trustees, 4

POLITICAL PARTIES, 102–03
See also Charitable Purposes

POUR-OVER WILLS (AKA POUROVER WILLS)
explained, 20–21
    facts of independent significance effect, 50

    incorporation by reference, 50
Uniform Testamentary Additions to Trusts Act, 20
    unfunded trusts, 20
validity problem, 20

POVERTY, 102
See also Charitable Purposes

POWERS OF TRUSTEE
See Administration of Trusts

PRECATORY LANGUAGE
express trusts, 14–15. *See also* Express Trusts
honorary trusts, 32

PREDECESSOR TRUSTEES, 132

PRESERVATION OF ASSETS, 135

PRINCIPAL AND INCOME
See Accounting for Income and Principal

PRIVATE SOCIAL CLUBS, XXII
See also Charitable Purposes

PRIVATE TRUSTS, 13
See also Beneficiaries

PROFIT-MAKING PURPOSE, 103
See also Charitable Purposes

PROPERTY OF TRUST
See Res

PRUDENT INVESTOR RULE, 135
See also Investments

PUBLIC BENEFIT, 94
See Charitable Trusts

PURPOSE TRUST
See Honorary trusts

QUANTUM OF ESTATE, 30

RACE DISCRIMINATION, 111–12
See also Charitable Purposes

REFORMATION, 163

REGISTRATION OF TRUST, 56
See also Trustee

RELATION BACK, 54–55

RELIEF OF POVERTY, 102
See also Charitable Purposes

RELIGION, 104–05
    See also Charitable Purposes
illegality or immorality, 100
irrational beliefs, 100
masses, 104
"religious" purpose, 104–05
spiritualism, 104

RES
alienability, 19
    inalienable property, 19
creditors, 22–23
defined, 12
identification, 12
    consideration, 57–58
    equitable interests, 2
    expectancies, 58
    fractional interests, 19

legal interest, 2–3
    quantum of estate, 30
    relation back, 54–55
  obligee as trustee, 20
  special deposits, 20
  Totten trusts, 20
life insurance trusts, 74–75
requirements, 52–53
revocable inter vivos trusts, 73–75
Statute of Frauds, 58

RESCISSION, 163

RESULTING TRUSTS
defined, 5
general nature, 5
  expressed trust fails, 22
    arises by operation of law, 5
    disclaimer by beneficiary, 178
    illegal, impossible, or impracticable, 177–78
    no express intent, 33
      excessive res, 22
      unanticipated circumstances, 176
  expressed trust unenforceable, 177
semi-secret trusts, 72
Statute of Frauds inapplicable, 63

RETRACTION, 54

REVOCABLE INTER VIVOS TRUSTS, 162
charitable bequests, 80 creditors, 85
elective share of spouse, 78–79
life insurance trusts, 74–75. *See also* Life Insurance Trusts
taxes, 79
testamentary character, 74
  retained powers, 23
Totten trusts, 75–77. *See also* Totten Trusts

RULE AGAINST ACCUMULATIONS, 13

RULE AGAINST PERPETUITIES
  See also Charitable Trusts; Duration of Trusts
charitable trusts, 110–11
honorary trusts, 42–43
resulting trusts, 113

SAVINGS BANK TRUSTS, 17
See Totten Trusts

SECRET TRUSTS, 70
constructive trust remedy, 71
  for whom imposed, 72
  no fraud requirement, 71
  no inducement requirement, 71
  Statute of Frauds compared, 71
intestate heir's breach, 73
semi-secret trusts compared, 72. *See also* Semi-Secret Trusts
voluntary performance, 71

SEGREGATION OF ASSETS, 53
See also Duties of Trustee

SEGREGATION OF RES, 108

SELF-DEALING, 121–22
See Duties of Trustee

SEMI-SECRET TRUSTS, 50
constructive trusts, 70–71
resulting trusts, 72

SENIOR CITIZENS, 107
See also Charitable Purposes

SETTLOR
  See also Express Trusts
bankruptcy of, 163
creditors of, 22–23
  asset protection trusts, 23
  corpus, 23
  fraud, 23
defined, 21
modification and termination by, 164. *See also* Modification
  and Termination
rights in trust property, 22
  fraud, duress, or mistake, 22
  modern trend—revocability presumed, 22
  reversionary interests, 22
  signature on trust, 60
Totten trusts, intent, 163. *See also* Totten Trusts

SPECIAL DEPOSITS, 20

SPENDTHRIFT TRUSTS, 85–89
argument for, 88
arguments against, 89
  social policy, 89
  symmetry of estates, 89
Claflin doctrine, 166
defined, 85–86
effect of restraints, 86–87
  assignments, 86
  attempted voluntary transfer, 86
  creditors' rights, 87–88
    "breaking through," XIX
    classes of creditors, 87–88
    distributions not protected, 87
    necessaries, 88
    spouse as creditor, 88
    tort creditors, 88
settlor's retained interest, 91
validity, 86–87
  bankruptcy, 86
  generally upheld, 166
  statutory limitations, 86
voluntary vs. involuntary transfers, 86–87

SPIRITUALISM, 104
See also Charitable Purposes

SPLIT-INTEREST TRUSTS, 108

STATUTE OF FRAUDS
enforcement of oral trust barred, 64
  bona fide purchaser, 63
  trustee willing to perform, 63
inapplicable to constructive and resulting trusts, 175
parol evidence rule, 2
  ambiguity, 21
  trust clearly stated, 20
  trust expressly excluded, 20
part performance doctrine, 64
  sufficiency of, 64
    beneficial use, 64
    trustee's acknowledgment, 64
  to cure defective transfer, 62
secret trusts compared, 72
  beneficiary, 61
  grantee, 61
  grantor, 60–61
  settlor and trustee, 60
status of res, 59–60
  personalty, 60

real property, 60
    proceeds, 60
        subsequent declaration, 60
type of writing, 60
unenforceable oral trust, 174
    constructive trust as remedy, 175
        confidential relationship, 180
        contemplation of death, 63
        fraud, 64
        intended beneficiary, 67
        mistake, duress, and undue influence, 64–65
        no wrongful conduct, 66
        unjust enrichment, 68
    parol evidence, 63
when writing required, 60

STATUTE OF WILLS, 71, 175

SUPPORT TRUSTS, 167

SYMMETRY OF ESTATES, 89
See also Spendthrift Trusts

TAXES
accounting, 158
revocable inter vivos trust, 79

TENTATIVE TRUSTS, 75–77
See Totten Trusts

TERMINATION, 164–66
See Modification and Termination

TESTAMENTARY ADDITIONS, 74
See Pour-Over Wills

TESTAMENTARY TRUSTS, 69–75
See also Creation of Express Trusts; Pour-Over Wills

THIRD PARTY, LIABILITY OF, 146–47
See also Administration of Trusts

TOTTEN TRUSTS
depositor's creditors, 77
depositor's death, 77–78
    intent, 77–78
    revocation by will, 77
presumptively revocable, 76
res, 20
termination if beneficiary predeceases, 78
validity and effect, 75–76

TRANSFER
See Beneficiaries; Creation of Express Trusts

TRUSTEE
        See also Administration of Trusts; Duties of Trustee
acceptance presumed, XV
    disclaimer of, 55
    relates back, 54
    retraction of, 55
as guarantor, 136
as sole beneficiary, 28
bonding, 24–25
constructive, 53
corporate, 132.
disclaimer by, 55
duties, 120–44. *See also* Administration of Trusts; Duties of
    Trustee
functions, 36
    preservation of res, 135
    productivity, 138

general responsibility and authority, 119. *See also*
    Administration of Trusts
indemnification, 131
interest of, 3
    death of trustee, 26
        sole trustee, 26
    merger of title, 28
    personal debts, 26
    relation back, 54–55
    source, 120
legal interest, 2
liability to beneficiaries, 137
    beneficiaries' remedies, 138–39
        breach of loyalty, 121–23
        damages, 138–39
            failure to make property productive, 138
            improper investment, 138
            interest and earnings, 140
            principal, losses to, 139
            profits, 139
        equitable relief, 138
            enjoin or compel trustee, 138
            remove trustee, 141
    defenses, 143
        exculpatory clause, 141–42
        insolvency of trustee, 9
        laches and limitations period, 142
    liability to third parties, 142–44
        contract liability, 142
            waste, 133
        indemnification, trustee's right, 131
            creditors' rights, 143
                defense costs, 124
    tort liability, 143
modification and termination by, 164–66. *See also*
    Modification and Termination
notice and acceptance, 55. *See also* Acceptance Powers *See
    also* Administration of Trusts
    capacity to administer, 23
    capacity to take and hold title, 23
    corporations, 24
        foreign, 24
    co-trustees, 24
registration of trust, 56
removal, 27–28
    animosity, 27
    by beneficiaries, 28
    insolvency, 27
    settlor-appointed trustee, 27
resignation, 26–27
    unauthorized reconveyance, 27
retraction, 54
unaware trustee, 54

TRUSTOR
See Settlor

TRUSTS
charitable trusts, 93–115. *See* Charitable Trusts
classification
    active trusts, 4
    constructive trusts, 63. *See also* Constructive Trusts
    express trusts, 5
    passive trusts, 5
    private vs. charitable trusts, 4–5
    resulting trusts, 5. *See also* Resulting Trusts
    trusts created by operation of law, 5
consideration not required, 13

defined, 2
discretionary trusts, 85
distinguished from agency, 7–8
    bailment, 6–7
    conditional fee, 8
    debt, 8–9
    equitable charge, 9
    other relationships, 10
elements, 13
legal and equitable interests, 2–3
mixed trusts, 40
parties, 21–22
private trusts, 13
protective trusts, 90–91
purpose trusts, 31. *See* Honorary Trusts
purposes, 12–13. *See also* Charitable Purposes
    impermissible, 40
        bequests compared, 41
        effect of invalid provisions, 42
        encouraging divorce, 41
        fraud on creditors, 40
        illegality, 40
        immorality, 40
        restraints on marriage, 40–41
    lawful and appropriate requirement, 39–40
        charitable trusts, 39
        honorary trusts, 40
        mixed trusts, 40
        private trusts, 13
    permissible duration, 42–43. *See also* Duration of
        Trusts
    savings bank trusts, 17. *See* Totten Trusts
    secret and semi-secret trusts, 73
    spendthrift trusts, 85–89.
    split-interest trusts, 108
    support trusts, 167
    tentative trusts. *See* Totten Trusts Testamentary Trusts,
        69–75. *See also* Creation of Express Trusts;
        Pour-Over Wills
registration of, 56

UNDUE INFLUENCE, 64–65

UNIFORM PRINCIPAL AND INCOME ACT
    See also Accounting for Income and Principal
        Accounting Rules, 151–52
prudent investor rule—1997 Act, 151
unproductive property, 156
wasting assets, 156–57

UNIFORM PROBATE CODE, 56

UNIFORM TESTAMENTARY ADDITIONS TO
    TRUSTS ACT, 20
See also Pour-Over Wills

UNINCORPORATED ASSOCIATIONS, 32

UPKEEP, 159
See also Accounting for Income and Principal

VESTING, 43–46
Rule Against Perpetuities, 42–46

VICARIOUS CONSENT, 164
See also Modification and Termination

WASTING ASSETS, 156–57
See also Accounting for Income and Principal

WILL SUBSTITUTES, 173
See Revocable Inter Vivos Trusts